The experience of adoption is far more common than is ordinarily thought. Conservative estimates hold that one out of five persons in North America is intimately linked to adoption – as adoptees, birthparents, adoptive parents, siblings, spouses, grandparents and as offspring.

In today's climate of controversy over the rights of adopted persons in North America, here finally is a book which brings solid facts to this area of deep emotion. In 1964 Kirk's highly readable book *Shared Fate* challenged the professional assumptions with research based on over 2,000 Canadian and American adoptive families. Now the author has provided an up-to-date review of the background for the current controversy concerning the civil rights of adopted persons. What he shows is that the difficulties peculiar to adoptive family life stem from well-meant but mistaken laws and administrative practices.

As in a detective story, *Adoptive Kinship* takes the reader through a gripping series of events. Eventually we discern the true sources of difficulty and also new directions for adoption, both as human relationship and as social institution.

Adoptive Kinship
A Modern Institution
In Need of Reform

H. David Kirk
University of Waterloo

With a Preface by Robin M. Williams, Jr.

Ben-Simon Publications
Port Angeles, Washington
Brentwood Bay, British Columbia

Ben-Simon Publications

USA: P.O. Box 2124
         Port Angeles, WA 98362

Canada: P.O. Box 318
         Brentwood Bay, B.C. V0S 1A0

Library of Congress Catalog Card Number: 83-670044
ISBN 0-914539-01-9
(original ISBN 0-409-84280-X)

Printed and bound in USA

To the memory of
Änny and Simon,
my parents

Contents

Acknowledgments

A book like this owes much to many people. First of all I must thank the publishers of the journals and books used here for their generous permission to quote from the works of their authors.

Among friends I want to give first place to Matille Rowan Rufrano who died an untimely death in 1979. In 1961, when she was a staff member at Vista del Mar in Los Angeles, she attended my public lecture series at Whittier College. The mimeographed summaries of those five lectures ultimately led to the writing of *Shared Fate*. I had not met Matille when she wrote to say that she had re-worked my ideas for staff training purposes, and had also used sections in group meetings with couples who had applied to adopt through her agency. It was the first time anyone had let me know that my work had utility for practitioners, and it was just the kind of encouragement I needed at the time. Years later we met and I came to appreciate Matille as one of those rare people who have eyes for the often invisible forces of social change. I believe that she was among the first of an older generation of social workers who came forward to try to understand the adoptee movement and its calls for institutional reform.

Then there is my colleague, Kurt Jonassohn. We worked together off and on between 1962 and 1972 on research that inquired into the health and behavior of 2,300 Nova Scotia children and their families. Kurt has been much more than colleague and friend: he has jollied and nagged, instructed and helped, always with his characteristic mix of dry humor and hard work. He and I are much indebted for the help we received in our work from the staff of the Nova Scotia Department of Social Services, and especially the then Deputy Minister, Dr. Fred MacKinnon, and the then Director of Child Welfare, Mr. Dan Johnson.

When I wrote *Shared Fate* I hoped that it would help to alert some members of the social work profession to issues in adoptive parent-child relationships which had largely been overlooked but which seemed vital to the wellbeing of the families in question. It was therefore enormously gratifying to receive communications from social workers who had found the work of value. One of these was Webster Martin, Jr., who was Director of Child Welfare for the State of Minnesota when he wrote to me in 1964. But Web Martin did more than write to say that some of the concepts like "role handicap" and "acknowledgment-of-difference" seemed to him pertinent to a wider range of social work activities than just adoption. He also challenged me to think through the application of my theory to the policies and practices of social agencies engaged in adoption work. That challenge led to a series of lecture and seminar workshops entitled "Adoption Services at the Crossroads" which, together with Ruth Kirk, I conducted in Minnesota, Ontario, Alberta, Quebec, Nova Scotia, and England between 1966 and 1968. I doubt whether I could have tackled the issues that make up the subject matter of the present book if I had not learned to think with Webster Martin about the problems faced by the administrator of an agency.

Among the mail I received after *Shared Fate* appeared was a letter from Michael Bohman, Sweden's indefatigable research psychiatrist who has himself been engaged in long-term social-psychological investigations of adopted children and their families. Although he has approached the problem from quite different vantage points, Dr. Bohman's meticulously designed and executed studies have served to supplement, support, and correct my own. I value his comradeship in this special area of work, and our friendship.

Among those whose scholarship and style of thinking especially enriched my development as sociologist was Robin M. Williams, Jr. He witnessed my groping for theoretical and methodological footholds in a subject area that then had few sociological precedents. I have remained immensely grateful to him for modelling so clearly his commitment to sociology as a discipline of intellectual integrity and craftsmanship.

Those of us who teach and use ongoing research in teaching will know how useful the critique of able students can be. Again and again I have found my work thus constructively challenged. I want to thank two of my recent students, Donna McGraw and A.K. Prempeh, who went with great care through the manuscript of this book. Their interest and that of many of their fellow students in previous courses and seminars serves to remind me of what a great privilege is to do work that one loves..

In looking back over many years I must also remember Ruth Kirk, my former spouse, with whom I was able to build a family of great value. In 1970, when our marriage came to an end, I feared the loss not only of a loved mate and companion but also the destruction of our precious family. I once voiced this fear to my son Peter. His response was enormously reassuring: "No, Dad, we children are the family now." Some weeks later the same issue came up in a conversation with my daughter Debbie. Though she put the matter differently, her meaning was similar to her brother's. "There are three families now," she said. "There's Mom and we children, there's the group of us children and you, and then there are the four of us by ourselves, and we'll be here after you and Mom are gone." While I speak of Peter and Debbie I must not forget Francie and Bill. All four have given me leave to speak of them by name in this book, to write parts of our family's history in so far as the events illuminate the ideas developed here.

Writing a book over a period of many months can be a wearying task for others than the person engaged in writing. Beve Tansey, my wife, has been an invaluable helper: with ideas, critique, and her wide-ranging reading through which I learned of references which to have missed would have been to this book's disadvantage. Beve's children, Ben and Lisa, suffered my presence through the long haul of writing, with a wit and generosity uncommon in two precocious teenage critics.

Sensible writers usually reserve at least a small corner for their editors, but a small corner will not do for Francine Geraci. Because of her forthright and clear-headed advice I can in good conscience face my readers with a book which, for all its shortcomings, is the book I very much wanted to write.

Addendum 1985
In this brief addition I would like to express my appreciation to Professor Clayton Roberts, my erstwhile brother-in-law. A historian at Ohio State University, and like others of his discipline not always supportive of sociological scholarship and writing, he said of this book: "As always you write with power and elegance, much better than any sociologist ought to. I especially like your plea to re-define the nature of adoptive kinship so as to conform to realities. I also like the way you connect this book with your earlier book, *Shared Fate*. I now have a clear idea what the Kirk thesis is on adoption, and what you have spent your career arguing." Clayton Roberts has been a kind of godfather to my work, though he has probably forgotten what he did. In 1961 I sent him copies of my five Whittier lectures "Parent-Child Relations in Adoption." He urged me to submit them immediately to a respectable publisher. That is how, a few months later, the Free Press of Glencoe (then one of America's most highly regarded social science houses) sent me a contract for a book that two years later became *Shared Fate*.

The following have granted permission for the use of excerpts:
— from Michael Bohman, *Adopted Children and their Families*, by permission: Proprius, Sweden, 1970.
— from Betty Dembroski and Dale Johnson, "Dogmatism and Attitudes toward Adoption" *Journal of Marriage and the Family* Vol. 31 No. 4. Copyrighted 1969 by the National Council on Family Relations. Reprinted by permission.
— from William M. Evan, *Law and Society*. Reprinted with permission of Macmillan Publishing Co., Inc. Copyright © 1962 by The Free Press.
— from Margaret Kornitzer, *Child Adoption in the Modern World*, Putnam, 1952.
— from E. Weinstein, "A Book Review of *Shared Fate*" *American Journal of Sociology* Vol. 71. Copyrighted 1966 by The University of Chicago Press.

Preface

For over three decades the author of this work has examined the social and psychological meanings of adoption. David Kirk has thought about the subject with rare persistence, clarity, and comprehensiveness — and above all with a humane skepticism concerning conventional beliefs and institutionalized assumptions. His first book, *Shared Fate,* was in every sense a pioneering study. Audacious at the time, it outraged some readers by its sharp challenges to both the biologistic and the sociologistic "received wisdom." But by now much of what it had to say has, in turn, become part of the accepted culture in the field of adoption. Perhaps *Adoptive Kinship* will share in the fate of its precursor.

Vigorously rejecting what he regards as the trivialization of adoption in the current literature of sociology, Kirk argues that adoption is a significant and integral part of basic kinship and family arrangements. This book, then, decisively moves the subject of adoption into a central place in the study of the institutions of kinship, and thereby, away from the traditional conception of adoption as a peripheral item among "welfare" or "social service" activities. Kirk estimates that no less than one person out of five in our society is "directly and intimately linked to the experience of adoption." As "reconstituted" households or families — formed by adoption, foster-parenting, divorce, remarriage — come to be a larger and larger proportion of all kinship units, the present study bears upon the daily concerns of many millions of persons in North American society.

The central, and massive, contribution of the book is to make it clear beyond doubt that: (1) adoptive kinship is not the same as consanguineal kinship; (2) the dogma of "no difference" leads to unnecessary inequities, felt injustices, and serious social tensions. A detailed examination of the differences between birth-parenthood and adoptive parenthood (pages 31-34) makes the sheer fact of important differences appear immediately obvious, and this work marshalls impressive empirical evidence to support this initial impression. All the more remarkable, then, is Kirk's account of the long, implacable resistance of many social work organizations — and of some adoptive parents — to the idea that acceptance rather than rejection of the differences would be appropriate public policy and beneficial to adoptive-family functioning.

It is important to note that in Kirk's conception neither rejection-of-difference nor acknowledgment-of-difference is merely a cognitive matter of just recognizing or not recognizing the sheer facts of similarities and differences between relations of adoptive and of consanguineal kinship. Both orientations involve complex and strong motivations and evaluations. What is advocated is a "consistently loving acknowledgment-of-difference" (page 72); a basic attitude that involves orientations toward openness, risk-taking, trust, clarity of expectations, and many other aspects of the "internal and continuing relationships" among adoptive parents and children.

The attentive reader — and this book is unlikely to have any inattentive readers — will be quick to appreciate how often the work confronts us with the hitherto unremarked significance of what previously may have seemed obvious or trivial. Thus, we are reminded that children do not remain children, they have the disconcerting characteristic of growing up and becoming adults. Surely this is obvious, but much social practice still is squarely premised on the conception that adoptees always remain children, as if a thirty-year old man or woman still has only the rights and duties of the same individual as an adoptee at the age of three years.

Now, David Kirk would never forgive me if this preface merely praised his work: for one thing, I must not spoil his cherished image of me as a stern mentor. Indeed, this book like any other is open to criticism. My own critique will not detract from its central findings but it may suggest possible lines of revision and development for future work.

Let us examine an instance in point. Since Kirk has based *Adoptive Kinship* so firmly on its predecessor *Shared Fate*, critical assessment of the earlier work seems in order even now. The data for *Shared Fate* were in large part derived from surveys conducted between 1952 and 1961. While some of Kirk's interpretations were based on relatively sophisticated scale analyses using multiple question items (see *Shared Fate* pages 29-31 and 175-176), other indicators of concepts in his theory of adoption were less sound, particularly when these indicators were based on interviewed persons' answers to single "attitude" questions (see *Shared Fate* pages 25-27). Nevertheless, Kirk's interpretations strike one as generally sound, largely because of his extraordinary sensitivity and his intimate knowledge of the domain, but I have sometimes found myself in the uncomfortable position of trusting the author of *Shared Fate* more than some of its data. Happily these strictures do not apply to most of the arguments advanced in *Adoptive Kinship*, for its crucial propositions rest on an impressive network of direct observations, systematic surveys, testimony, public records, and well-grounded theory.

A second point: I am somewhat less confident than Kirk that the purposively-constructed social forms and relationships are necessarily any more "rationally contrived" than the older "traditional" forms. One reason for this skepticism is doubt as to the meaning of "rationality" in the case of social relationships that are inherently more than purely instrumental. Certainly, however, there are more reasonable and less reasonable ways of constituting adoptive relationships. Arbitrary and stereotyped placement practices are not reasonable, nor are laws that proclaim the adoptive family as the social equivalent of its consanguineal counterpart when such claims fly in the face of other laws that apply to all families. Thus *Adoptive Kinship* demonstrates that the "rationally contrived" form of modern adoption is internally contradictory: while it seeks to promote values implied in all kinship institutions it does so by inhibiting the voluntary characteristic of these values. In modern, secular social life, the kinship values of enduring commitments, which are of necessity diffuse and collectivistic rather than specific and individualistic, nevertheless are largely voluntary rather than imposed by law and social pressure. These values, implying continuity between generations, also imply in modern families deep respect and active concern for the feeling states and the personal sentiments of individual members, for their unique histories and relationships. If such respect and concern often seem deficient among members of mainstream families, these values would appear to be at even greater risk in families constituted by adoption. There the continuity between generations is inhibited by the knowledge that the relationship has been artificially created, and that beyond the adoptive family there exists another generational line to which the adopted person might have belonged. This complex circumstance, peculiar to adoption, would seem to produce conflicting feelings in adopted persons, especially when they compare their life histories and family relationships with those of mainstream family members. Thus, in spite of his apparently confident view of the rationality in new purposively-constructed social forms, Kirk nevertheless infers from his book's data that in the case of the modern institution of adoptive kinship thoroughly rationalized reform steps are evidently needed. What rationally contrived reform would have to provide is an institutional recognition of the complexity of adoptive relationships and thus of special requirements for respect and recognition of adopted persons' life histories.

Adoptive Kinship could not do everything at once. A needed addition is the further testing of the Shared Fate theory. What is lacking is information on how adoptees, raised in families that emphasized rejection-of-difference, fared as compared with other adoptees raised in relatively acknowledgment-of-difference oriented homes. Such research would seem highly desirable, since it could shed light on questions of "outcome" under conditions of differing values and practices in adoptive families. But not all social research plans can be carried out. At the time Kirk collected his data on the families in his studies, the adoptees were still children, so that the proposed outcome studies would have been both ethically and practically questionable. Now that all the adoptees in Kirk's samples are adults, the omission might well be rectified: certainly follow-up research is now feasible, timely, and scientifically desirable.

Short of such further research, however, *Adoptive Kinship* gives us a much more complete analysis than hitherto available. This comprehensive view is developed by meticulous unfolding of one facet after another of the central actors and relationships: birthparents, adoptive parents, adopted children, adoptees as adults, relations among adoptive siblings, social work agencies, the courts, legislatures, inheritance, incest prohibitions. Thus chapters 6 and 7 give a remarkable account of how the ideologies and practices of social work agencies for many years unwittingly perpetuated contradictions and "false consciousness" among many adoptive families. Chapters 8 and 9, similarly, point out glaring inconsistencies and omissions in U.S. and Canadian laws and court decisions concerning adoptive and stepchildren, e.g. questions of incest, marriage, "extended family" relations, insurance, and inheritance. The documentation in these chapters convincingly shows the precariousness created by imperfect institutionalization of adoptive relationships. In an age of "reconstituted families" resulting from frequent divorces and remarriages, these analyses are relevant to millions of non-adoptive family units.

Many other readers will share in my fascination with the account in chapter 10 of the emergence of organizations of adult adoptees "concerned with liberty, identity, linkage and the rights to find one's own way as adults, as "yesterday's children" (page 127). It has taken a long time, but finally there is growing public recognition of the ubiquity and strength of the urge to know one's origins, to have roots, to feel a sense of continuity with past and future. Kirk gives us a penetrating, judicious and well-grounded interpretation of the complex interplay of "contracts" ("a mental construct that derives from the culture of the social work agency") and "entitlements" of birthparents, adoptees, and adoptive parents. Obstacles that still bar specific institutional reforms are reviewed in chapter 11. The picture of legislative recalcitrance thus sketched leads Kirk then to suggest (chapter 12) that the greatest hope of constructive change may rest in the child welfare and adoption agency system, for that system no longer is seen by him as the former monolithic, monopolistic advocate of policies of sealed records, invisible origins, and rejection-of-difference. Thus Kirk arrives at the perhaps surprising position that "the child welfare apparatus might, through the considered application of its legal system, become the mainspring of institutional reform of adoptive kinship" (page 150). Although Kirk's optimism may appear as problematic to you as it does to me, he gives us at least a refreshing account of reasonable possibilities. In any case, the author lays out with admirable conciseness in his concluding chapter an illuminating map of the possible parallels between parent-child relationships and the "macro" institutions of law and practice that define and constrain those relationships.

Adoptive Kinship saves its strongest card to the last: the suggestion that "mainstream" Western kinship-units more and more have taken on qualities similar to adoptive kinship. Traditional norms are not enough. For strengthening all families and for enhancing the life-experience of all individuals, it is necessary to institutionalize new supports for authenticity, empathy, and communicative abilities.

We all are indebted to David Kirk for this careful, far-ranging and humanly sensitive study. The work is a happy marriage of deep personal concerns with scholarly objectivity. It is a civilized contribution to the public and private life of today and tomorrow.

Robin M. Williams, Jr.
Ithaca, New York
January 1981

Introduction

Adoptive kinship is a pattern of social relationships as well as a legally established social institution. It can therefore be studied within either perspective. This book does both, but it also combines the two approaches, demonstrating the interdependence of both. But this interdependence becomes reasonable only when one divests oneself of a common misconception concerning adoptive kinship. That misconception holds that contemporary adoption practices have a direct link with the far away past of Western societies, that they are traceable to ancient Greece and Rome. The facts are quite different. While in ancient Greece and Rome adoption was principally animated by religious and property interests of kin groups, contemporary adoption, certainly as practiced in English-speaking and some other West European societies, has very different functions and rationale. Besides, English common law made no provision for legal adoption. Between the adoption laws and practices of ancient Rome and our own society there lies a thousand year gap. Thus the first adoption legislation in North America, not based on Latin precedents, was enacted in Massachusetts in 1851. Adoption legislation came seventy-five years later in England and Wales, in 1926, and in Scotland only in 1930. These laws are modern in more than chronology: they place the adopted child into the center of the institution, manifestly at least making the adoptee's interests the primary concern of the institution, more important than the interests of birthparents or adoptive parents. It is in that sense that contemporary adoption, in contrast with adoption in the antique world, can be viewed as modern.

The subtitle also claims that this modern institution is in need of reform. It is a judgment based on systematic inspection of the connections between the interpersonal and the institutional contexts of adoptive kinship. My research, begun in 1951, started as an inquiry into the social and cultural settings in which adoptive relationships develop. This meant learning how people surrounding adoptive families — neighbors, doctors, teachers, and other members of the public at large — viewed the meaning of the relationships established through adoption. Later studies inquired how the parents and children themselves experienced both the relationship and the attitudes of other people. Pursued with the tools of sociological investigation, such questions led to data which eventually suggested a fascinating picture of adoptive kinship. That picture turned out to be rather different from the one which was then projected by professionals and by the media. In that picture derived from a decade of research — in the resulting theory of adoptive relations — it was evident that modern adoption is typically associated with a particular pattern of strains and tensions, peculiar to the adoptive parent-child relationship. But the theory also suggested potential avenues to strain reduction, made possible through the adopters' sensitivity to the special needs of their children. That sensitivity was in turn motivated by the memory of problems which had led the parents into adoption in the first place. The theory and the book reporting the researches were therefore called *Shared Fate*.

The theme of that book coincided with the major themes of several popular movements which arose about the same time, the mid-1960s. What these movements emphasized was a realistic assessment of minority group circumstances, as for instance in the case of black people and of women. I suspect that it was this cultural climate that helped make the Shared Fate theory both reasonable and acceptable to many professionals engaged in adoption work. But hardly had these new perceptions of adoptive kinship begun to take hold when demographic changes in North America greatly reduced the supply of adoptable infants. While the adoption agencies cast about and found new clients in handicapped and older children and in more risk-accepting and even single people as parents, a further cultural development threatened the equilibrium of institutionalized adoption. Groups of adopted adults, hitherto not numerically significant as a political factor, suddenly became highly organized and vocal. They rapidly gained in numerical and ideological strength throughout North America, pointing publicly to inequities which present adoption laws and professional practices create for the adopted.

As the chorus of voices for institutional reform swelled on this continent, some of the changes they advocated were written into law in Great Britain in 1975. When that happened I became fully aware that my work, begun almost a quarter century earlier, was not yet complete. I had come to see a possible connection between the strains that appeared endemic to the situation of the adoptive families I had studied, and the institutional arrangements that made those families possible. Could it be, I asked, that the institution itself was faulty, that it was productive of the strains experienced by its main participants? Such questions led to further inquiries which have in turn provided the data for the present book.

This book has been organized in two parts. The first part considers the place of adoptive kinship in the context of interpersonal relations, tracing crucial steps that led to the Shared Fate theory. The second part has as its focus the institutional arrangements — social services and laws — which make adoptive family life possible. Now it becomes evident that there are links between interpersonal strains and institutional contradictions.

Here then is this book's thesis about adoptive kinship: given that the adoptive situation at the interpersonal level is objectively different from the situation of the family based on consanguinity, the solidarity of the adoptive family's membership is enhanced when their atypical reality is acknowledged in their daily relationship. These findings from *Shared Fate* have here been given more firmly founded verification. In addition, we have now the background picture showing that the institutional arrangements which were intended to create solid and satisfying new family relationships, are not without responsibility for the strains inherent in modern adoptive kinship. Thus while legal and administrative dogmas assert that adoptive kinship is to be the social equivalent of consanguineal kinship, a number of aspects of family and property law, as well as administrative practices, create results that belie these dogmas. Such contradictions make the present circumstances of adoptive kinship untenable for millions of adult adoptees in the United States and Canada, and also for many birthparents and adoptive parents.

While the substantive focus of this book is adoptive kinship, the underlying theme refers to institution-building and thus modernization. We recall that modernization involves more than technological change and urbanization, but that it calls into being transitions from status-based social relations to relations and arrangements mainly organized around contract. Modernization and the institutional apparatus it brings with it thus involves shifts from traditional social forms to rationally contrived ones. Such shifts occur in the circumstances of modern adoption. In the strains and contradictions that are here shown to accompany adoptive kinship one may see intimations of the kind of hidden results that accompany modernization. With its theme of reform of a modern institution, this book reminds that in the open society rational planning is necessary and possible, but never final or conclusive.

Addendum 1985

That reminder is of course applicable to the family in general, and therefore to family policy. While modernization of the family as institution has in recent decades advanced, that has been principally true for the institutional arrangements of marriage, divorce, and cohabitation. How little the laws of North American jurisdictions have done to modernize the institutional arrangements of family-building after divorce becomes evident in the drama of the ever-increasing phenomenon of remarriage. Where children from a previous marriage obtain a new parent through the custodial parent's remarriage, should the law simply allow adoptions to be made automatically, as if the arrangement were "all in the family"? That is one of the questions that have not been properly confronted in either Canadian or United States jurisdictions. Here, in the larger field of family policy, we see a critical case of hidden forces resulting from modernization – in this case the modernization of divorce law. The focus of this book is then indeed a focus of social change and rational planning, with special emphasis on family policy.

Part I

Shared Fate
Revisited

Chapter 1

Up From Trivia

"The adoption of children is a major means by which adults can alter the membership of that basic social unit, the elementary family. We may consequently expect that, where adoption is frequently resorted to, it will have important effects on the structure of the society and the personality dynamics of the people involved. The comparative study of the role of adoption in diverse societies will increase our insight into the functions of the family in society." With these sentences began an article in the *American Anthropologist* more than 25 years ago. (Weckler, 1953: 555) The author of that article reported there his study of the people of Mokil, a tiny Oceanic island which in 1947 had a population of 425. Weckler found that for almost two centuries the people of Mokil had practised adoption so frequently that it is not uncommon for as many as one third of all children born on Mokil to be adopted by households other than those of their birthparents. Weckler's interest in adoption was not new in anthropology. Scholars like Boas (1888), Lowie (1930), and Firth (1936) had decades earlier recognized the importance of adoption for the understanding of preliterate societies. More recently Dunning (1957, 1962), Spencer (1959), and Willmott (1961) have observed and commented on the apparent functions of adoption in the life of Inuit peoples.

In contrast, sociologists have seldom dealt with adoption as an issue worthy of their consideration. Even textbooks on the family seldom show adoption as an entry in their subject indices, and then almost exclusively in terms of social welfare arrangements for the parentless child.[1] Only in one specialized area has there lately been some evidence of sociological interest, namely the adoption of children across racial lines.[2]

How is this difference between two sister disciplines, so similar in outlook and method of study, to be understood? One possible answer may be found in the fact that kinship arrangements are central in preliterate societies and of far less importance in urban-industrial ones. Anthropologists have traditionally concerned themselves principally with the former, sociologists with the latter forms of human association. When I began sociological research into adoptive kinship almost three decades ago, I may have tried to understand the discrepancy in interest among different branches of social scientists in this way. Also I probably reasoned that, whereas preliterate peoples readily shifted children between nuclear families, making adoption a common practice, among us it has mainly been practised as an emergency measure, and so is

3

far less frequently resorted to. Although reliable adoption statistics are not generally available in North America, it has been estimated that between two and four per cent of the population is adopted. Thus the phenomenon of adoption may properly have seemed sociologically trivial when seen in the context of numbers in modern kinship and family life.

For some time, I have been less than satisfied with this explanation of the discrepancy between anthropological and sociological degrees of interest in adoption. We know that for several decades there has been a remarkably sustained interest in adoption among wider publics, perhaps animated by news stories involving war orphans, teen-age pregnancies, abortion and related issues. And this interest has most likely a far sounder and more permanent motivating force than news stories or soap operas. The five, six, or seven million adoptees estimated among the child population become much enlarged when we consider the number of people who are intimately linked to each adoptee. Let me estimate for each adoptee a birthmother and two adoptive parent figures, one sibling, and one adoptive grandparent. With the adoptee, that makes six interested parties. When the adoptee is 30 years old, let us have him or her live in a household with a marriage partner and one child. The number of people directly and intimately related to adoption has now become eight. Assuming a low figure of five million adoptees, that figure can be multiplied by eight, so that in a population of two hundred million, one fifth of the people are directly or intimately linked to the experience of adoption. For urban and suburban areas, where it is believed that adoption is more concentrated than in rural ones, the proportion of the population thus connected to adoption is even higher. In the light of such numerical significance, how is one to account for the trivialization of adoption among sociologists? For a tentative answer, let me refer briefly to that well established guide to cultural meanings in our society, the Dewey Decimal Index.[3] It tells us how librarians have for some time classified the entire range of our cultural life. There we find "Marriage and family" to be classed under the Social Sciences (300) and Sociology (301). In contrast, "Adoption and placement services" is classed under "Welfare services to special groups — Scope: rehabilitation" (362):

362.1 welfare services to the physically ill
362.2 . . . to the mentally ill
362.3 . . . to the mentally retarded
362.4 . . . to those suffering physical handicaps and disablements
362.5 . . . to the poor
362.6 . . . to the aged and infirm, to survivors and dependants
362.7 . . . to the young (Child welfare)
Aid to infants, children, adolescents through aid to mothers, *adoption and placement services*, child guidance clinics, junior republics.

In other words, adoption is not classed as a cultural item with "family" or "kinship" but with "welfare services" and "rehabilitation" of people in need.

This fact may shed some light on the peculiar myopia which makes adoption appear sociologically trivial. "Welfare" and its professional exponent, social work, have long been less than attractive companions for sociology. Social work emphasizes practicality and application; sociology emphasizes theory and research. If both deal with the human condition, they do so in very different contexts. Sociology had just become academically respectable when professional schools of social work first made their way into the American universities. The former discipline was concerned with its academic purity, the latter with its prerogatives as a nascent helping profession. Neither wished to be confused with the other, but both were. Thus, as long as adoption stood for "welfare," it denoted an identity which made it less than attractive to sociologists.

A personal encounter illustrates how this rivalry seems to have worked. During the summer of 1958 I had presented a paper at the annual meetings of the National Council on Family Relations, held at Eugene, Oregon. There Professor Harold T. Christensen, then editor of *Marriage and Family Living,* asked me to submit my paper to his journal for possible publication. I agreed, and on returning to McGill University I made some minor revisions, whereupon the paper was accepted for publication.[4] However, to my surprise the editors asked me to furnish the name of a social work specialist in adoption, who might in the same issue of the journal comment on my paper. I suggested Henry S. Maas,[5] then Professor of Social Welfare at the University of California, Berkeley. At the time I was startled by the request, for it was not common for such discussions to appear in the journal. Looking back, I find the editor's action entirely in keeping with the circumstances surrounding adoption, which was then seen as the professional preserve of social welfare. To a very large extent it has remained so.

In light of the almost universal lack of interest by the sociologists of the early nineteen fifties, it becomes pertinent to ask what brought me to this inquiry and what kept me engaged in it for so many years. I had begun graduate studies in 1948, assuming that training in sociology would equip me for helping to build a more humane and peaceful world. In that assumption I was probably not so different from others who had been aged and motivated by the war years, and were now returning to university to complete their studies. Looking back, I realize that I was naïve in what I expected to learn from graduate training in social science. But this naïveté may also have stood me in good stead. It made me formulate ideas for research which, while far beyond my own capabilities and perhaps those of my discipline, were informed by the great questions of classical sociology. One could not have seen the rise and impact of the Nazi juggernaut and not have longed for a world in which human beings counted as intrinsically valuable rather than as mere commodities. As a teenager, I had been strongly influenced by the romanticism of the German youth movement, with its emphasis on interpersonal relations and community. Once I read Tönnies and Weber as an undergraduate, I seemed to rediscover these values in academically acceptable form. This is how I came to concentrate my last two years as an undergraduate in trying to understand the problems of flagging solidarity in contemporary parliamentary democracies.[6] In more specific terms of national allegiance and loyalty, this question then informed my first two years of graduate study and the resulting thesis.[7] By the summer of 1950 I had begun the next phase of graduate study, research for the doctorate. Yet the old question was still with me: in a world which had only recently freed itself from the irrational ideology and the divisive power of Nazism, how might inclusive human community life be rationally advanced? This question, which was on many minds at the time, seemed especially urgent in light of the heterogeneity, intergroup conflict, and competitive social mobility which characterized American society in the post-war era.

During that summer, a personal issue lent new poignancy to the old political question. My wife and I had long hoped for children, but had been unable to produce them. So we applied to adopt, and while waiting, had taken two little girls as foster children. The two sisters would join their own family again within a year; we were anxious for a baby by the time they were to leave. I had begun to think about my experience as a foster father and in what ways this would be similar to or different from my future as an adoptive parent. This kind of questioning sent me in search of literature about adoption. I soon found that between romanticized popular accounts ("adopting is such a wonderful experience") and professional warnings ("social work investigations seek to prevent people with the wrong motives from getting children"), I was not really being educated. I therefore decided to try to think the matter out as best I might on my own. It was in this way that I thought I saw a connection between my earlier research and my newer personal questions about adoptive parenthood. I asked myself what the principal characteristics of social relationships are in adoption. Thus I became aware that the microcosm of adoptive kinship also contains heterogeneity, conflicting interests, and social mobility. Here the heterogeneity is given by the differences in backgrounds and genetic histories of adoptive parents and children. Conflicts of interest arise between birthparents, mediating professionals, and adoptive applicants. Social mobility is evident when unwed mothers can begin a life without the responsibilities of a baby to care for and support, when children with the stigma of illegitimate birth are legitimated through legal adoption, and when involuntarily childless people move by adoption into the status of parenthood. But what intrigued me most, beyond these similarities of a large-scale modern social organization and the micro-system of adoptive kinship, was the utility expected of adoption as a social device. Was it not intended as a means for creating that most elemental type of human community, namely kinship, out of a medley of previously unrelated persons and backgrounds? Furthermore, was this not to be achieved through the application of instrumental rationality — by legal and social contrivance — in lieu of the process of nature?

Here, then, seemed to be an opportunity to study the problem of rationally devised community in minute detail. So I began to plan a doctoral investigation around the intriguing possibilities of adoptive family relationships. Looking back on those days, I must admit that once again I was less astute than my previous sociological education and training should have made me. I failed to recognize that sociological theory did not provide the knowledge necessary for translating information from small-scale social systems to the situations that apply to large-scale systems. Yet had I been fully aware of my error, I would most likely not have undertaken the long trek into this relatively unknown territory.

What fascinates me in retrospect is that years later I learned that my sociological hunches about adoption as involving community-making were not so far-fetched. Thus Dunning (1962: 259) quotes Spencer's observations on North Alaskan Inuit adoption, and his view that the practice served to "extend the kinship circle and hence the bonds of cooperation" (1959: 87). Moreover, much more recent data on adoption in Alaska bear out this view of its function. Thus in 1974 of 320 white children, 80 or 25 per cent were adopted by unrelated persons, while of 203 native children, 147 or 72 per cent were adopted by persons previously unrelated to the children.[8] While these observations refer to a preliterate group, a surprising parallel was noted as applying to a developing but essentially modern society. In 1968 I received a communication from Mrs. Aviva Lion, Head of Adoption Services in Israel's Ministry of Social Welfare. She wrote: ". . . we are faced in Israel with the immense problem of integration of immigrants and to me the task seems to be not to eliminate the differences, but to bridge over them, so that my interest in the concept of 'acknowledgment of difference vs. rejection of difference' is self-evident." Elsewhere she said: "In Israel it seems that adoptive parents (and children) are faced with an additional strain and this is an ethnic disparity between the two groups. . . 75 per cent of unwed mothers are of Afro-Asiatic origin, [while] 60 per cent of the adoptive parents are of European-American-Oceanic origin. . . ."

But I seem to be getting ahead of my story. First I must deal with research questions which my peculiar position as adoptive parent opened up for me. In my early notes there are recurrent observations to the effect that adoptive family relations do not have the same connotation of "kinship" as do those based on consanguinity. Clues leading to this realization came from many sources — from the remarks of outsiders as well as our relatives, from experiences with social work investigations and writings, and from an inspection of legal statutes regulating adoption. My doctoral thesis was mainly based on a study of public opinions and attitudes as these relate to adoption. I recall very clearly how I felt during 1952 when I had collected 183 interviews with householders in a small city of upstate New York. These interviews centered on attitudes toward family life and children, and also touched on infertility and adoption. The respondents were carefully selected to exclude people who had adopted children or were themselves adopted. When I analyzed the results from these interviews, it became apparent that along a number of value and attitude lines the adoptive relationship was not seen as the equivalent of the procreative family. For me, just then beginning life with a small adopted daughter, it was a hard blow, for I knew full well that we do not make our own environment. Other people, and their attitudes and views, are the social environment which in large measure directs our thinking of ourselves and our lives. I knew that I wanted to be a father; I did not want to be reminded of the fact that I found myself as parent in an atypical position in social life. This event draws attention to a conflict between my manner of working and the then dominant view among social scientists that the researcher ought to be emotionally detached from the subject of his inquiry. Thus I was not unaware of the risk which the link between my theoretical interests and my personal involvement posed for me as professional sociologist. If the early studies of adoptive kinship yielded discoveries that were personally disturbing to me, this fact was grist for the mill of "affective neutrality," the warning against personal involvement. The blow to my aspirations for full and unqualified parenthood, deriving from the discovery that the adoptive family was not regarded as the equivalent of the mainstream family, led me temporarily to abandon this type of research. In 1953 I reported my findings in a doctoral dissertation and then turned to academic activities less threatening to me personally.

This "holiday" from studies of adoptive kinship lasted about a year. Then a number of circumstances turned my attention back. During the latter part of 1954 I had a request from the Child Welfare League of America, which had initiated an inquiry into current adoption practices and was planning a National Conference on Adoption, to be held in Chicago in January 1955. I was asked to prepare a paper based on my doctoral research. My paper dealt with community values as an aspect of the adopted child's heritage. The result was that I received offers from several social work administrators in different parts of the United States and Canada for their agencies' cooperation in continuing research. I picked up the thread of adoption research by designing an inquiry into the ways in which adoptive parents experienced the attitudes of others, and how they adjusted to these experiences. When it was undertaken, this research involved more than fifteen hundred adoptive family households in two Canadian provinces and three U.S. states. What their reports showed was that the majority of adopters seemed to deny what had to me become so painfully clear: the culturally given difference between our kind of parenthood and that of the mainstream family. This fact I came to call "rejection-of-difference." I wondered how this false consciousness among adopters came about, what forces fed it. In answer I formulated the idea of "role handicap"[9] or barriers to the enactment of socially required actions. I surmised that limitations to role enactment such as those experienced by involuntarily childless people, might lead to a false consciousness, or "sour grapes" attitude. At the same time I asked myself what the consequences of such false consciousness might be for the parent-child relationship in adoption. I suspected that it was not good for that relationship, and that rejection-of-difference, or false consciousness on the part of adoptive parents, would tend to disturb their relationship with the adopted child, since it probably inhibited their capacity for empathy with the special problems that only the adoptee experiences. The result, I argued, would be diminished communication with the adopted child, and therefore probably less strong solidarity between the members of the adoptive kin group.

There in a nutshell is the theory which was developed in *Shared Fate*. The theory became widely known and accepted, at least in English-speaking countries, during the sixties and seventies. I had not expected such results; of course they were gratifying, especially when I found continuing scholarship based on my pioneering studies and formulations. But there were other developments resulting from the theory which were at least as exciting as having one's work publicly acknowledged and used.

During 1962, while beginning the manuscript which became *Shared Fate*, I recalled an insight of mine that adoptive kinship seemed cognate to certain common aspects of modern social life. But whereas earlier I had principally considered the heterogeneity of modern society, now I thought about the ubiquity of drastic change. Technological and attendant social changes are the everyday experience of human beings in contemporary social life. In adoption studies I had seen how drastic changes led people into building their families by artificial means, and that even when the families had been constituted, drastic and unexpected changes were part of the members' lot. As in the larger society, change meant role handicaps for the members of adoptive families, and role handicaps called for ingenuity to cope with the impediments. I had discussed such thoughts with a colleague, George K. Zollschan, who was in the process of putting together a book on social change. He asked whether I would provide a chapter, and that is how in 1963, about the time *Shared Fate* was finished, I produced the article for the Zollschan and Hirsch book.[10] In it, I sought ways in which the role handicap insights I had gained in the adoption studies could be applied to other change-induced human predicaments.

Early in 1964 both *Shared Fate* and the Zollschan and Hirsch book were published. I had left McGill and joined the fledgling sociology department at the University of Waterloo. By 1966 I had begun to introduce my ideas on social change and human coping behavior into my courses. That year I had a young woman student with a congenital defect: she had been born without a right hand. I noticed that she kept her right arm carefully hidden under the table, and wrote with her left. Toward the end of the term, this student came to see me. I saw the stump where a right hand should have been, and wondered why she would expose it now. Then she said: "I want you to know that your book made me aware of the fact that I was rejecting my physical difference from others." Yet she had resisted pressure from various sources to wear a prosthetic device, pressure which had come not only from lay people but from members of the helping professions. She especially recalled a school nurse who had counseled wearing an artificial hand. Now, years later, my former student is married and has two pre-school children. She remarked to me recently how important this openness is for her relationship with other people, especially her children, for they must deal with other children's inquiries. Not long ago she showed her arm to a neighbor's four-year-old daughter who had asked about it. The neighbor is a social worker, but was nonetheless surprised at such candor. Thus my former student's insightful application of the social-change-in-adoption theory to her own different predicament eased her relationship with others for whom her defect might otherwise have been an obstacle.

The paper for Zollschan and Hirsch's book had at the time been a minor issue for me. Hearing my student's moving story that day in 1966 made the question of human coping with drastic change into a major and long-term interest.[11] Such events are as important for keeping up one's commitment to inquiry, as the public acceptance of one's work.

In coming to the end of this first chapter, I want to note that I have already begun to report here in a manner that shall be maintained throughout this book. I shall move back and forth in descriptions and analyses between relatively objective data and subjective, phenomenological ones. In that sense my writing will reflect the research on which it is based. Once I made up my mind in 1955 to pick up the threads of my research, the work became increasingly useful to me personally. What I learned now was no longer so much threatening as challenging; it suggested new ways of approaching problems associated with adoption in the context of my life in the family. The work provided me with increasingly exciting ideas for the pursuit of systematic sociological research. Thus what had occurred was far from the feared contamination of the scientific character of my work. But for all the benefits that experience and insight provided to the large research undertaking to which I was now so clearly committed, there continued to be serious obstacles to its acceptance by fellow sociologists. Thus during the nineteen fifties and well into the next decade, it was generally understood in our discipline that the editors of respected journals expected from contributors a particular style of reporting. That style tended to emphasize the "scientific" character of data, generally precluding the recall of the rich, if less systematic, realm of personal experience. Not only my very subject matter, but the manner in which I approached it, tended to reinforce the impression that I was engaged in work which was sociologically trivial. It is therefore not surprising that when I wrote *Shared Fate* in 1962-63, I de-emphasized the personal side of my inquiry. Now, a good many years later, the atmosphere in academic social science has radically changed. The dynamic interplay between the observer and the world of external social facts is now given increasing and dignified recognition. Participant observation, once a respectable method widely used by Chicago's urban sociologists, had for four decades been eclipsed by more structured methods of social research. Lately it has come back into favor. Works like Goffman's *Asylums* (1961) and the methodological treatises by Cicourel (1964) and Glaser and Strauss (1967) helped to relegitimate the inductive approaches of the phenomenologist as part of the systematic work of social science exploration. As there is now more openness and less cant in social science writings generally, I feel encouraged to speak in more personal terms also about my work.

NOTES

1. Floyd Martinson's *Family in Society* (1970) discusses adoption in a section labelled "Family Welfare Services"; Gerald Leslie's *The Family in Social Context* (1973) has four entries about adoption, the first one on ancient China (p. 100), a second on ancient Rome (p. 173), and a third among Germanic tribes (p. 179). Only the fourth entry (p. 673) refers to adoption in contemporary North America, but the reference is embedded in the report of a study on the relationships of older parents with their children. Leslie notes that among other circumstances "the late adoption of a young child. . . [prolonged] the years of parental responsibility in some cases." Thus the interest in adoption was either antiquarian or utterly oblique.

2. Diana Conway Robertson. "Parental Socialization Patterns in Interracial Adoption," unpublished Ph.D. dissertation in Sociology, University of California at Los Angeles, 1974; Rita James Simon and Howard Alstein, *Transracial Adoption*, 1977 and Arnold R. Silverman and William Feigelman, "Some Factors Affecting the Adoption of Minority Children," *Social Casework* 58 (November 1977): 554-61.

3. Melvil Dewey, *Dewey Decimal Classification and Relative Index*, 1965.

4. H. David Kirk, "A Dilemma of Adoptive Parenthood: Incongruous Role Obligations," *Marriage and Family Living*, Vol. XXI, No. 4 (Nov. 1959), pp. 316-328.

5. At the time I was troubled by Maas' discussion of my paper; today I recognize his critique to have been generally sound. Furthermore he saw what many of his colleagues in social work did not: that the adopted experience special troubles in spite of all the benefits:

> . . .I do not mean to deny the potentially difficult psychological situation of "revelation" for the child who is seeking to establish his identity. "Who am I?" is a central psycho-cultural problem of our times.* For the adoptive child, the question, "Where did I come from?" has a far more complicated answer than most children discover. But the immediate issue is the role of adoptive parent, and if in this special type of parental role the mental health assumption of human imperfection and the mental health principle of acceptance of such imperfection were deeply implanted as a basis for expected behavior, wherever "non-fecundity" and "revelation" were at issue they would be accompanied by some kind of (sad?) acceptance. It may be that it is the effort to present our children only with the myth of parental perfection which is socially dysfunctional. Where this occurs, painfully honest adoptive parents and children may, by comparison, have the advantage.

> *See Allen Wheelis, *The Quest for Identity*, New York: Norton, 1958.

6. I wrote a somewhat labored undergraduate honors thesis, in the course of which I became acquainted with much of the literature later required in graduate work: H. David Kirk, "Some Aspects of the Problems Caused by Weakened Social Ties," unpublished Sociology honors thesis, The City College of New York, 1948.

7. "The Loyalties of Men in Crisis," unpublished M.A. thesis, Cornell University, 1950.

8. I am indebted to Janice Rae Cole, Research Analyst in the Health Information

Systems Section, Department of Health and Social Services, State of Alaska, for making this previously unpublished information available to me.

9. First used in my paper "A Dilemma of Adoptive Parenthood: Incongruous Role Obligations," 1959, *op. cit.,* the concept was given professional recognition when in 1968 it appeared as an entry in G. Duncan Mitchell's *Dictionary of Sociology.*

> **role-handicap.** A term introduced into sociological literature by H.D. Kirk (see his *Shared Fate: A Theory of Adoption and Mental Health,* 1964) to point the contrasts between people in certain kinds of situations, where the culture provides in the one case for behavioural expectations, and in the other case it does not do so, or does so inadequately. Thus, for example, adopting parents are role-handicapped as compared with natural parents in some instances, such as the death of child, for natural parents will receive the support of understanding and sympathy of family and friends readily and firmly, whereas there is no great likelihood that an equivalent degree of support would be forthcoming to help adoptive parents, whose grief may be no less. Again, the situation of people facing disaster is different if the disaster occurs during war-time, when the populace is prepared for hardships, than it is in peace-time, when they are less prepared psychologically, and we may say that the latter represents a case of role-handicap. G.D.M.

Although "role handicap" is cognate to Professor Goode's concept of "role strain," there is also a significant difference between the two ideas. Whereas "role strain" was defined by Goode as "the felt difficulty in fulfilling role obligations" (William J. Goode, "A Theory of Role Strain," *American Sociological Review,* 25, No. 4, 1960, p. 483), I have defined "role handicap" as the objective condition which stands in the way of fulfilling role obligations, whether or not the role incumbent or aspirant feels it or is aware of it.

10. H. David Kirk, "The Impact of Drastic Change on Social Relations," published in George K. Zollschan and Walter Hirsch, *Explorations in Social Change,* 1964.

11. I had come to the conclusion that my attempt at creating a useful model of generic role handicap types had not been successful as developed in the 1964 paper (see Note 10 above). When Zollschan and Hirsch decided to bring out a new edition of their book, they asked whether I wanted to update my paper. Except for a similar introduction, the paper which appeared in 1976 is new and lays the groundwork for systematic theorizing about the impact of drastic change on social structures, social relations, and social selves. H. David Kirk, "Toward a Taxonomy of Social Discontinuities," in Zollschan and Hirsch, *Social Change,* 1976.

Chapter 2

Social Ground for Human Identity

In the stories and myths of humanity one finds a recurring question. It asks who we are, whence we come and whither we are bound. It is the question of meaning and destiny, inherent in the lore of primitive people as well as in our own. The reply may be,with equal justice, "We are descended from the Sun," or "We are created in the image of God." The question, so posed, concerns our collective identity, at least to the extent of our vision of community.

This corporate identity has its counterpart in questions of private identity. "Who am I?" Here no myth and no cosmology can fully solve the problem. I must have some sense of my personal identity to carry on social intercourse, and to live with equanimity and effectiveness I must have an assured knowledge of self, the bases of which are never seriously questioned. This view of the social nature of the self has only recently been rediscovered by the disciplines which deal with the emotions. It holds that disturbances in the psychic life of persons are often, even typically, reflections of faulty or disturbed interpersonal relationships; thus the self is created in the context of interpersonal relations, and the success of our early relations within the family determines the success with which we become fully human.

Myths and fictions flourish in the realm of the collective; in the private world of the individual, however, such "misperceptions of self" are generally not tolerated. If a man were to think himself into being a king or deity, he would likely be cut down, if not physically, then to his native dimensions. What the crucial persons around us, in our groups, "the significant others" as they have been called, define as our real selves must be adhered to fairly strictly if we want to remain members in good standing.

Yet many of the positions we are called on to fill require of us, in the beginning at least, some sort of fiction. We may have thought about parenthood long before we became parents, yet on the day we ourselves entered that new position for the first time, we had to make believe that we knew how to enact it properly. The majority of people know something of what parenthood is about — we have mostly experienced life with a father and/or a mother — yet on the day we ourselves become either father or mother it has a novel quality, so we invent the fiction that we know what it is like and can act it out in confidence. This kind of fiction is both necessary and allowed, for it enables people to learn the ropes of some newly acquired position in social life.

Thus our self-conception, our identity as seen from the inside, is at times in flux, however secure it needs to be over the long haul. Our identity changes with new situations. Of course some center of organization remains, for otherwise we would be lost, and others who have to deal with us would find it hard to recognize us. But given drastic changes in our life situation — changes in which it becomes necessary to perform novel tasks, or in which we are threatened with difficulties hitherto unsuspected — in such circumstances one may be forced to review one's identity and summon all intuitive forces to the task of reorganizing the field of inward forces.

Identity is a part of selfhood: every self-conscious human being must have an identity of some sort. What we learned from anthropology is the fact that there are common expressions of identity or personality within cultures, that the social self is in part derived from the milieu in which it is embedded. In that sense we no longer talk glibly about "human nature," realizing that the elements which are common to us are also elements of a potentiality which is enormously flexible and variable. At the same time we recognize that selves are manifold and different from each other.

How do our identities come into being? How do we learn to become the people we become over a lifetime? The sociological view, first fully formulated by G.H. Mead, is that it begins by what he called "role-taking," namely taking the attitudes and views that others have of us as our own, by learning to see ourselves through their eyes, and acting by means of their standards. This view makes the process of socialization, of child-rearing and later adult learning, into the mechanism by which personal identity is shaped. Since the family is the forum in which, for the majority of people, these early learnings take place, we can regard the family as crucial for the creation of individual identity. There the person is given those earliest significant experiences, which make up the core of the social self. The family provides for the developing person a matrix of belongingness. One becomes similar to the others in the family because one is considered to belong with them, and accepts that view.

When an infant is born into a family, he is typically besieged by the members with one query: whom does he resemble? It has often seemed to me that these people are not so much concerned with some particular likeness as with membership and belongingness. They may really be asking whether the new member resembles others in the group sufficiently to become one of them. I suspect that their concern with resemblance conceals questions like these: will the new member come to act like one of us? Will she or he come to feel, think, and respond to the world's and our own stimuli as we would? Any external likeness is taken as reassurance that all is well. Nonetheless, the questioners would probably admit that they themselves are not unimportant in making the new member into the likeness of the group. They would probably recognize that their ways of speaking and walking, their gestures and their preferences enter the life of the newcomer so that in this way they themselves are crucial in helping to form his or her identity. Of course what also irritates some of them is that the new member does not simply become a composite likeness of them all, but that, for all the socializing influences of the group, he also remains to an extent new, separate, and strange — forever defying their inquiries and marking him or her as an individual.

In fact, once the ground of belongingness has been assured, the growing child can afford to note and act out his or her own separateness and individuality with impunity, perhaps even with pride. The family is thus of prime importance as the setting in which one becomes identified with a group of special people, people among whom one gains an identity both as a member and as a separate person. Let us consider a factor that aids in this process: human beings who find themselves in the relationship of parents and children have a strong tie to each other, a tie that they know existed before their social intercourse began. That is so because they have in common a bio-social past which makes them each part of a long line of kin. It is this *prima facie* connection that the adoptive parent-child relationship lacks. In societies where adoption is a valued and common pattern of parenting, the lack of the blood tie may mean little; in North America it has in recent years meant a great deal, surprising as that may appear. Thus adoption must in some way reflect this lack. Meanwhile, let us return briefly to the question of identity in the context of the family, but with special emphasis on adoptive kinship.

At this point I want to tell of an event which occurred in my own family. In my notes from the latter part of 1955 there is an entry that much later helped me formulate a theory of adoptive relationships. In *Shared Fate* I told the events impersonally, for my children were still too small to give their consent to such personal revelations. Our daughter Francie, then not quite five, had pressed to have the story of Cinderella read to her at bedtime. Evening after evening she asked for it, and then she would have nightmares and wet her bed. Ruth Kirk began to suspect a connection between Francie's insistence on the story and her nightmares and bedwetting. But before Ruth could decide how to deal with it, Francie made the overture herself. She said casually, "Mommy, if I had a stepmother, what would she do to me, would she be cruel?" Recognizing in this question our little daughter's struggle with the meaning of her adoption, Ruth replied: "Francie dear, I too am someone like a stepmother. I was unable to bear you in my body, but I love you very, very much. Perhaps there are stepmothers who are bad, who would be mean to their children. Cinderella's stepmother *was* a very bad mother, but only because she did not love Cinderella."

Why bring up such dangerous stuff, I thought at the time. Who knows what Francie might make of it? Why emphasize a difference that we all know too well is real for adoptive parents and children? I had wanted to interrupt Ruth and change the subject, but somehow I thought better of it. And it was good that I held my peace, for after a pause during which Francie seemed occupied with her toys she said: "Now I can have a *good* dream." And so it seems to have happened, for the bedwetting and the nightmares did not recur. I was aware that something important had occurred, but did not realize that this event was a preview of what subsequent research was to tell me impersonally: it was really a demonstration of Shared Fate in action.

Between 1957, when the bulk of my Canadian and U.S. survey data had been processed and analyzed, and 1963, when *Shared Fate* was completed, I conducted follow-up studies of subgroups of survey respondents and field investigations of adoptive parent groups. The most important achievement for me during those years, however, was not in the empirical research, but in making sense of the multitude of information gathered. During 1959 I saw for the first time that my data could be sorted, in jigsaw-puzzle fashion, to make sense of the complex set of circumstances that had begun to emerge. Actually, I first discerned a series of events which drew my attention to the riddle that was formulated later. The finding was that adopters engaged in behaviors which seemed puzzling: why should they want to deny differences which were all too apparent? If I were to point to any one principal event in the long research sequence which was to prove seminal for the entire enterprise, it was when I discerned certain patterns of conduct among adopters which required explanation. I tried to look behind the behaviors to possible causes, and it seemed to me that adopters were experiencing structural constraints that hindered the performance of tasks socially required of parents generally. This was the phenomenon to which I gave the name "role handicap."

Now it was possible to think about a theory of adoption — a theory that would try to explain adoptive parental behavior. Such a theory was indeed not far behind. With this theory in hand, one could now ask how different structural arrangements of family life, among them adoption, influence the social and perhaps even physical development of children. These questions became the focus of a study which, together with Professor K. Jonassohn, I conducted in Eastern Canada during the mid-nineteen sixties. With this I had expected to conclude my many researches into the dynamics of adoptive kinship.

By the beginning of the past decade, a development led me to rethink much of what I had done over the years. By then the small and few groups of adopted adults which had existed since the nineteen fifties had grown and proliferated, and in Jean Paton's prophetic words, the adopted had indeed broken the silence. What the old and newer organizations of adopted adults were saying was in effect that they considered themselves inequitably dealt with by the legal and administrative arrangements that surround adoptive kinship. I had been generally aware of this movement before, but had not asked myself what its increasingly insistent calls for justice meant from the point of view of my previous work. At about that time, two different events coincided to focus my attention on the issues raised by the adoptee associations. My publisher had just suggested a revised edition of *Shared Fate*, which would include information from the more recent studies. A month or so later I met a Californian who had found *Shared Fate* of special value in her search for understanding her own adoption. She was adopted shortly after birth by a couple in comfortable circumstances. As adolescent and young woman, she had felt keenly the confusion about her background, wishing for a more intimate knowledge, but sensing that her adoptive parents were anxious for her to leave things well enough alone. Being an avid reader, she scoured the public libraries for better knowledge about adoption and the cultural world in which her adoptive parents had been formed. She sought to know what had made them so anxious to keep uncomfortable questions from being raised. One day she came across *Shared Fate*. We met through a mutual friend to whom she had confided her sense of discovery. My book had, she said, for the first time revealed to her some important parts of the inner world of her parents. Her anger over their anxious silence concerning her origins had lessened once she understood what had led them to where they were, why they had acted as they had. She had begun to make inquiries about her background. When her curiosity was satisfied, she was able to make her peace with her own history and accept her adoptive parents as her parents, "warts and all."

These events combined to urge a new rendering of the Shared Fate theory. I came to realize that what I had done earlier pointed the way to an understanding not only of the role handicaps of adoptive parents but also of adopted persons. I decided therefore to write not a revision of *Shared Fate* but a new book which would take account of the newly evolving circumstances. Yet, however much there are now new conditions in which adoptive kinship must be viewed, the central premises of the Shared Fate theory remain; if anything, the new circumstances have strengthened the theory's arguments. At the heart of these arguments is the fact that every human being requires social ground in which to develop and on which to stand.

One of the social scientists who worked most creatively with this premise of "social ground" as the matrix of human identity was Kurt Lewin. He regarded social ground to be vital for all children, and especially for those of minority status. He believed that such social ground was more readily provided where the significant others — particularly the child's parent figures — could deal realistically with their minority circumstances and explain their own and the child's life situations as impersonally (e.g., historically) shaped. In the main these views are strongly supported by all the research findings which I made since 1955. But as we know, human consciousness does not revolve around stark impersonal reality alone. Our minds, our inward worlds, and our social actions tend to transform historical reality into explanations that make stark necessity more meaningful perhaps, certainly more livable. I want to illustrate this process with two stories of children who, in their own way, sought to deal with the problem of social ground, when that ground was not firm enough for them.

In the fall of 1949 Ruth Kirk and I agreed to make a temporary home for two little sisters, aged five and six, whose mother was hospitalized and whose father was finishing his professional training in another state. Let me call them Wendy and Rose, the latter being the older sister. The two children had been with us for a few weeks when one afternoon, after they had come home from school, I asked them to accompany me on a brief shopping trip. I was walking faster than Wendy and Rose, who were a couple of yards behind me. I had been thinking my own thoughts when I heard Wendy say almost plaintively, "He does *so* look like Daddy." (The girl's father is a six-footer while I am short; he is blonde while I am dark.) Rose's reply to her sister was a slap and a reminder never to confuse the two of us! I was both surprised and dismayed at the time, but held my peace. I did not turn around or enter the conversation, but I remembered it often in the ensuing months. Wendy and Rose were our foster daughters for two years, during which time Wendy sought, time and again, to create for herself the illusion that we were her real parents, while Rose stood sturdily for her true family membership. I remember how much I felt with both girls. It would have been lovely had they been able to remain as our daughters. But we knew from the beginning that this was impossible, and so Rose's definition of the situation was the one which we helped to emphasize for both children. Here is a case of two developing human beings needing social ground on which to affirm their identities. Wendy sought to do so by myth, Rose by her fierce remembering where they belonged and would in time return.

A second case has to do with two women students whom I was able to interview early in my work for the doctorate. I had put an advertisement in the personals column of the university student newspaper, making it known that I was beginning research into adoptive kinship and asking students who had been adopted to contact me for some exploratory interviews. One of the students was Laura. She appeared poised and self-confident, but was not particularly helpful when I asked her about other people's attitudes toward adoption. Not until I dropped the subject of community attitudes completely would Laura speak freely about herself as an adoptee. She told how her mother had avoided speaking of the adoption and how the first inkling she got of it was when her father called her into his study and told her about it. She was then eleven years old. "For two days I stayed in my room and cried — I felt as if all the ground had slipped out from under me. But after that I found myself again." Laura added that she thought adoptive parents should not wait as long as hers did to tell the child the truth, but should do so while the child is still very young — as soon as the words can be understood.

My next notes of the interview refer to some remarks of my own. Apparently I said: "As you may know, adoption is very common among certain preliterate peoples. Anthropologists have recorded such practices and have noted that under circumstances of widespread adoption, some persons may never know whether they are members of their kin group by birth or by adoption. What would you say to that situation? Would you say that there, too, adopted persons should be told as early as possible about their position in family and society?" Laura's reply was, "No, I don't think that would be necessary." When I asked why not, she added: "Well, I think in such a society it does not really matter." I noted the discrepancy of this and her earlier statement about our society. She acknowledged the discrepancy, but explained it by saying: "You see, here, among us it *does* matter." Laura's viewpoint will become more understandable as we move through the next two chapters. For the time being, I note that she dealt here with reality, but almost immediately thereafter moved into myth. Laura continued her remarks spontaneously, telling me about an older sister who is also adopted. "Olga is two years my senior. We are not at all alike. Where I'm fastidious, she's rather sloppy. Our mother is a good housekeeper as far as she goes, but I am different also from her in my insistence on order. When I come home on holidays from school and I open my closet, I can tell when a single item has been moved." Then she added as an afterthought: "I have an aunt, however, who is much like I am." She was referring, I found, to her adoptive father's sister. I was struck by that remark and probed a little into the relationship with the aunt. The lady lived in a town fairly far away both from Laura's home and from the college she was attending. She saw her aunt only occasionally, when members of the extended family might get together. I gathered that Laura was somehow trying to bolster her membership in the adoptive family by a myth of likeness with some member outside the nuclear family, seeing that there she found differences rather than similarities.

A second adoptee, also a young woman, said when interviewed: "I am an individualist, that is all an adopted child has to stand on." She felt herself only a marginal member of her adoptive family. She could think of no good reason why she should belong in that family rather than some other. Here the sense of realism was not, as in Laura's case, supplemented by myth.

At this point let us think briefly about myth, what myth implies in social life. The distinguished anthropologist Malinowski, speaking of myth in primitive psychology, notes with respect to legends:

> Whatever the hidden reality of their unrecorded past may be, myths serve to cover certain inconsistencies created by historical events, rather than to record these events exactly. . . . The historical consideration of myth is interesting . . . in that it shows that myth, taken as a whole, cannot be sober dispassionate history, since it is always made *ad hoc* to fulfil a certain sociological function, to glorify a certain group, or *to justify an anomalous status.*[1]

Lewin and Malinowski — reality and myth — what part do they play in an understanding of social life, of kinship, and in particular the understanding of adoptive kinship? It is this question of reality and myth which has enticed me again and again into the study of family bonds created by legal and social contrivance. It is this question which, if followed through for adoptive kinship, promises to illuminate also the mainstream family. With that as our long-term goal, let me now proceed to a summary of my first decade of research into adoptive kinship.

NOTES

1. B. Malinowski, "Myths in Primitive Psychology," *Magic, Science and Religion,* 1948, p. 125 (emphasis added).

Chapter 3

Exploration and Discovery

The Shared Fate theory of adoptive relationships tries to piece together and explain how myth and reality have combined in the lives of hundreds of adoptive parents, and how the mix of myth and reality affects the bonds they have formed with their children. When I first planned to explore the world of adoptive kinship, I did so with the insights as well as blindspots of a would-be adoptive parent. Perhaps it was not surprising that I assumed fellow adopters would be willing and able to shed light on the interactions and experiences people have in adoptive families and beyond. As a first step I therefore decided to locate some adoptive parents among my acquaintances and sound them out: what were their lives like? If from them I could learn what they regarded as most significant in their family life experience, it might give me beginning hints for more systematic research. In this way I approached one of my professors whom I understood to be an adoptive father. On the occasion of discussing my doctoral research plans with him, I asked whether he might tell me some of his own experiences. He became reticent and suggested that this was properly a topic to be raised with his wife. A few days later I went to see her; almost from the beginning of our talk the atmosphere between us was tense. She kept asking what I thought the problem was; what did I *really* want to know? The interview never got off the ground. The woman stressed that she had never encountered anything that had in any way made her feel adoption to be a problem. When I made reference to an episode between a neighbor and my wife, during which the neighbor had suggested that adoption posed a certain risk, my professor's wife laughed, saying: "It's all in your mind," adding that there was no problem unless we made it.

At that time I did not understand that this woman's attitude was typical of those from whom I wanted information. Luckily, I was not deterred from trying to locate adoptive parents through another route. I inquired of social workers in adoption agencies how I might reach into the interpersonal world of adoptive parenthood. Now I was told that it was neither possible nor desirable, that adoptive families should not have their privacy disturbed and that they must not be made to feel different from other families in the community. I did not yet understand that modern adoption arrangements had been institutionally organized so as to create the strictest anonymity for the principals. Only the legal and administrative intermediaries between the adopting family and the surrendering birthparents would know the details of the transaction. Furthermore, all records that could in any way shed light on the arrangement were to be sealed and made inaccessible to the prying eyes of outsiders. It was all planned to be of benefit to surrendering parents, adoptive families, and of course to the children. But over the years less beneficial consequences of this anonymity have become evident. It is now clear that as adopted children grow up into adulthood, the secrecy surrounding their past can be more of a hindrance than a help to many of them. But the institutionalized invisibility of adoptive kinship also has problematic consequences for the social researcher. If all records are sealed, amended birth certificates issued, and adoptive relationships merged in the census with those of the mainstream family, then any systematic research into adoptive kinship is seriously inhibited.

Research Phase I: A Cultural Climate for Adoptive Kinship?

In the face of such obstacles, I had to rethink my plans for research. At that time my sociological training was in large part directed by a group of scholars whose principal methodological interest and forte was survey research. Graduate students, if they want to maximize their professional opportunities, must link their interests to those of their professors. It is therefore not surprising that I came to define my research problem initially along lines that could be investigated by survey techniques. I now began to study the cultural climate, i.e., the ideas, beliefs, values, and attitudes that surround adoption and set the tone for adoptive relationships. I took steps planning survey research which was to assay attitudes and beliefs attached to illegitimacy and sterility, as well as parenthood by birth and by adoption. I read popular and technical works and sought out novels and plays with themes of family substitution. My goal was to obtain a many sided picture of adoptive kinship in our culture, past and present. Slowly I began to create ideas for systematic sociological inquiry — a pattern of questions for interviewing adults who were to have had no direct contact with adoption themselves. In other words, I wanted to tap public opinion, not intimate knowledge, concerning adoptive kinship. It took months to develop and pretest this interview instrument — so long, in fact, that one of my professors became irritated at my slowness. I had taken seriously his admonition that a sociologist must so carefully construct his survey tools that the questions in it refer as precisely as possible to some clearly articulated ideas. Equally important was the task of finding out what the items in a questionnaire meant to the people to whom they were to be directed, i.e., how the respondents interpreted what they were being asked.

By the end of 1951 I finally had what appeared to be a sensible and workable interview schedule, and so I began in 1952 a series of 183 interviews with adult householders in Ithaca, N.Y., then a city of some 20,000 inhabitants. Even from the pretests of the final interview instrument, it became clear that adoptive kinship was not regarded as the equivalent of kinship based on consanguinity or shared ancestry. Analysis of the final interview results showed that such bias as was expressed against adoption was most closely associated with attitudes toward illegitimacy and toward the meanings of motherhood. In other words, people who tended to discriminate in their judgments against adoptive kinship were also likely to make discriminatory judgments against illegitimacy and to devalue motherhood which is not based on having given birth. The Ithaca study (called "Eastern City" in *Shared Fate*) was partially replicated in an eastern Canadian metropolis four years later. Both studies showed that, while age and socio-economic status of respondents influenced their replies, adoptive kinship was generally regarded as inferior to consanguineal kinship, a "second best" decided on last.

Research Phase II: Culture Themes and Personal Themes

It was this pattern of attitudes which, during the years 1951-53, had become increasingly disturbing to me personally. In the process of completing my research for the doctorate, I had come to realize the power of public opinion as it dealt with adoptive kinship, and accordingly I shied away from further studies in this area of social life. But by 1954 I had moved to Canada with my family and was teaching at McGill University. My association with social work professionals and the results of the 1955 paper to the Child Welfare League's National Conference on Adoption provided a renewed impetus for adoption research. Offers of agency cooperation across the United States and Canada to enlarge the perspective of my earlier work helped overcome my hesitation. I had begun to develop a questionnaire that was to ask adoptive parents about their experiences with the attitudes of people in the wider community, when I ran into renewed and familiar obstacles.

In Chapter 4 of *Shared Fate* I described how a certain core part of the 1956 mail questionnaire came to be constructed. I told of a group meeting of adoptive parents, held on the premises of Montreal's Children's Service Centre. Eleven adoptive parent couples had answered the director's invitation to help pretest the main items for a new questionnaire to be sent to adopters through the mail. The most important of the items to be tested in that evening's meeting referred to the experience of adopters with the attitudes of other people — whether the adoptive parents had experienced disconcerting questions or remarks. The couples present were for a long time unwilling to deal with the issue, either on paper or verbally. But from the anecdotes eventually reported that evening by the participants, I was able to construct questions which were later incorporated in a mail questionnaire. This questionnaire was answered by hundreds of adoptive parents in Quebec and Ontario, New York, Ohio, and California.

Two important findings emerged from the mail questionnaire: first, it showed that adopters in all the regions of North America where questionnaires had been sent reported very similar patterns of experience with the attitudes of other people (see *Shared Fate*, Chapter 2, esp. Table 4, p. 30). This meant that there appeared to be a common value system in the local and regional life, defining adoptive kinship in very similar terms from east to west, in Canada and the United States. The thrust of this value system might be termed "benevolent discrimination," for it was discriminatory against adoption, however benign the words and phrases in which it might be couched. The pattern of other people's attitudes reported by more than 1,500 adoptive couples across this continent in the mid-nineteen fifties makes it possible to speak of certain themes as typical in the cultural experience of North American adopters at that time. But what is the relevance of such data for the present? Why is this being recalled here, a quarter-century later? The fact is that the cultural climate of that time is part of the social ground in which the identities of people adopted then were formed. For the children adopted during the nineteen fifities, the experiences which their adoptive parents had with the attitudes of others will have been of considerable importance. If public opinion defined adoptive kinship as different, then it set adoptive parents and their children apart from the mainstream. This then was the first of two major findings derived from the mail questionnaire of 1956.

The second finding, which turned out to be at least as important as the first, came to light in the course of what I had planned as a minor part of the mail questionnaire. While pretesting it, I had noticed that adopters became very tense while they checked items which stemmed from the anecdotes revealed during the evening at the Children's Service Centre. So I experimented with a blank page following the list of those apparently disturbing items, hoping thereby to reduce the respondents' strain. The blank page was headed: "Please add here any other experiences regarding the adoption which were especially important to you, and indicate how you felt about them at the time. Also note any important matters relating to adoption which you would have liked seen included in this questionnaire."

This page clearly served its purpose, which was to help the parent-respondents blow off steam after the pressing chore of recalling and documenting any experiences similar to those reported at the Children's Service Centre. But as the questionnaires came back in the mail — daily in batches of twenty or more — the contents of that page became more and more intriguing. It became evident as one read the entries on page 10 (the "blank page"), that the respondents had there aired some of their deepest feelings and revealed some of their genuine interests and wishes. For me as researcher, this growing awareness of material originally thought to be of little substantive importance was exciting, but also vexing. Each of the entries was personal and different. Perhaps here was a hidden goldmine of information which I would bypass at great risk to my research goals. But what was to be done with the material, how would I be able to break through the multitude of different entries to see such characteristics as they might have in common?

I knew of the method of content analysis developed by Harold Lasswell (1946, 1949) during the nineteen forties and codified by Bernard Berelson (1952, 1954). So, late in 1956, I organized a student research team. During the next two months we developed a 30-page code book for analyzing the material from page 10 of the mail questionnaire. This minute and meticulous code led us exactly nowhere. Statistical analyses of what words had been used, and with what feeling tone, broke down the unity of the individual statements, but did not help to reveal any common messages.

After some weeks I decided that instead of the minutiae of the Lasswell-Berelson method, I ought to look for recurring themes which I suspected were buried in these questionnaire entries. The idea for such a theme analysis stemmed from an article by Opler,[1] who had suggested themes as key elements in the understanding of a culture. If I could identify theme patterns in these writings by adoptive parents, I might then gain more intimate insight into the special subculture of adoptive kinship as experienced by the parents. Looking for someone to help me with the gigantic task of reading more than 1,500 questionnaires for thematic contents, I located a capable graduate student who would within another month or so have to leave Montreal to begin his field work in an Inuit village. William Willmott[2] and I divided the question-naires between us randomly, but in such a way as to assure that each had a similarly sized sample from each of the five regions. We agreed to read the contents of page 10 for possible themes, and decided not to communicate with each other until one of us thought he was in possession of a thematic picture. Only when both us had such results would we meet and share the information. It happened that three weeks after we began this work, Bill Willmott phoned to say that he thought he had got hold of something. Shortly afterwards I also felt sure enough of my material to call for a meeting between us. We had previously agreed to keep such themes as we thought there were in the form of examples from the questionnaire entries. When we met at my office, each of us had brought a list of such examples. As we compared them we discovered that we had identified what appeared to be a dichotomy — two sets of responses which were logical opposites. One of these implied that the adoptive experi-ence was essentially not different from that of the mainstream family, while the other set of responses recognized real differences. Because Bill Willmott and I had quite independently noted the same patterns, and especially because we each had a set of different questionnaires more or less randomly dis-tributed among the regional samples ("split-half" method), I felt confident that we had struck pay dirt. As I now considered this two-sided or bi-polar pattern more closely, there came to mind a name for each of the different definitions of adoptive kinship which seemed to inhere in the themes we had discovered. I called one side "rejection-of-difference" and the other "acknow-ledgment-of-difference."

Research Phase III: The Meaning of the Personal Themes

The single page in the 1956 mail questionnaire had now yielded its secret. There appeared to be two antithetical themes by which adoptive parents defined their situation. But what was the meaning of that finding? Was it perhaps just a chance event that had no special significance for understanding the inner workings of adoptive relationships? Having come this far, I found it an irritatingly pressing question. I went about trying to find an answer by ruminating in my workshop of sociological ideas. What did I know with some degree of certainty about adoptive family and kinship? I knew something now about public attitudes which did not appear to concede to adoptive parents a full place in the cultural sun of family life. This, after all, had not been an isolated finding but one which was similar in New York and Quebec, Ontario and Ohio, and even as far west as California. Here were these bi-polar, antithetical definitions of adoption *by adopters*. It was as if some of them wanted to close their eyes to what was clearly before them. The rejection-of-difference theme was reminiscent of the interview with my professor's wife back in my graduate days, and also of the evening with the eleven couples at the Children's Service Centre in Montreal during the winter of 1955. What had these people been up to, why this pattern of denial of what was so evidently a part of their social world?

What then did the polar types of answers, the duality of themes of rejection-of-difference (R/D) and acknowledgment-of-difference (A/D) imply for the adoptive parent-child relationship? This was what I had to find out next. As I reviewed the various findings of my previous studies, trying to fit into some kind of meaningful whole what I thought I knew and what was unclear and called for answers, I remembered what had happened in my family in the winter of 1955, two years earlier. That event now acted like a trigger: I saw a way to explain the R/D and A/D themes. I recalled the story of my daughter Francie and her temporary obsession with the Cinderella tale. As I thought back to Ruth Kirk's creative way of dealing with that difficult situation, several pieces of the puzzle seemed to fall into place. First of all I realized that she had pioneered in a complex and threatening circumstance, acting out an acknowledgment-of-difference suitable to our little daughter's problem and her capacity to understand. The child was struggling to grasp her own situation and she had fastened on that of Cinderella — an explanation which, at the same time, was deeply disturbing to her. What Ruth Kirk had done was to acknowledge the fact that both mothers — Cinderella's stepmother and she — were substitute mothers, but that their respective interests in their daughters were very different, the former being malevolent, the latter, loving and concerned. Thus I discerned that Ruth Kirk's response to our daughter's pained and painful inquiry about her place in our family had required a reference to the reality of loss and pain which are inevitable concomitants with the joys of adoptive parenthood.

Confirming this interpretation of Ruth Kirk's actions was the fact that the R/D and A/D themes appeared immediately following the questions about experiences with remarks made by outsiders. These questions appear to have acted as stimuli to release the thematic entries encountered on page 10. These stimuli were threatening: in previous research steps it had become clear that adopters resisted revealing their experiences with unfriendly or merely insensitive encounters. Now they had been led into admitting such threatening events, so that when they turned the page of the questionnaire they not only blew off the accumulated steam, but tried to shield themselves against any more intrusions. The themes we had discerned on page 10 of the mail questionnaire could therefore be thought of as defensive reactions to the role-impinging memories evoked in the preceeding part of the questionnaire. In other words, I came to think of the thematic entries which we had classified R/D or A/D as means of coping, serving adopters as mechanisms for dealing with strains they had encountered in adoptive kinship. But what was their coping to address, beyond those immediately annoying reminders of other people's uncouth remarks? Was there some more profound basis for their discomfort? Could that basis be connected with the unpalatable attitudes and behaviors of outsiders?

In pursuing this line of inquiry, I did what I have often done when faced with vexing sociological questions. Rather than take myself out of the picture, I'd place myself squarely into it. I would ask myself what the theoretically vexing circumstances would mean to me as a participant. In the situation of the adopters who had answered the mail questionnaire, I had no difficulty in taking their place. But being a sociologist as well as an adoptive parent, I reasoned this way:

As members of a society we learn the ways and means of a culture. These learned ways and means are like the script of a play, except of course that much of the cultural script is not on paper but in our perceptions of the world, our feelings, and behaviors expected of us in our social roles. Once a member knows the role, assigned or chosen, it is easy enough to manage the part as long as fellow actors carry out theirs. But what if one of them were to fail, were to change drastically the lines or actions for which the script calls? Then the first member would find his or her part in jeopardy; in other words, the companion actor or actors would find themselves at considerable loss to keep the action going. This was the kind of circumstance I came to call "role handicap," in contrast with socially and culturally provided "role supports."[3] Note that role handicaps are not derived from the actor's subjective disposition to like or dislike the plot or the lines. It results from an external interference with the actor's capacity for carrying out the part as indicated in the script.

Such a train of thought implied that the themes Willmott and I had discerned could have been ways of coping with role-handicapping conditions in the adoptive parents' lives. I reasoned that, with fellow actors not appreciating the adoptive situation as they themselves did, the adopters tried to shield themselves with a form of deviance disavowal, or even avowal. While I felt confident that my observations corresponded to the social reality of adoptive parenthood, and that my interpretation of the observed behaviors made good theoretical sense, I knew that I had to put both to more stringent tests. I had to ask whether adoptive parents would respond to specific role handicap cues by means of the R/D and A/D themes we had noted.

Research Phase IV: Verifying Role Handicaps and Coping Mechanisms

For this purpose I designed an interview schedule which was to be administered to adopters who had previously answered the mail questionnaire. This was deemed necessary because it would enable me to link the information from the latter to more pointed question-and-answer data gathered in the new interviews. But such follow-up was possible only for those 1956 respondents who had volunteered their names and addresses. In 1956, 407 couples had made up the Montreal sample of adoptive parents. Of that number a total of 243, or 60 per cent, had responded, but of these only 100 of the 243 had volunteered their name and address for a possible follow-up study. When we checked on those 100 adoptive couples in 1958, we could locate only 86, and of these we eventually interviewed 70.

In the 1958 follow-up interviews with the 70 adoptive parents, I was principally interested in knowing whether they readily responded to questions tapping specific instances of role handicap, and whether their answers were of the R/D and A/D types. Here is a selection of questions and answers from an interview with an adoptive mother of two pre-schoolers:

Questions with Role Handicap Content	ANSWERS
14. How did you feel about the interviews you had at the agency before you were given a child?	"They were fair and right."
15. Couples who have their children by birth don't have to ask anywhere for permission to start a family. Does it seem reasonable or not so reasonable to you that only couples who want to adopt have to be approved for good parenthood?	"It is wonderful. They have to look after the infant's interest."
16. It is probably true that people generally get satisfaction from being parents. In your opinion do adoptive parents get some satisfactions which other parents do not get?	(Respondent seems to have misunderstood the question:) "They miss the birth experience which is part of the adventure."
17. And now what about other parents? Do you feel that they have satisfactions that adoptive parents don't have?	"Just the pleasure of having the child from a younger age. They are able to notice family traits. This is a pleasure." (Respondent said that she likes to gloss over things that make them different.)

22. Some adoptive parents complain that there is no dignified public ceremony at the time of adoption. Have you or your wife/husband ever wished that there were such a ceremony?
    c) Why would some people want such a ceremony? That is, what would it give the people involved, do you suppose?

(They must think about the "adoption" angle rather than the "family" angle more than she does. She doesn't like to emphasize the link with blood parents. She likes not being able to tell the child who his real parents are. She says that their mother was a good person. You can paint them as you wish if you don't know.)

28. In many situations the feelings of an adoptive parent are just like those of any parent; in other situations the feelings of adoptive parents may well be different. (After a list of interviewer-given situations, respondent is asked to indicate one or more that occur to her or him. Then interviewer asks:) Do you think the feelings would be the same or different here?

(Respondent volunteers the situation of christenings in church. She was not anxious to face church with an older child. But she saw the christening of an adopted older child and thought it was very touching. She didn't want to do anything to make a scene or be different. Therefore one child was, and the other will be, christened at home.)

30. Many of those parents who tell their children that they are adopted, find the telling difficult. Why do you suppose it is so hard for these adoptive parents to tell their children of their adoption?

"They are masquerading, even subconsiously. They are trying to pretend the children have been born to them. Although (R. mused) they forget that their children are adopted."

34. Now a question about your child's original parents. How often would you say you think about them — frequently, just once in a while, or never?

"Just once in a while. Especially on birthdays." (She wonders if the mother wonders about the child's appearance.)

35. Do you find that there are certain matters which come up in adoptive families and which you and other adoptive parents find it difficult to deal with?

"Not so far, maybe when they are teenagers."

An inspection of these questions and answers immediately reveals that the respondent moved back and forth between R/D and A/D poles, sometimes in the same reply. This mixing of coping mechanisms had already been observed among the respondents of the 1956 mail questionnaire. Mixed or not, even this abbreviation of one interview demonstrates that the themes of R/D and A/D coping were real enough, that they corresponded to activities and sentiments of one particular adoptive parent. What I needed further was some indication that the role handicap concept was anchored in structural reality, that back of this purely theoretical concept lay an observational one.[4] Some weeks after the follow-up interviews had been completed in Montreal, an event occurred which led me to just such an observational concept.

Every experienced researcher knows that discovery does not follow neat, orderly lines, as the following episode will illustrate. Early in 1959 I received a telephone call from Washington, D.C. The caller was Richard Barker, a lawyer, who during World War II had founded a child-placing agency, the Barker Foundation. I had been in touch with the foundation some months before, having been asked to exchange research ideas and findings. Now Mr. Barker asked me to address the annual meeting of the foundation on January 23, 1959. I indicated my willingness, but could not on such short notice give him a title for my talk. I said however that I would base it on my recently completed interviews with the 70 adoptive parents in Montreal.

Mr. Barker was prepared to leave the matter somewhat uncertain, while I assumed that in the intervening fortnight I would be able to extract from my 1958 study data an interesting topic for my talk. It turned out that those two weeks were full of unexpected pressures at university and at home, so that I found no time to put together the notes for the address to the Barker Foundation's membership. But since the date was firm, there was no way out but to try writing the talk on the journey down from Montreal to Washington, D.C. I flew to New York and took a train from there, hoping that the longer journey would give me enough time to do the job. With my briefcase crammed full of statistical tables and notes relating to the study of 1958, I sat on that train, papers spread out on several vacant seats, trying to select data that could serve in giving an interesting talk. But my hopes were frustrated. I arrived in Washington no better prepared for that evening's address than I had been when I left Montreal early that morning.

The foundation had booked me into the stately Hay-Adams hotel, where Mr. Barker was waiting for me. He offered to look after me for the rest of the afternoon, before I was to join him and the members of his board for dinner. I pleaded fatigue and asked to be excused until it was time for the meal. Mr. Barker agreed to call my room in two hours. So that was the time I had to put something together for the talk. In those two hours I finally managed to solve my problem, but without any reference to the research data I had brought with me. What I wrote down in my hotel room that afternoon was, in rudimentary form, an inventory of the objective circumstances that make up the difference between natural and adoptive parenthood. My notes for the evening's talk began with the observation that adoptive parenthood is objectively different along several points of reference from parenthood by birth, and that this difference is echoed in the attitudes and sentiments of other people in the community. I noted that adoptive parents react to this manifest difference by making use of the themes of rejection-of-difference and acknowledgment-of-difference. Then I proceeded to list in two columns the contrast between natural and adoptive parenthood. In the left-hand column I wrote down what seemed to me the promises and consequent expectations concerning parenthood in our cultural script. In the right-hand column I entered the actual events encountered by involuntarily childless people who move into adoption.

In those two hours I was able to produce a listing that made sense. At the time I thought it was luck, but in retrospect I realize that had I not already known much about adoptive parenthood — especially the types of role handicaps adopters experienced — this inventory would most likely not have come into being. That day I felt otherwise, however: the inventory could not be shown to be directly based on research findings which I brought down to Washington for that purpose. I was therefore concerned how it would be received by the group of Barker Foundation parents and professionals. Still, by then it was too late to worry. Shortly Mr. Barker came to fetch me to dinner, where I began to realize that I had come into elite circles of Washington society. I sat next to Linda Burgess,[5] then the acting executive director of the Barker Foundation. When she identified herself as the daughter of the great physiologist Cannon, I felt as if he himself had put the seal of approval on my notes for that evening. His famous work *The Wisdom of the Body* seemed to say to me: "Go to it! You produced your notes from your guts." After dinner we moved to a nearby church hall where I was to address an audience of 100 or so adoptive parents and professionals. My heart sank once more when I saw this elegant and sophisticated audience. Would they not think that my simple, non-technical rendition of everyday facts was unworthy of this occasion? What actually occurred was quite different. These people honored my presentation with so much interest and enthusiasm, with examples of their own in the discussion that followed, that I could not doubt that I had struck pay dirt. When I returned to Montreal the next day, I set to work systematically on the two-column inventory I had begun in Washington under those peculiar circumstances.

What was produced that day was the idea of situational discrepancies — i.e., contradictions between culturally promised events and personal encounters with a very different reality. The inventory of situational discrepancies provided me with a picture of the structural underpinnings of role handicap. Once I saw that connection, I did not have to question further the reality of role handicap in the lives of adopters.

Situational Discrepancies

BIOLOGICAL PARENTHOOD	ADOPTIVE PARENTHOOD
1. Preparation for adult life presumes that there will be children. This implies that persons moving into marriage ordinarily take for granted their potential fertility. They have thus a mental link between marriage and the ability to have offspring.	While the cultural script prepares people to expect fertility, for sterility and its interpersonal consequences there is little if any preparation. Interviews with 70 adoptive parents showed that only 9 of them could recall ever having considered the possibility of childlessness before they encountered it in their marriage.

BIOLOGICAL PARENTHOOD	ADOPTIVE PARENTHOOD

2.

The relative certainty of the child's coming makes possible an early sharing of news with parents and friends. Their rejoicing will be supportive during some of the trying times which may be part of the pregnancy.

The considerable uncertainty connected with adoption plans frequently inhibits sharing of plans with family members or friends. Thus, at the time of the adopting couple's other difficulties, there is the additional fact that others, through ignorance, may be unable to rally and support them.

3.

In our society, biological parenthood is sanctioned and rewarded by a variety of benefits which are conferred on the new parents. For instance, medical and hospital care plans recognize and help pay for certain costs involved in the child's arrival. Further, welfare state tax laws allow medical costs of pregnancy and birth to be deducted from taxable income.

For adopting couples there are few equivalent arrangements to take care of the costs of the child's arrival. Tax laws have seldom provided for the deduction of expenses involved in adoption. As late as 1980 the Canadian federal bureaucracy would not recognize an adopted child's coming into the family as an equivalent time problem as that of post-natality. As a result, the new adoptive mother cannot collect unemployment insurance if she elects to stay home for a while with her new infant or child.[6]

4.

Once licensed to marry, the couple have no further requirements to meet to make them eligible for parenthood.

Adopters have to show authorities that they are fit for parenthood. Eligibility must usually be proved along lines of economic, psychological, and marital stability, and membership in religious organizations.

5.

The biological parents are ultimately *independent* in the procurement of their child. However much they may utilize the technological services of medicine, surgery, and hospital, they know that procurement is possible without all these services. Essentially they are *not in need of a middle man.* (Note here the importance of relative independence and autonmony in the middle-class value system.)

Adopting couples are ultimately *dependent* on the services of a middle man, whether this helper is professional, or friend, social worker, physician, lawyer, minister, or black marketeer. (Note that relative dependence may be increased in agency adoptions, partly because there is here no direct transaction between parent and adopters, but also partly because the latter are frequently not clear about the agency's criteria for evaluating applicants.)

BIOLOGICAL PARENTHOOD	ADOPTIVE PARENTHOOD

6.

Parental status is initiated during pregnancy and fully secured at birth. All rights, duties, and privileges of parenthood accrue to the new parents at that time. This fact aids them in directing all their feelings to the infant as a *member* of their family unit.

Parental status is not fully secured at the arrival of the child in the adoptive household. Adopting parents are responsible for the child's maintenance and safety, but guardianship rights remain in the hands of others who are still in *loco parentis*, i.e., either the natural parent(s) or the agency.

7.

With the child's coming, parents are fully expected to do everything in their power to make him one of their group, to integrate him into their midst. Only after he has become fully a member need they give any thought to his participation in groups outside the family circle.

For over four decades, adopters have been advised that they must tell the adopted child about his adoption. Although this professional prescription has been surrounded by assurances that it will not be a problem if started very early in the child's life, this very aspect of the prescription makes it especially problematic. It means that adopters are confronted by conflicting role obligations — the first to integrate the child fully before he is allowed to find other membership and reference groups; the other to begin his differentiation out of their midst simultaneously as they are seeking to integrate him.

8.

Preparation for biological parent roles is *gradual* — the period of pregnancy provides the couple with a known timetable which moves them imperceptibly toward progressive involvement in their coming parental tasks.

Preparation for adoptive parenthood tends to be *abrupt*, with no clear-cut timetable by which they can shape their feelings and thoughts about their hoped-for parenthood.

9.

Maternity clothing begins to be worn about the mid-term of pregnancy. This clothing is an external sign to others and to the couple of their changing position. It thereby assists the couple in moving into the path of developing parenthood. (Note also the folklore about irrational food cravings which suggest that the culture gives the pregnant woman much latitude in her concern for herself and her role.)

For adopters there are few signs to impress on others and on themselves the changing position for which they are reaching.

BIOLOGICAL PARENTHOOD	ADOPTIVE PARENTHOOD

10.

At the time of the child's birth the family usually gathers around the new parent couple, looking for family likenesses in the newborn, remarking on the choice of name, and are frequently participants in religious ceremonies whereby they assert the new member's part in the group.

In adoption there are no ceremonies of this order to mark the new member's arrival in the family. Knowledge of the rupture of the family line precludes looking for family likenesses.

With this inventory of situational discrepancies, here abbreviated, I had identified structural sources of role handicap — at least as they apply to the circumstances faced by adoptive parents. Now I had made a number of discoveries that specified the nature of adoptive kinship from the point of view of adopters. These discoveries were starting points for a theory of adoptive relations, since they sought to explain the function of the themes as differential patterns of coping with role handicap. But the larger theory of adoptive kinship, the theory to which I have given the name "Shared Fate," had not yet come into being. Early in 1959 I may have had the basic building blocks for constructing such a theory, but I had not asked the crucial question that was to lead me to a rearrangement of the known variables, of the points of reference on my map of adoptive kinship. That crucial question was not asked until the fall of 1960, during a two-year study sojourn in Southern California. Because the California project proved essential for the development of the Shared Fate theory, I must now recall some of its most important and seminal events.

Research Phase V: California Sojourn

Sometime early in 1958 I had learned from a letter by Professor Lee M. Brooks[7] that in California there were several local associations of adoptive parents. I wondered about the functions of such organizations: what did they seek to do and what did they in fact accomplish? Professor Brooks' letter also mentioned that the three associations — in Los Angeles, Redlands, and Whittier — used the label "Adopted Children's Associations." Since they were really groups of adopters and not of adoptees I wondered whether they might be serving their members as self-help organizations, somewhat like Alcoholics Anonymous. Perhaps the "Adopted Children" label permitted the parents to hide their identity as adopters. Such misplaced labelling might have implied a form of R/D coping with the role handicaps of adoptive parenthood. On the other hand, the very fact that the members were officially joining a group that was concerned with adoption should mean that they were coping along lines of A/D, of acknowledgment of their position in society. I decided to select certain key questions about role handicap and coping patterns from the 1958 questionnaire I had just constructed for the 70 Montreal adopters. I wrote and asked Lee Brooks to administer my mini-questionnaire to the Whittier group's membership at their upcoming meeting, which he did. Now I had a basis of comparison between the adopters in Montreal who did not belong to a parent association, and the ones in Whittier who did. The results seemed instructive: the Whittier parents — quite similar in age and socio-economic position to the Montreal parents — were in some respects quite different. The California group expressed much more of an A/D oriented view of adoptive kinship than the Quebec parents.

On the basis of this information, I felt that the adoptive parent groups in California presented a remarkable opportunity for studying role handicap and coping patterns *in process*, i.e., in the very circumstances of day-to-day social interactions. I therefore applied to the National Institute of Mental Health, United States Public Health Service, for a research grant that would enable me to spend some time in the field, doing participant observation and developing other study programs. I approached both the Whittier Adopted Children's Association and Whittier College with requests for sponsorship of my study. The grant and the sponsorships were obtained in early 1959 and by fall of that year my family moved with me to Whittier.

In *Shared Fate* (pp. 108-111) I dealt with a small part of the work in Whittier, mainly showing that the actual behavior of the membership of the local Adopted Children's Association was by no means A/D oriented. The year 1959-60 was principally devoted to unstructured interviews of members and their families, and to participant observations of group meetings and committees. However, my participant observation work did not produce the quick and dramatic results that were obtained by a study I had not even planned to do. A few days after I set up my office at Whittier College, a tea was held for new faculty, and having come there as a visiting professor of sociology, I was one of the small group being welcomed. As I was being introduced, and the purpose of my temporary research connection with the college was mentioned, a woman member of the education department came over to me with some interesting news. Had I seen the current issue of *McCall's*, the nationally distributed women's magazine? If I had not, I would find it very interesting from the point of view of my research. I thanked the lady and as soon as I could free myself from the collegiate tea-and-cookies scene I rushed to the nearest stationery store to pick up a copy of *McCall's*. Indeed, my informant had not overstated her case. Here was an article — boldly announced on the cover — entitled "To My Adopted Daughter: I Wish I Hadn't Told You." Written by Henrietta Sloane Whitmore, this piece represented the ultimate in a rejection-of-difference position.

I went back to my office and telephoned New York. Would the editor of *McCall's* permit me to read and analyze the letters the magazine would undoubtedly receive in answer to the article? I explained that I was directing a research program funded by the federal government, and that I would be happy to share with the editor's office what I found. I obtained permission and in due course received by special delivery a number of letters. Eventually

I was able to analyze a total of 184 letters to the editor of *McCall's,* and reported my findings not only directly to the magazine but later on in an article in a Canadian professional journal.[8] Here I want to note that almost all of the 84 adoptive parents who wrote to the editor disagreed with Mrs. Whitmore's point of view. But they also indicated their belief that her problems, which she claimed to have encountered in telling her daughter about adoption, were of her own making. Thus they did not allow for problems of "telling" to stem from the nature of the adoptive situation, i.e., from the reality of adoptive parental role handicap. Here then was not only a challenge to the professional prescription for adoptive parental conduct, but also a defense of it, and perversely both the challenge and the defense were characterized by rejection-of-difference!

This chance event, this unexpected appearance of the *McCall's* article, served as a proper opening to my work in Whittier, for it set me increasingly in the direction of asking: what happens when adopters engage in R/D or in A/D modes of coping? Mrs. Whitmore had told her daughter and wished she had not, thinking that it had done neither of them any good. As the parents who wrote to *McCall's* said in their letters, perhaps her difficulties had all stemmed from Mrs. Whitmore's ineptness. But what was it that made a person successful as an adoptive parent, and what did "success" mean in the first place? Slowly my interviews with adopters in the Whittier and Los Angeles areas came to have that kind of focus, so that by the end of the first year I had formulated a number of ideas that came to make up the basic framework for a theory of adoptive kinship. With these ideas I went back to the data from the 1958 interviews with the 70 adopters in Montreal, interviews in which I had sought to test the reality of the coping mechanisms. Now I used the questions asked of those adopters to try to test my notions of a theory of coping in adoptive parental role handicap. Limited though these data were, they suggested that I was in fact on the right track.

In *Shared Fate* (Chapter 6, pp. 89-95) I made use of those still rather primitive data to test the hypotheses which underlie the Shared Fate theory. But during my second year in Whittier (1960-61), I prepared the ground for a much more stringent test of the theory. A series of pretests with the Whittier membership led to the construction of a tightly organized questionnaire which adopters could fill out themselves in group meetings. Because in the meantime I had learned of other adoptive parent associations in other parts of North America, I was able to gain the cooperation of some of these groups for administration of my new questionnaire. Thus in 1961 the Los Angeles, Washington, D.C., and New York City groups participated in a study that provided me with 283 questionnaires filled out by adoptive couples. That questionnaire served as a further test of the theory, but also as a means to the construction of a final interview tool which was used two years later in a study of parents in Nova Scotia.

Let me briefly take stock. I have tried to recall certain critical moments in the first journey of exploration. I did not intend to cover all or even most of the details, for these are given in *Shared Fate.* But I wanted to share the sense of excitement that is part and parcel of such a journey, with all its uncertainties, and the rewards of persistence when the course of events cannot be plotted beforehand.

For me, much of the previously hidden nature of adoptive kinship was now laid bare, especially as it concerns the world of the adopters. At the opening of the decade of the nineteen fifties I had known little of that world; at its close I knew much of it. Moreover, I had begun to conceive and formulate a theory of adoptive kin relations which proposed to explain the denial that I had first encountered in my professor's wife. But the theory went beyond an explanation of adoptive parental strains and coping: it sought to interpret what occurred as a result of different coping patterns.

NOTES

1. Morris E. Opler, "Themes as Dynamic Forces in Culture," *American Journal of Sociology*, LI, No. 3 (1945), pp. 198-206.

2. William E. Willmott is at present Professor of Sociology, University of Canterbury, Christchurch, New Zealand.

3. In my paper "A Dilemma of Adoptive Parenthood: Incongruous Role Obligations," 1959, *op. cit.,* I defined "role support":

> By "role supports" I mean all those intra-psychically, inter-personally, and collectively derived gratifications which aid in the enactment of role expectations. The "good conscience," the reputation of "good parent" among neighbors, and the "Mother-of-the-Year" award are types of parental role supports on these three levels respectively. Conscience, reputation, and award each draw the actor's attention to the normative expectations involved and support his readiness for further acts in the required direction.

4. For the distinction between "theoretical concepts" and "observational concepts" see Abraham Kaplan, *The Conduct of Inquiry,* 1964, p. 296.

5. Mrs. Burgess has recently written an interesting book, based on her extensive knowledge as administrator of an adoption agency: Linda Cannon Burgess, *The Art of Adoption,* 1976.

6. The *Kitchener-Waterloo Record* of March 29, 1980 had this news item:

UIC refuses support to moms on adoption

Toronto (CP) — Several appeals have failed to persuade the Canada Employment and Immigration Commission to allow adoptive mothers of infants to be eligible for unemployment insurance benefits, even though natural mothers can receive full benefits for up to 15 weeks.

Roger White, public affairs officer for the commission, said Wednesday that claims involving "the eligibility of adoptive mothers for benefits come up often."

White said he knows of six cases that have been rejected recently at the appeals level. He said that under existing rules, the only way mothers can claim maternity leave is to provide proof of pregnancy, which "automatically excludes adoptive mothers," or they must be ready and available for work.

"In many cases, they cannot make themselves available for work because adoption agencies require that the mother stay at home for a prescribed period of time with the baby," said White.

Dan Doctor, spokesman for Lloyd Axworthy, minister of employment and immigration, said a review committee within the department is looking into the matter.

7. Lee M. Brooks was at that time Professor Emeritus, Department of Sociology, University of North Carolina. He and his wife Evelyn Brooks, themselves adoptive parents, had in the 1930s co-authored a book on adoption (*Adventuring in Adoption*).

8. H.D. Kirk, "Guarding the Ramparts: Reader Reactions to a Magazine Article Challenging a Social Work Prescription," *The Social Worker,* (Canada), June-July 1962.

Chapter 4

A Theory of Bonding

Early in the nineteen fifties, the idea had occurred to me that adoptive kinship simulates, in microcosmic form, certain essential features of modern society. Modernization implies more than industrialization and urbanization; essentially it involves critical transitions from status-based social relations to social arrangements principally organized around contract. It involves a shift from traditional social forms to rationally contrived ones. When adoptive kinship is initiated, that is exactly what happens. Contrivance and contract establish human associations normally initiated by nature and confirmed by tradition. But then something remarkable occurs, for the contractually formed structure of contrived kinship typically becomes molded into the nuclear family of everyday life. The erstwhile artificial unit will feel and appear to its members entirely natural, a circumstance in which myth and reality have mingled and are now indistinguishable. This was the idea which had drawn me into the study of adoption, and which had faded as I became absorbed in the details of day-to-day researches. Over the years of the long journey of exploration, I had lost sight of the original quest. When at the end of the decade it reappeared, it did so in less grandiose form, reshaped by the knowledge I had gained in the intervening years. Now the question had become not only researchable but also crucial for the construction of the Shared Fate theory.

This question asked about the possible effects of the R/D and A/D coping patterns on the adoptive parent-child relationship, on the success of bonding between members of the adoptive kin group. In particular, which of the parents' coping ways would have the best chance of furthering the child's attachment to and integration in the adoptive family? It was toward the end of the first year of my Whittier sojourn that this question formed in my mind, probably stimulated by the analysis of letters to the editor in answer to the Whitmore article in *McCall's*. In addition, the Cinderella story kept coming up. Could it be that Ruth Kirk's answer to our little daughter's pained inquiry, and the child's reply, "Now I can have a *good* dream," was pertinent to my theoretical problem? One day during the spring or summer of 1960 I was asked to address the staff of a Los Angeles child guidance clinic on the subject of my research. It was in the preparation of that paper that the main pieces of the puzzle fell into place for me. At this point I reasoned that acknowledgment-of-difference facilitates empathy with the child's circumstances, that empathy in turn facilitates the parent's readiness to let the child freely inquire about the meanings of adoption, and that such communication between parent and child would firm up the bond between them.

As noted earlier, I went back to the data of the 1958 follow-up study of 70 Montreal parents for a first test of that hypothetical chain of events. In Chapter 6 of *Shared Fate* I spelled out my reasoning for believing that empathy and communication are key requirements for dynamic stability of families not regulated by tradition. By "dynamic stability" I meant social relationships which are both reliable and flexible, which provide a secure base for the small child's growth and development while making allowance for changes, for maturation, and the child's need to become an independent adult. In traditional kin groups, dynamic stability is furthered by myth-backed rules of conduct which tend to emphasize collective interests. In the precarious family of urban-industrial societies, the old rules of conduct are weak or absent, and the dominant interests tend to be the individual's rather than the group's. In such circumstances it may be argued that empathy and communication become needed substitutes for commanding rules of conduct, since empathy makes the members sensitive to each other's circumstances and open channels of communication let them express what they understand to be going on in their world.

Such was the reasoning with which I approached the link between ends and means of the adoptive parent-child relationship. This is how I prepared the way toward a theory of bonding. What I had to do next was to try and translate these ideas into behavioral terms, i.e., into terms for which quantifiable and therefore measurable indicators could be found.

The Problem of Measurement

I would like to be able to say that my early attempts at testing the hypotheses were satisfactory and persuasive. Some of the reviewers of *Shared Fate* were more perceptive, some more generous than others in the assessments they made. I may be forgiven here if I admit that one or two of them made me hopping mad at the time. Looking back, I now find one of these very thoughtful and incisive. I refer to the review by Professor Eugene A. Weinstein (1966: 577), himself one of the very few sociologists who had taken adoption seriously:

> *Shared Fate* is an interpretive synthesis of some nine studies about adoption conducted over a ten-year period. The subjects of the studies range from community attitudes toward adoption to content analysis of letters in response to a magazine article to several surveys and interview studies of adoptive parents about their attitudes and experiences. From these sources the author, an adoptive parent himself, develops what he calls a theory of adoption. *Whether he develops and tests a theory or generates a comprehensive post factum interpretation, I would rate as a toss-up.*

His central thesis is that adoptive parents suffer from role handicap. Whatever little cultural script may be available for playing the role of adoptive parent is full of built-in inconsistencies and ambiguities. These are reinforced by the attitudes of the large community that adoption, while acceptable, is an inferior (perhaps slightly stigmatizing) alternative to the enchantment of natural parenthood. These attitudes may be internalized by the adoptive parents themselves. On these points, Kirk and his data are quite convincing. It is what follows that is somewhat less solid, somewhat more speculative. Kirk notes that there are two major modes of coping with role handicap among adoptive parents, "acknowledgment of the difference" and "rejection of the difference." He argues theoretically (perhaps implicitly autobiographically) for the superiority of the "acknowledgement of the difference" approach and tests this supposition on the basis of questionnaire data from adoptive parents. *The tests involve highly dubious operationalization so that the items presumably indexing empathy with the child could as easily be indexing parental conceptions of the child's being different because he is adopted. The relationships he finds seem built in because of similarity of item content.*

The book is somewhat axe-grinding, somewhat preachy. It claims to establish a theory of adoptive relations, but the adopted child is most conspicuous in his absence as a source of data. Nevertheless, it is head and shoulders above the bulk of the literature in the area of adoption and the first piece that brings sociological perspectives to bear in any comprehensive way.

I have emphasized part of his critique of my methodology, because that is where I must now start. I was not unaware of the problem that Weinstein raised in his review, but when I was finishing *Shared Fate,* I was in the middle of studies which were designed to provide sounder tests of the theory.

As it happens, the theory emerged in my mind only as more and more data about the experiences and attitudes of adoptive parents became available. Of course facts never speak for themselves, one must ponder them. During 1957-58 I had come to suspect that the themes identified earlier in 1957 implied means of coping, and in that context I had asked myself, "Coping with what?" In this manner, sometime between 1958 and 1959 I realized that the ideas of cultural discrepancies and role handicap could be linked to the acknowledgment-of-difference and rejection-of-difference modes of coping. I gather that Professor Weinstein considered my theorizing to that point persuasive. It is the subsequent thinking about the effects of different coping patterns that my critic called into question. And he was not wrong in that, for some of the items which were used to represent empathy were indeed not clearly differentiated from those which were taken to represent acknowledgment-of-difference. Accordingly, a correlation between the two is to be expected "because of similarity of item content."

I was not unaware of the difficulty inherent in the indexing I had done. But years of participant observation had given me the assurance that the many research data which I had linked into a theory of adoption provided a correct picture. The trouble lay partly in the fact that I was writing *Shared Fate* relatively impersonally. As a result I could not make the point that I, as long-time and intimate observer, could phenomenologically validate much of what my sometimes weak data had suggested. But there was another reason for the use of data which I knew were not fully satisfactory. By 1963, when I was completing *Shared Fate,* I had almost uninterruptedly been carrying on adoption research for more than 10 years. Yet I had published only three papers, two of them theoretical. It was time to report substantive information on the many studies which had been funded by outside agencies over the years. So it was a choice between getting on with a book which would be in places uneven, or continue still longer in the hope of plugging all the holes. But holes inevitably show up in one's work, and since grant support for research demands comprehensive reporting, *Shared Fate* appeared when it did.

In returning to Professor Weinstein's review of that book, let me say that he surmised correctly that part of my theory was based on *post factum* interpretations.[1] As I had said in *Shared Fate,* the test of the hypothesis concerning the utility of different coping patterns was based on data which had come from a study not designed for that purpose. Let me quote the relevant passage (*Shared Fate,* p. 91):

A FIRST TEST OF THE HYPOTHESIS

In this chapter we shall want to formulate our total theory and are therefore eager for a preliminary test of our key hypothesis. Such a test is possible with the aid of information from a questionnaire interview study of 70 adoptive parents. These parents had answered the 1956 mail questionnaire, so that considerable information from them was already available. When they were interviewed in 1958, the main object of the study was to ascertain whether the "rejection-of-difference" and "acknowledgment-of-difference" concepts could be further validated. The subsequent analysis of these interviews furnished opportunities for a test of our hypothesis.

In retrospect, it might have been well had I warned my readers of some of the pitfalls frequently encountered in the use of secondary data. Be that as it may, the Shared Fate theory has stood the test of time, as we shall shortly see.

Lest my readers gain the impression of a researcher who was satisfied with partially weak data, trusting time to mend things, let me at once disabuse them. By 1961 I had begun to develop more satisfactory indices for the concepts that make up the theory. The study of 283 adoptive couples[2] located in Los Angeles, Washington, D.C., and New York City was intended to produce better indices of acknowledgment-of-difference, empathy and communication. In addition, I had decided that we needed an index of family stability or solidarity. The 1961 study might have furnished the data I needed for *Shared Fate,* but since they derived from volunteer respondents who could not be considered representative of adopters, I reported instead the earlier data based on the 1956 Montreal sample. With the new instruments which the 1961 study had helped to create, it was now possible to plan a new piece of research which would allow a stringent test of the Shared Fate theory.

In 1963, together with another sociologist, I initiated a large-scale study of child health and behavior. Professor Kurt Jonassohn and I had obtained grants for such a study from two sources[3] and in 1963-64 we carried out field research in Nova Scotia. There we gathered data on 2,294 children between the ages of 3 and 16. These children resided in 1,352 households. The larger part of these households represented a random sample.[4] To it we were able to add a series of households with adopted children, and these children represented not a sample but a universe of all children adopted in the jurisdiction of Halifax and Dartmouth, and who belonged to the same age groups as the children in the sample. While this study was designed to furnish other kinds of information,[5] it provided me with a large and representative group of adoptive mothers whose data enabled me to test the Shared Fate theory with the instruments devised in 1961.

The 1961 study had not only provided me with better instruments for indexing the concepts I was using, but it had also served to validate these concepts. With the use of the Guttman scaling method,[6] it was possible to test whether a group of items belonged to the same dimension of meaning. Based on those tests I treated the items as scalar scores, applicable to the Nova Scotia population several years later. In the Halifax-Dartmouth study of 1964 the index scores obtained by any one adoptive mother represent a simple sum of all the affirmative replies given by her. Let me illustrate this with reference to the index of acknowledgment-of-difference. That index was constructed out of five questions which referred to thought and memory factors concerning the respondents' adopted children. A sixth question referred to interpersonal actions (discussions) between adoptive parents. The index items are shown below and followed by an explanation of the scoring procedure.

Index of Acknowledgment-of-Difference

Since the adoption became legalized, have you:

	No	Yes
Wondered whether the biological mother ever thinks about the child?	0	1
Wondered whether the biological father ever thinks about the child?	0	1
Remembered child's original name?	0	1

	No	Yes
Recalled that at one time the child legally belonged to someone else?	0	1
Wondered whether the biological mother worries about the child she has given up?	0	1
During the past year, have you and your husband talked together about your child's biological mother or father?	0	1

Total A/D Score = Sum of "Yes" Answers

Thus, if the responding adoptive mother said "no," that she had not wondered whether her child's biological mother ever thinks about the child, she got a score of 0. Whenever a respondent gave an affirmative answer to any of the questions, she received a score of 1. The total score for the index represented the sum of all the affirmative answers given to questions relating to that index. The range of possible scores for acknowledgment-of-difference was from 0 to 6, there being six items or questions in that index. Next I shall produce here the indices of empathy and communication.

Index of Empathy

Since the adoption became legalized, have you:

	No	Yes
Wondered what your words about adoption mean to the child?	0	1
Tried to imagine how the child feels (or will feel) about being adopted?	0	1
Thought that the child might some day worry about his (her) background?	0	1
Wished that you might understand adoption from the point of view of the child?	0	1

Total Empathy Score = Sum of "Yes" Answers

Index of Communication

	No	Yes
Have you told your adopted child that he has been adopted by you?	0	1
Have you talked with your adopted child about the difference between birth and adoption?	0	1
Have you ever celebrated the anniversary of the day the child came or of the day the adoption became legalized?	0	1

Have you personally been asked by your child for the reason why his (her) biological parents did not keep him (her)?	0	1
What answer did you give, or do you plan to give, if asked? (Illegitimacy part of answer?)	0	1
Have you told your child whether his (her) biological parents were married?	0	1

Total Communication Score = Sum of "Yes" Answers

While the foregoing indices of acknowledgment-of-difference, empathy and communication were relatively self-evident, the index I employed in 1961 and 1964 to stand for the cohesion or solidarity of the parent-child relationship requires some explanation. I was confronted with the problem of how integration or solidarity could be measured when we were dealing with children between the ages of 4 and 17. Pre-schoolers would clearly express their sense of belonging in very different ways from 12-year-olds, and these again from late adolescents. I needed a question or questions that somehow applied to all the age groups and that at the same time represented a sense of the children's attachment to the adoptive parents. I had to decide on a compromise solution: questions asked by children concerning their origins require trust in the adoptive parent. When our son Peter was 14, Ruth Kirk asked him one day: "What does it take for an adopted child to be able to ask questions about himself or his background?" Peter's answer was: "First, trust; he has to be able to trust his parents. Second, courage; it takes courage to start to ask." Ruth Kirk wondered out loud: "To say it takes courage must mean that there is something scary about it. What is it that is frightening?" Peter answered: "To know that this is a part of your life, that to learn about it is the basic foundation, that it is what will help you grow up." Then he added an afterthought: "The parents have to have the something or other to understand what the child is trying to get across." So this is where I got the notion of using trust as an index of integration. But it was a compromise. If a mother reported having been asked one or more types of questions about the child's birthmother, we could accept the information at face value. But if she said she had not been asked by the child — what did that mean? Did it mean that the mother could not recall these events in the life of the child, or did it indeed mean that the child did not trust, did not have the courage to ask? This one could not tell, and so the data from this question cannot be as convincing as I would like them to be. Of course I would like to say to my readers: "See, we have here very firm evidence that certain kinds of coping activities favor the ultimate integration of the adoptive kin group. I believe that everything I know points in that direction." But in fairness I must say this: the trust index of integration is interesting, it produces fascinating results; but they must not be taken as proof. It is the sum of many pieces of evidence which gives the Shared Fate theory its credibility.

Index of Trust

Some children seem to be more curious than others about their biological parents. Which of the following questions has your child asked?

	Has NOT Asked	Has Asked
Whether biological mother is alive	0	1
What she looks like	0	1
What her name is	0	1
Where she lives	0	1
What other questions has child asked? (number of additional questions child has asked)	0	1

Total Trust Score = Sum of types of questions child is said to have asked.

Let's see what the new indices of our concepts show when they are being statistically related one to another. In Table 4.1 we see that the greater the adoptive mother's readiness to acknowledge the difference between birth and adoption status, the more likely she is to be empathic with her child's atypical situation. Thus while 86 per cent of the mothers who scored low on acknowledgment-of-difference also scored low on the empathy index, only 4 per cent of the high scorers on acknowledgment-of-difference scored low on empathy. Our evidence then is not absolute, but based on probability. We find that the likelihood is much greater for acknowlegment-of-difference to be associated with empathy than for rejection-of-difference.

Table 4.1

Relationship Between Indices of Acknowledgment
of Difference and Empathy

Acknowledgment of Difference

		Low					High	
		0	1	2	3	4	5, 6	
Empathy								
low	0-1	86.2	52.8	35.0	18.4	9.5	4.4	(286)
medium	2	5.6	17.6	29.9	28.4	16.2	15.2	(112)
high	3-4	8.2	29.7	35.1	53.3	74.3	80.3	(234)
		(195)	(91)	(117)	(109)	(74)	(46)	(632)

Now let me turn to the relationship between the mothers' capacity for empathy and their readiness to communicate with their children about issues involved in adoption. Table 4.2 shows that the greater the degree of the adoptive mother's empathy with the child's background situation, the more likely it is that she will also communicate more readily with her child concerning the adoptive situation. But what is also of considerable interest in this table is that mothers, who represent the highest empathy scorers, do not supply a commensurate proportion of high communication scores. We are reminded here of Alexandra McWhinnie's finding that her Scottish adoptees reported that the adoptive parents waited for the children to ask, and the adopted children waited to have the adoptive parents explain.[7] Verbal communication in the context of adoption has clearly been a difficult task for the adoptive mothers in the Nova Scotia group. This suggests to me that adoptive parents have in the main been ill prepared for the essential task of communicating with their children concerning the expanding meanings that knowledge of their adoption necessarily produces as the children grow up.

Table 4.2

Relationship Between Indices of Empathy
and Communication

		Low 0	Medium 1-2	High 3-4	
			Empathy		
Communication					
Low	0-1	80.2	38.4	26.0	(303)
High	2-5	19.7	61.5	74.0	(329)
		(213)	(185)	(234)	(632)

Next we come to Table 4.3, which shows the relationship between communication and trust. Here one sees a very strong association between the

Table 4.3

Relationship Between Indices of Communication
and Trust

		0	1	2	3-5	
			Communication			
Trust i.e., Number of types of questions mother recalls child has asked						
Low	0	96.5	87.9	63.1	44.4	(482)
Medium	1-2	2.4	9.0	26.2	39.0	(107)
High	3-6	1.2	3.1	11.6	16.7	(32)
		(171)	(132)	(293)	(36)	(632)

adoptive mothers' readiness to communicate and their children's readiness to ask a variety of questions about the birthmothers. Thus of the adoptive mothers who score low on the communication index, 93 per cent said that their children had asked no questions at all. But once mothers scored high on communication, they were much more likely to recall having been asked questions about birthparents by their children.

From Data to Theory

In all science, theory represents attempts at interpreting and explaining observations. Here we are on a threshold of a theory of adoptive relations. What are the puzzling observations that are in need of explanation? We have seen that adoptive parents are in some peculiar ways handicapped, but also that, because of the rewarding aspects of adoption, these handicaps are not readily visible to the adopters themselves. I noted that adoptive parents tend to shrink from facing this handicap in their situation. I puzzled over this observation; as I carried on my researches, there slowly emerged a pattern that lent itself to an explanation of adoptive parental behavior. Here then is this explanation, this theory of bonding, much as it was developed in *Shared Fate*:

1. Couples entering on adoption are confronted by a series of difficulties that appear to stem from the fertility values of our culture.

   Involuntary childlessness implies severe deprivation, especially for wives. In planning adoption, the couple face new difficulties: they are dependent on outsiders in getting a child, they are uncertain as to the meaning of their coming status, and they often find that members of their kin group are less enthusiastic about adoption than about the pregnancies of their peers.

2. These experiences become handicaps in the satisfactory performance of parental roles, and the initial role handicap is further reinforced by the attitudes and behaviors of other people.

   After the arrival of a child in their home, the adopters tend to discover that other people view neither their motives nor their experiences as equivalent to those of natural parenthood.

3. In the form of parental dilemmas, the adopters' role handicap is carried into the evolving family relationship.

   Adopters are typically instructed to tell the child of his adoption. As he grows and learns increasingly complex concepts, he will want to understand the social and personal implications of adoption. At that point the professional prescription to explain his position to him conflicts with the adopters' desire for full and exclusive parenthood.

   This conflict poses a number of dilemmas for them, whereby their role handicap is carried into the evolving parent-child relationship.

4. When confronted with obstacles to performances of valued roles, people will try to cope as best they can: so it is with adopters.

   To cope with their role handicap, the adopters take recourse in various supports for their parenthood as they understand it (which is principally as they have learned it, i.e., in terms of biological parenthood). Their coping methods appear to be of two types: those that serve them in denying that their situation is different from that of biological parents ("rejection-of-difference") and those means that serve them in affirming the peculiarity of the adoptive situation ("acknowledgment-of-difference").

5. The same culture that has so strongly emphasized the value of fecundity has not seemed to provide non-fecund people, especially women, with equally sanctioned and meaningful values for self-fulfilment. In the absences of clear and supportive cultural alternatives, denial may be a way of seeking to adapt to unpleasant circumstances.

   The greater the original deprivation that the adopters have suffered, and thus the greater their original role handicap, the greater also the likelihood that they will lean toward the use of mechanisms of coping by rejection-of-difference.

6. It may safely be assumed that having stable and cohesive family relationships represents universal goals of parenthood. But when the culture does not provide clear lines of conduct toward such goals, considerable inventiveness and interpersonal competence are called for.

   For all parents in our society, certain cultural goals may be assumed. Adopters, along with other parents, seek to have families of dynamic stability and relative permanence, yielding personal satisfaction. Stability requires rules of conduct. Families not regulated by tradition must depend for internal order on the interpersonal skills of their members. These skills imply empathic and ideational communication. In adoption, such empathy and communication necessarily refer to the child's original parents and other aspects of the child's background, such as the meaning of illegitimacy.

7. Coping activities of the rejection-of-difference type may aid the adopters in assuaging the pains of their own deprivation, but these means of coping do not in the long run further the achievement of their family's integration.

   Adoptive parents' coping behavior of the order of acknowledgment-of-difference is conducive to good interpersonal communication and thus to order and dynamic stability in adoptive families. Coping activities of the rejection-of-difference type, on the other hand, can be expected to make for poor communication, with subsequent destructive consequences for the integration of the adoptive parent-child relationship.

I believe it is correct to say that this seven-point theory is of the type which Kaplan (1964: 298) calls "concatenated":

A *concatenated* theory is one whose component laws enter into a network of relations so as to constitute an identifiable configuration or pattern. Most typically, they converge on some central point, each specifying one of the factors which plays a part in the phenomenon which the theory is to explain. . . . This is especially likely to be true of a theory consisting of tendency statements, which attain closure only in their joint application.

Another philosopher of science, Braithwaite (1953, 1960: 365) warns that in "sciences like psychology and the social sciences which make great use of tendency statements [one should note]. . . that to assert an isolated tendency statement is to say very little." In other words, to find a statistical relationship between two variables like empathy and communication would not be saying much in the way of a theory of adoptive kinship. But a set of interconnected tendency statements which culminates in the explanation of rejection-of-difference type behaviors does provide such a theory.

Three Modifications of the Theory

As presented here, the theory applies principally if not solely to adopters who were involuntarily childless prior to adoption. It also suggests that all myth-making by adopters is rejection-of-difference and thus undesirable for the long-run goals of parent-child solidarity. Finally, the theory is monolithic in a third sense, in assuming that parental coping must be oriented toward acknowlegment-of-difference, and consistently so from beginning to end. For purposes of clarity, I have let the theory stand in this monolithic manner, but now it is necessary to let the reader see that I am aware of at least three modifying circumstances which gives the Shared Fate theory a more human, less mechanistic, character.

The first modification has to do with the person of the adopter. Must he or she be unable to have children of the body in order that the memory of deprivation and sorrow might become an asset in making for an increased awareness of the adopted child's special needs? I think that I first became alerted to the possibility of the memory of pain as the adoptive parent's empathy mentor in connection with Ruth Kirk's response to our daughter's anxiety around the Cinderella story. Only much later did I conceive the idea that the adopters' sense and memory of deprivation might become an asset for them in their attempt at creating a stable and cohesive relationship with their children. But I kept thinking that I ought to look for a similar mechanism to aid all adopters, not merely those who had once been involuntarily childless. All adopters should really be similarly equipped for empathy with their children's genealogical bewilderment. One day I recognized that there is a universal deprivation that affects all parents by adoption, the fertile as well as the infertile, those who adopt out of their own needs and those who come to adoption by other routes, such as stepparenting.

I noted this universal condition of deprivation when I heard a woman acquaintance speak of her children. She was the mother of five — the first four had been born to her and the fifth had recently joined them when he was nearly four years old. She was telling a group of us what it had been like, how her other children had welcomed the little boy, how he had taken hold in the unfamiliar setting and begun to make a place for himself. One of the other women in the group asked about the new adoptive mother's experiences: what was it like for her with the new child? How did she feel about motherhood by adoption when she had already been raising a large family born to her? Did she think that her feelings were the same as with the others? I was familiar with such questions, but I was not prepared for the adoptive mother's reply. She hesitated a bit and then said almost defiantly: no — she did not feel as she had with her other children. People were very quiet and attentive. "You see, not only was Tim so much older when I first set eyes on him, but he had already lived a life without us for quite a time. And more important, I missed all the experiences of carrying him and caring for him in infancy. I feel a great loss; however much I shall get to love this child, I can never expect wholly to become his mother." She looked surprised at her own revelation. We were all touched. For me it was a revealing statement. By it I became aware for the first time that all adoptive parents are deprived in the sense that they have not had the full experiences of natural parents. Why should not the memory of this deprivation become the vehicle for being sensitive to the child's deprivation and need? With these thoughts, the Shared Fate theory became applicable to all adoptive parents and all adopted persons, whatever the ways by which they originally came together.

The second modification of the Shared Fate theory has to do with the mix of myth and reality which the parent-child relationship can accommodate. When he was 11 years old, my son Peter remarked one day: "The child who is born into his family is like a board that's nailed down from the start. But the adopted child, him the parents have to nail down, otherwise he is like a loose board in mid-air." The amazing thing, aside from the way Peter articulated his insight, is the succinct manner in which his pronouncement summarized the Shared Fate theory. Looking at the way the adopters writing on page 10 of the 1956 mail questionnaire moved back and forth between R/D and A/D modes of coping, I became convinced that many parents sensed this need for "nailing the child down." But at the same time, the very mix of their coping orientations showed that they had no clear idea as to how this "nailing down" was to be accomplished. This observation at first meant to me that adopters ought to be taught to be consistent in their adherence to acknowledgment-of-difference ways of coping, and that is how I presented the theory in *Shared Fate*. But this may have been a utopian view, a standard set so high that it could not be reached. Furthermore, I made a discovery some months after *Shared Fate* had gone into print which made me wonder whether myth and reality could be so carefully separated.

In Chapter 3 of the present text I mentioned that the Whittier sojourn of 1959-61 culminated in a more stringent test of the Shared Fate theory. For this test, I had developed a questionnaire which was administered to adopters who were members of adoptive parent associations in Los Angeles, Washing-

ton, D.C., and New York City. One part of that questionnaire was filled out
by husband and wife jointly, the other part consisted of identical forms which
husband and wife filled out separately in different rooms. Each of the three
forms had the same identification number pertaining to one couple. This
permitted me to link the information for subsequent analysis. In late 1962 the
bulk of the analysis was completed, but some of it came too late to become
available for inclusion in *Shared Fate*.

Among the as yet unreported data was one which sharply contradicted the
interpretation I had made of one coping theme which Willmott and I had
discovered on page 10 of the 1956 mail questionnaires. In *Shared Fate* I placed
that theme item under "Patterns Suggesting Rejection-of-Difference," thus:

> The adopter who wishes to define his own role as that of the true parent
> figure, can remove the natural parent by the invention of a myth: "We
> were very elated that our daughter accepted us as Mother and Father
> from the very first day she came to live with us. She was three and a half
> years old and we believe that she was meant for us and that God had a
> hand in bringing us together." (pp. 62-63)

Assuming that this statement implied an R/D orientation, I included it with
other items intended to measure degrees of acknowledgment-of-difference
and empathy in the 1961 questionnaire form given separately to husbands and
wives. On it I had accordingly asked:

> Since the child's legal adoption, have you:
> felt that God or fate had a hand in bringing you and the child together?

When all the items intended to test for A/D-R/D and for empathy were
analyzed by the Guttman Scaling and factor analysis methods, a peculiar
and at first disturbing discovery was made. While all the other items were
shown to belong together in the two categories of orientation toward A/D-
R/D and empathy, the item dealing with God or fate did not belong to either,
certainly not to the one to which I had hypothetically connected it. In other
words, feeling that God or fate had a hand in bringing one's children into one's
adoptive family was not, at least in terms of statistical checks, an indication of
rejection-of-difference. But if it was not R/D, what was it? Here I can resort
only to conjecture: I suspect that some myth, however much it may imply
rejection-of-difference, may be needed for what Jaffee and Fanshel (1970: 13,
14) have termed "entitlement":

> After a review of the professional literature and after discussions with
> persons close to the phenomenon of adoption, the concept of *entitle-*
> *ment* emerged in our thinking as providing a useful perspective for
> understanding the dynamics of adoptive parent behavior. While the
> adopted child may be viewed as typically facing the task of resolving
> complex identity problems with respect to the two sets of parents who

have played major roles in his life, we also considered it useful to think of a parallel identity challenge facing the adoptive parents. It was our conception that the typical adoptive parent is faced with the primary task of developing a feeling of entitlement to his child.

Finally, there is this modification of the Shared Fate theory: as I had originally formulated it, the theory had a distinct all-or-none character. A/D modes of coping were always to be preferred to R/D modes. Then I discovered a possible exception.

I had been speaking to a small group of people at an agency; they were couples each of whom were shortly to receive their first child. I had tried to tell them a little about my research findings and their implications for adoptive parent-child relationships. As I listened to the content of their remarks and the level of their excitement, I began to suspect that most of these parents-to-be had heard little or nothing of what I had tried to tell them. Some time later it occurred to me that the circumstances of that evening at the agency could be understood by an analogy. I thought about starvation victims: would people who had long been deprived of food, who were ravenously hungry, be concerned with getting a balanced diet or just anything that was edible? The answer was obvious, and so was its meaning for understanding the adopters that evening.

That is how I came to realize that there might be exceptions to an all-or-none mode of coping. I came to think about people who took a very young infant and who could, for a while at least, indulge in all the long-desired experiences of being parents pure and simple. Tiny infants are not ready for language; one need not verbalize to them any particular set of ideas. Until the toddler's concepts form with language use, the adopters can indulge in the immediate gratification of rejection-of-difference. They can do so with impunity as long as they are aware of the necessity to shift their behaviors to A/D patterns when the time comes. And the time will come soon enough — as soon as the child becomes adept with words. This view then modifies the Shared Fate theory by allowing for a transitional period when the child is young enough. When the child who comes into the adoptive home is older, the parents have none of this opportunity. Then A/D oriented coping must begin forthwith.

I have sought to show how the Shared Fate theory was formally tested in the course of studies designed by myself and carried out with students and assistants over a number of years. But an investigator's work must be replicated by others if the results are to become fully authenticated. Unfortunately, proper replication seldom takes place in sociology, partly because stringent laboratory controls are seldom possible, or at least very difficult to duplicate. That is why cognate researches by other investigators are strategically important. Let us now look to such studies, as well as to more homely settings in which the Shared Fate theory has been put to work.

NOTES

1. Dr. Weinstein's comment, "Whether he develops and tests a theory or generates a *post factum* interpretation, I would rate as a toss-up," seems to me even now to have been specious. It is unlikely that in the history of science one would readily find many instances in which purely inductive reasoning, which Weinstein here evidently equates with "theory," remained uncontaminated by deductive (*post factum*) reasoning, i.e., after the facts were in.

2. Actually not all of the respondents were married. Of the 283 couples who volunteered to participate, one lost a husband before the research meetings were held. For obvious reasons, the widow was included when she indicated her desire to remain part of the research group.

3. The Foundations' Fund For Research in Psychiatry, and the Department of National Health and Welfare.

4. Perhaps it would be more correct to say that it was a "systematic-random" sample. The main sample was drawn from the birth records and consisted of every 20th birth that was either a first or a second child born in the cities of Halifax and Dartmouth in the years 1948-1960. See: H.D. Kirk and K. Jonassohn, *Halifax Children,* 1973, pp. 3-8.

5. We were interested in the organization of families in terms of such variables as family size, geographic and social mobility, socio-economic status, and age-sex distribution as well as the health and behavior of the children in the families studied. For the rationale of our interest in the health of adopted children see: H.D. Kirk, K. Jonassohn, and A.D. Fish, "Are Adopted Children Especially Vulnerable to Stress?" *Archives of General Pschiatry,* Vol. 14, March 1966, pp. 291-298.

6. Guttman scaling is a statistical technique which orders the responses of people answering an opinion or attitude questionnaire in such a way that the numerical position of any respondent indicates the strength with which a particular attitude or opinion is held or has been expressed. If the items to which responses are given form a so-called "scalogram" pattern, that fact is taken to imply that the items represent a common dimension of meaning.

7. A.M. McWhinnie, unpublished Ph.D. dissertation, Edinburgh University, 1958.

Chapter 5

Shared Fate Put to Work

In the Scholarly Community

At the conclusion of a 1964 review essay[1] of *Shared Fate* by Professor David Fanshel, there was this revealing passage:

> In the absence of *any* theory of adoptive family relationships, the fact that we now have available a carefully thought-through theoretical formulation is a welcome development. That it is out of contact with much of the thinking in today's adoption agencies need not diminish its value as a provocative stimulus for the creation of other theoretical formulations about adoptive family life.

Had the thinking in adoption agencies been changing during the early and middle nineteen sixties? There is no doubt of it. Whereas during the previous decade most North American agencies seem to have agreed with religious and racial adoption restrictions demanded by churches or state jurisdictions, more daringly liberal points of view began to prevail in the agency policies of the nineteen sixties. That there were forward-looking social work staffs in organizations from the east to the west coast I saw in the many contacts I had with agencies in New York, Quebec, Ontario, Ohio, and California during my years of research there.

It was not so much that I was out of touch with the thinking of people in the agencies or of writings in their journals. It was much more that my work was so little known prior to the appearance of *Shared Fate* that it had almost no impact on the practitioners. As a matter of fact, I had written the book as a research report and theoretical work. It never occurred to me that it might have a future as a stimulus to changing modes of adoption practice. However, that is exactly what it became.

It seems to me true to say that by the end of the nineteen sixties, when adoption itself began to decline as a prestige activity in social work, the Shared Fate theory had gained wide acceptance. It was quoted in most publications dealing with adoptive parent-child relations, and almost invariably with agreement. But it would be arrogant and probably mistaken of me to assume that this pleasant result had come about in the course of critical reassessments of adoption policies and practices. I suspect that quite different, less personal and intentional, forces were at work. I believe that the theory became widely accepted not only because of its scientific or utilitarian merits, but perhaps even more because of fortuitous circumstances of social change. The decade of the sixties had seen the growth of a number of popular movements, each of which challenged certain traditional values: sexual, racial, and political. I think that in such a cultural climate a new generation of adopters became readier to take risks, accept uncertainty, and experiment. Likewise, a new generation of social workers began to look more to learning and systems theories than to the so-called psychodynamic theories of personality when trying to understand the behavior of their clients. *Shared Fate* had more in common with the former models than the latter so that, without assuming an overwhelming persuasiveness of my theory, there came to be a certain amount of elective affinity between it and the younger practitioners. This kind of critique is not based on invidious judgment of social work as against the theoretical social and behavioral sciences. It is based on the observation that in the absence of the cumulation of knowledge that marks the physical sciences, the acceptance or rejection of new theories in the applied as well as theoretical social sciences will depend more readily on fashion and chance than on stringently replicable and monitored tests.

Did the Shared Fate theory have "value as a provocative stimulus for the creation of other theoretical formulations about adoptive family life?" Aside from Fanshel's "entitlement" concept, I do not recall any attempts from within social work to bring alternative formulations into the picture. And concepts alone, however imaginative and germinal, must first be fitted into a larger framework of ideas to be recognizable as a theory.

Reflections in Two Apprenticeship Works

One indication that a theory has come of age is that it is taken seriously in the scientific or scholarly community, appearing as a key issue in postgraduate dissertations. The candidate for a higher degree is typically very much dependent on the judgment of academic supervisors. Thus their views of the candidate's investigative problem or chosen methodology will usually feature importantly in what finally appears in the thesis.

Before the end of the nineteen sixties, two postgraduate theses in Psychology were built around the Shared Fate theory. In 1968 Jerome F.X. Carroll[2] obtained a doctorate from Temple University for a thesis entitled: "The Acceptance or Rejection of Differences Between Adoptive and Biological Parenthood by Adoptive Applicants as Related to Various Indices of Adjustment/Maladjustment." Carroll had studied "94 married, childless men and women who had applied to adopt through the Catholic Charities Adoption Department in Philadelphia." He had developed an Adoptive Parent Questionnaire (APQ) based in large part on the research work that had led to *Shared Fate*. "The APQ was designed," says Carroll in Chapter I of his thesis, "to measure the direction and intensity of A/D and R/D tendencies." This 92 item, forced-choice questionnaire was to test "Kirk's role theory of adoption and its specific tenet relating to two coping mechanisms, A/D and R/D (acknowledgment-of-difference and rejection-of-difference)." Carroll also hoped to extend the theory "by examining the relationship between these two coping mechanisms and the concept of adjustment/maladjustment."

Dr. Carroll says of his findings:

What had been hypothesized was that the A/D oriented subjects would be well adjusted, while R/D oriented subjects would be less well adjusted. However, two unexpected findings were observed. One was that *both* A/D and R/D subjects appeared "normal" as this term was operationally defined by scores on the Tennessee Self Concept Scale. Secondly, subjects who tended to be more A/D than R/D were more inclined to describe themselves in a more realistic, although less socially desirable manner than subjects oriented toward R/D. The latter tended to be more guarded and less critical in their self-appraisals, at least in so far as they had to communicate their self evaluations to others.

When the relationship between the Adoptive Parent Questionnaire (APQ) and the Tennessee Self Concept Scale (TSCS) scores was examined, for example, it was observed that subjects who had obtained the highest APQ scores (i.e., A/D) were better able and more willing to acknowledge and report dissatisfaction with selective aspects of their self concepts than subjects with low APQ (i.e., R/D) scores. The intensity and scope of their expressed self dissatisfactions however were well within the limits of "normality" and seemed logically to reflect a more realistic and genuine self appraisal. . . .

These observations were described as being congruent with Jourard's (1963) model of a well integrated personality. Therefore, the data were interpreted as indicating, not so much that the A/D subjects were adjusted and the R/D subjects maladjusted, but that the A/D subjects were *better* adjusted than the R/D subjects. Better adjusted in the sense that their means of maintaining their adjustmental status was characterized by a more stable and realistic self concept and "genuine," "transparent" mode of disclosing this self to others.

The R/D subjects, on the other hand, seemed to sustain their "adjusted" status by denying and distorting selective aspects of their self concept and the environment. Further, they appeared to be more defensive and concerned about creating a favorable impression when describing their self-concept to others than [was the case with] the A/D oriented subjects. *Thus confirmation was demonstrated for Kirk's theory as it relates to the A/D and R/D coping mechanisms.*

A Master's thesis in psychology which relates closely to my adoption work was produced by Betty Giles Dembroski at the University of Houston, Texas. In a paper by Dembroski and Johnson,[3] the results of her research were reported in 1969:

Rokeach's notion of dogmatism viewed as a system or network of beliefs and attitudes was related to the area of adoption attitudes. The Dogmatism Scale and an Adoption Attitude Scale[4] were administered to 113 college students. Hypotheses that dogmatism would be positively related to intolerant attitudes toward adoption and areas related to adoption were almost wholly supported for the 61 males in the sample, but not for the females. The results are interpreted as suggesting that the emphasis on the maternal aspects of the feminine role in our society makes attitudes toward adoption an exception to Rokeach's theory of dogmatism.

The degree to which Dembroski's research relied on methods, findings and interpretations from our adoption studies can be gauged from these excerpts from her 1969 article:

The present study is an inquiry into the attitudes of others toward those involved in the adoption of a child who is not biologically a member of the family, and areas generally related to extra-familial adoption such as illegitimacy and infertility of the adopting parents. Since adoption is a relatively unusual situation in that it calls for the acceptance of an outsider into the intimacy of a family, the question of ability to accept the unusual is raised. That is, can a closed-minded person accept an unusual state of affairs as readily as a more open-minded person?

HYPOTHESES

The first hypothesis was that open-minded persons are tolerant of a wider range of adoptive practices than closed-minded individuals. This hypothesis stems from Rokeach's notion of attitude systems and belief systems.

The second hypothesis was that sex differences in attitudes toward adoption will appear when dogmatism is held constant. That is, when the males and females who score highest on dogmatism are compared with respect to their attitudes toward adoption, the females will be more accepting of the adoptive situation. Similarly, when the males and females who have the lowest dogmatism scores are compared with reference to adoption, the females will again reflect more tolerance. This hypothesis stems from Kirk's findings that the period of child deprivation before adoption was felt more keenly by the prospective mother than the father. This finding is in line with what might be expected as a result of the socialization process in our society, where motherhood and the maternal role are emphasized for the female. In fact Kirk found that this relationship extended to another generation in that potential grandmothers on both sides of the family were more accepting of adoption for their children than were the potential grandfathers.

METHOD

The measure of adoption attitudes used was a combination of a pencil-and-paper adaptation of Kirk's schedule and items from an especially devised questionnaire about attitudes toward adoption.

Dembroski found that "hypothesis 1 was supported almost entirely by the males in this study rather than the combined male-female sample." Thus the dogmatic men will likely show themselves less hospitable toward adoption than dogmatic women. Dembroski concludes: "Implications which might be drawn from the results suggest looking to the father for strain in the adopted child-parent relationship." What is so interesting about this finding and interpretation is that both align closely with my discovery about husbands from relatively tradition-oriented sectors of North American society. Such men were more likely to state a preference for a girl as a first or only adopted child than did men from more secular, less traditional backgrounds. In *Shared Fate*, Chapter 8, I brought together evidence for the view that preferences for female children in adoption contradicts a common preference for boys as first children when people are or expect to be fertile. I was also able to show that preference for girls by adopters is associated with various indicators of R/D coping patterns. I noted (*Shared Fate*, pp. 140-145) that men tend to be more hesitant than women in approaching adoption, and that this hesitancy appears to derive principally from the traditional values of their kin group relationships. A girl represents less of a threat to the lineage interests of the traditional kin group, and at the same time she provides role meanings and companionship to the otherwise childless wife.

In bringing this discussion of two postgraduate degree studies to a close, I note a certain congruence. Independently both investigators showed that those of their subjects who had an A/D orientation were, in normative terms, "more adequate." Both Carroll's "better adjusted" and Dembroski's "less dogmatic" subjects confirm the view that adoptive kinship represents in microcosm certain normative aspects of modernity: a permissive secularism vs. dogmatic orthodoxy, and social competence (adjustment) vs. rigidly ascribed role definitions.

Reflections in Two Journeymen's Works

Besides these doctoral theses, there are two scholarly and complex follow-up studies of adoptive families which reflect the ideas of the Shared Fate theory. One of these studies was conducted by applied social scientists in the United States, the other in Sweden. Both research reports appeared in 1970. The American one was written by Benson Jaffee and David Fanshel, who are university teachers of social work; the Swedish study is the work of Michael Bohman, a professor of psychiatry.

The Jaffee and Fanshel volume[5] sheds light on the Shared Fate theory rather obliquely. Central to their work is a sample of 100 adoptive families formed into three sub-groups for purposes of assessing the outcome of the adoptions. The authors had hoped to interview not only the parents but also their teenage and young adult children. But it appears that two thirds of the adoptees could not be interviewed.

Referring to the inability or unwillingness of adoptive parents to arrange to have their young people interviewed, the authors say: "This posture is reminiscent of the "denial of difference" orientation of adoptive parents described by Kirk, and it is difficult to appraise its latent meaning and the thinking and feeling underlying it" (p. 335). Yet five pages further, one finds some revealing information: Here Table B-3 (p. 340) shows a "Comparison of 33 interviewed and 67 noninterviewed adoptees with respect to eight background variables." In that table there is information on religious affiliation of the adoptees' families:

	Protestants (N=42)	Jews (N=25)	Catholics (N=30)	Mixed (N=3)
Adoptees who were interviewed	43%	32%	20%	—

When I tried to explain the phenomenon of differential sex preference (*Shared Fate,* Chapter 8), I made use of the index of traditionalism based on religious affiliation, developed in their student study by Dinitz, Dynes, and Clarke.[6] Like these investigators, I treated Protestants as more secular, less traditional, than Catholics. When that same index is employed in the Jaffee-Fanshel data, it is possible to make an educated guess about the structural source of refusal to have the adoptees interviewed. Catholic adoptees were said to be considerably less ready to be interviewed than were Protestant ones, with Jewish adoptees somewhere in the middle.

Had Jaffee and Fanshel understood the differential sex preference data of *Shared Fate*, they would probably have had less difficulty in understanding the "latent meaning and the thinking and feeling underlying" the adoptive parents' reticence in having their young people interviewed.

The second of the journeymen's works cited is that by Bohman.[7] His book represents an ambitious "social-psychiatric follow-up of a representative group of adopted children and their families. . . ." Bohman says that:

. . . The planning of the study and the collection of data were governed by two main questions:
1. How have the adopted child and the adoptive family developed after the placement?
2. Which factors (if any) in the biological parents, the child, the pre- or postnatal environment or the adoptive parents are relevant for the behavior and adjustment of the child. . . ?

Throughout Bohman's report, he identifies links to the *Shared Fate* data:

1. How adoptive parents manipulate an adoption will depend to a large extent on how they see themselves as parents as well as on their ability to communicate with their children. (p. 13)
2. The adoptive family as a minority group has been studied in terms of

social psychology by Kirk, who holds that adopters in general are unprepared for their roles as parents. (p. 28)

3. Kirk refers to the incongruent role-obligations of the adoptive family, its character of a minority group that lacks the support of social conventions. (p. 31)

4. Many adoptive parents. . . find it difficult to talk "naturally" with the child about its past, i.e., its biological parents and adoption. Part of the difficulty lies in the lack of tradition and "cultural script" in this sector of parenthood. (p. 33)

5. . . . Men appear to be more hesitant about adopting than women. . . . (p. 97)

Bohman also brings together considerable information to show that in his Swedish sample adoptive applicants tended to prefer girls:

6. When they applied to the adoption agency, about half of the adoptive parents expressed a definite sex preference, two thirds of these preferences being for a girl. (p. 188)

In his general discussion and conclusion, Bohman remarks:

7. [The adoptive parents'] immediate attitude as a rule was that there is "no difference" between being adoptive parents and "ordinary" parents but contrary feelings were often expressed. . . during the course of the interviews. Many adoptive parents no doubt had to struggle against their own and other people's prejudices against adoption. . . . (p. 208)

The four studies cited here indicate different ways in which the Shared Fate theory was put to work by different investigators. My personal preference would have been to see systematic replication of some of my work, for that is the route along which theories in the exact sciences have been attacked, demolished, and verified. Having to depend on my own perceptions and judgments without the critical but informed assessment of the work by colleagues, I used what opportunities offered themselves to validate the results of my work. One such opportunity was the life within my family.

The Theory on Home Ground

Long ago I learned at home the value of equity, of fair play. Looking back, I think the most powerful lesson was taught me by my son Bill some time after he had joined our family in October 1956. He was just three years old, a plump little boy whose speech I found difficult to understand. The social worker had brought Bill to us for a first visit the week before. It was agreed that on the second visit he would come to stay overnight and then return once more to the foster home. Only the third time would he be told that we were to be his new family. "We" meant Peter and Francie, both not quite six at the time, Debbie who was three years and four months, and Ruth and I. Debbie had for some time been pestering us for a brother: "I want a boy like Francie has a boy." So we finally consented to look and learned about Bill, who needed a permanent family. Somber but very agreeable, he was delighted with the idea of making cookies on this, his first visit to our house. Debbie was at nursery school when Bill arrived; an hour later, he was just settling down to some cookies and milk when the doorbell rang and Debbie entered. She had anticipated Bill's visit, and on coming up the stairs called out: "Billy, mine Billy!" But once in sight of him she slowed her approach, for she saw Bill perched on her own chair. Her welcome changed momentarily to jealous rage and she moved to pull Bill off her chair. But Bill would have none of that. He merely emitted a low growl, the kind one might hear from a lion cub in the zoo. Debbie withdrew; apparently she had found her match in Bill!

When he was brought to our house for the second visit, he came with more clothes than an overnight trip seemed to warrant. When we asked the social worker over tea about the clothes, she said casually, "Well, I thought he'd better stay on permanently as of today." Then she explained that the foster father had made a scene, calling on the little boy to make a choice between the foster home, where he had been since infancy, and the new people he hardly knew. The worker had felt that this was unfair to the little three-year-old, and did not want him subjected to an emotional tug-of-war. She decided that he would not return to the foster home. Bill stayed that night, but in the morning he came out of his room with his shopping bag stuffed full of his clothes. Asked what he was up to, he mumbled that he was going home. We all tried to tell him we wanted him to stay with us, that we were his new family, that life would soon be full of good times. But he cried bitterly. After some time he became more cheerful and seemed to settle in well. We assumed that his anguish of the first night in our home, his disappointment in not being able to return to his foster home the next day, was over and done with. Much later we discovered that we had been wrong. One day, 9 or 10 months after he had joined our family, Bill and I were strolling along the streets of our neighborhood. We were holding hands and I was absent-mindedly humming, when I became aware that Bill was trying to tell me something. At first I had difficulty in understanding him; he seemed to be saying something about wanting to "go home." Could he really be talking about his erstwhile foster home? I decided that I'd have to find out: was he talking about the family where he had lived before he had come to us? He nodded his head in affirmation.

I remember being taken aback. Bill had been doing so well among us. Why was he now, so much later, trying to reopen the past? Still walking hand in hand, I tried to put myself into the little boy's shoes. I asked myself how I would feel if I had been told that I was coming on a visit to these people, and without any further warning found that I was not to return to the place I regarded as home, where my bed and toys were, where I knew the people and where I was known. I realized that I would have been angry and very upset.

Why should it have been different for Bill, though barely four years old? True, it was surprising that he hadn't said anything about it before this, but perhaps better now than to keep silent even longer. So I asked aloud: would Bill want to go back once more to the foster home, which had been promised him long ago? Maybe this could be arranged still. In response, he squeezed my hand. When we came home I talked with Ruth and we called the social worker. She didn't like the idea but agreed to arrange a final visit to the foster home. A few days later, when it was to take place, Bill asked for Peter to come along. The foster parents had tea for Ruth and the social worker; the little foster sister was there and played with the boys; when it was time to go, Bill said his good-byes, took Ruth's hand and came home very contented. What he evidently had been wanting was equity, fair treatment. Once it was given, he was free to make his break and affirm his new connections.

Some recollections of the Shared Fate theory on home ground are more painful. By 1957, Bill had been with us a year and had settled in well; there was no thought in our minds that we would further enlarge our family. Then an old friend approached us about a girl who was close to our older children's ages. Heather (not her real name), aged seven, had a history of such childhood miseries that we wondered what, if anything, could be done for her. We tried to assist in finding another family for Heather, whom we thought in need of more parental attention than she could get with our large and often boisterous group of children. But all our efforts were in vain. Eventually we reluctantly agreed to have Heather come to us on a trial basis.

At the beginning it seemed a foolhardy venture for us all; Heather was a small and frail child. We wondered how she would fare among the other children, who were sturdy and active. To our surprise and delight, she blossomed. Heather had been with us a year when, late in 1958, with hardly a warning, a relative appeared and claimed her. We had no right to hold on to her; it all happened so quickly that none of us even had time to say decent good-byes. In some ways it seemed worse than a death in the family, for in addition to the loss and grief we felt deceived and humiliated by the friend who begged us to take her. Only three weeks later Heather would have been legally a member of our family. Suddenly she was gone, and we could not even reach her by letters or telephone. Because of the peculiarities of the circumstances, we had no legal rights in the matter and all our efforts to regain custody of Heather were in vain. All these events were terrible enough in themselves. Their effect on our children's peace of mind was devastating. Peter and Francie were eight, Debbie and Bill were five years old. For them the sudden removal of Heather from our midst spelled calamity; again and again they asked about themselves. Could this happen to them? I tried to explain that Heather did not yet have papers to prove she was one of us, while they all had their adoption papers. One day we went to the bank together, got into the safe deposit vault where all our documents were kept, and I showed each of them their papers. They seemed reassured.

Then, one day at dinner, Debbie asked: "Dad, could you ever give *us* away?"

I understood the question in the context of the devastating events surrounding our loss of Heather. I sat awhile, wondering how to answer such a terrible question. I felt a simple but forceful NO would not have been sufficient, for in the little five-year-old's mind there may have been moot difference between "letting Heather be taken away" and "giving Heather away." I must have been lost in my own thoughts and worries; when I looked around me I saw the children had stopped eating and everyone was looking to see what I'd say. I have always liked riddles and it occurred to me that I could make my reply in that form. So I said, "Yes, I suppose I might, but only for an incredibly large sum of money." The children were stunned; Ruth looked at me as if I'd gone out of my mind. I continued: "Try to think for a moment about all the money that until recently has been anywhere in the world. Let's say all that money from everywhere, all through history, has now been piled up in this one big heap. Would that money be enough? No, it wouldn't. And now let's think of all the money that is now in the world, and let that be piled up in a second heap. Even that wouldn't be enough." "Why are you making things so complicated?" Ruth asked. "Well, let's imagine now all the money that will ever, ever be in the world from this moment on till the very end of time. That would be an enormous mountain of money, wouldn't it? Let's imagine that it is being piled up in a third heap. Now we have all the money that *has ever been* in the world, all the money that *is now* in the world, and all the money that *will ever be* in the world. Would that be enough for me to be willing to give you away? No, it wouldn't. I'd want one more penny."

Obviously my riddle had been too complicated and too long. Debbie seemed confused. Peter helped out: "Never mind, he's just being clever. He wouldn't give us away." Thanks to Peter I could at least try to explain that since there couldn't be any extra penny, there was no way anyone could possibly pay enough! It wasn't very clever of me; looking back, I think I was myself so unhappy and confused during those weeks that the riddle was a way for me to escape the impact of Debbie's question. I was glad when someone changed the subject and we finished our meal. Eighteen years later, while I was temporarily living at the other end of the continent, Debbie sent me a birthday note that said: "I love you always plus one more day." At the bottom of the note was a P.S.: "Remember all the money in the world, plus one more penny?" You see why I think that while we may err in taking risks, our children are likely to sense our intent, and go on with us from there.

There are two more incidents of risk-taking I want to describe. One of these occurred on Francie's tenth birthday. It was late December 1960. We were living in Whittier, California where I was engaged in studying adoptive parent organizations. My work had earlier that year led to the formulation of the Shared Fate theory; I was full of my discovery and perhaps more confident than I should have been. Early that morning I had gone into the garden to pick a flower. There was a splendid hibiscus bloom on the bush — tan into tea-rose yellow. I went into the kitchen and put it into a shallow bowl and, knocking on my daughter's door, called out: "Happy birthday!" Francie said that she had forgotten what day it was. I remarked that another person would most likely be remembering her today. Who? she wanted to know. At that point I began to feel uncertain, but having opened the matter up, I was unable to stop there. "Your first mother who gave birth to you is surely thinking of you today, and this flower is for her as well as for you." To my dismay, Francie's instant response was: "I don't want to think about that today; it would make me too sad." After some time, seeing her enjoy her birthday. I came to understand that her remark had not been evidence of upset or anxiety, but a simple matter-of-fact statement of her limits. She had let me know that thinking about her origins on that day, however natural it may have seemed to me the grown-up, was not what she wanted to do. It was I who felt the pangs of anxiety. She evidently did not.

Finally, there is an episode I have told impersonally in *Shared Fate* (pp. 164-5). By 1961 I had the theory clearly in mind and was able to put it to work with determination. But even then it involved risk. I was never quite certain what the impact of my words on my children might be. The theory gave me general directions but no specific indications of correct action. In July, with school out, the family travelled by car back across the continent to Montreal. There is something unsettling in leaving behind the companions of playground and school, perhaps never to return. Perhaps such uncertainties triggered Peter's many questions that year. He was going on 11, and his questions showed how preoccupied he was with matters of his origin. At one point he demanded of Ruth Kirk that she tell him what his birthmother's name was. Ruth hesitated and asked me how I felt about the issue: what were we to do? On the basis of what I had learned, I replied that we must take the risk and tell him what he wanted to know. Ruth did so the next time Peter raised the matter. His reply was startling. He said: "When I'm older, I'll change my name to hers." Then he challenged Ruth to tell me what he had said. A few days later, Peter asked me whether I had received his message. I replied that I had and that I understood his feelings at least a little: "A name is a very personal possessions. The name you had before you came to our family was taken from you without you having had any say in the matter. But a name is also a way of saying where we belong. So, if you should decide to change your name when you are grown up, and if I'm alive then, I will add your new name to our family name so that all of us can continue to belong together."

During the following weeks there was a noticeable change in Peter's behavior. He had been inattentive at school and irritable at home. Now his teacher revealed that he no longer played hooky; he got down to his school work again and seemed generally more agreeable. Some weeks after the confrontation about his name, we were playing handball in the field behind our house. Passing the ball to Peter I called out half in jest: "You know what — I'm getting all ready to change my name." Peter's laughing retort was: "That won't be necessary now." When I wrote this encounter down in my notebook, I observed its similarity to Francie's Cinderella episode. As in Francie's story there was in Peter's an objective consequence that told of the child's increasing comfort with himself as an adopted person.

In these four anecdotes from the home front, I have stressed the issue of risk-taking that is unavoidable for the A/D oriented adopter. But a word of caution is in order concerning my interpretation of events reported out of the life of my family. I would not want anyone reading this to set about trying to imitate; nothing I said here is to be taken as a formula. I have wanted to say that both in the world of social science and the world of family living, the Shared Fate theory has given a good account of itself. Still, I am fully aware that I was immensely fortunate. The research had alerted me to the realities of adoptive kinship. For a time I was unable to accept these realities as applicable to myself and my family. Nevertheless, I returned to the task of research, and of applying its discoveries at home. Thus I was most fortunate that I had the research data to guide me and the stimulation of the work to urge me on toward the theory's finish line. I was fortunate in comparison with other adopters, who were entirely dependent on their own counsels. My fellow adopters, left to their own devices in circumstances of considerable uncertainty, made the best of it. Many of them seem to have veered between the poles of rejection-of-difference and acknowledgment-of-difference, similar to the adoptive mother whose interview was partially reported in Chapter 3. But why did they have to be ignorant of the nature of adoptive kinship, and uncertain about the outcome of their actions? Were there not competent social workers and legal professionals to set their minds to the needed attitudes and tasks? In the second part of this book, I shall try to show that the professional services were and remain less helpful than they were intended or thought to be. In fact, these services have added to the role handicaps unavoidably given in adoptive relationships. We will therefore see that myth and reality combine in the institutional arrangements of adoptive kinship much as they do in its interpersonal relationships.

NOTES

1. David Fanshel, "An Upsurge of Interest in Adoption," *Children,* September-October, 1964.

2. Jerome F.X. Carroll, "The Acceptance or Rejection of Differences Between Adoptive and Biological Parenthood by Adoptive Applicants as Related to Various Indices of Adjustment/Maladjustment," unpublished Ph.D. dissertation, Temple University, Chapter V, pp. 114-115, emphases added.

3. Betty Giles Dembroski and Dale L. Johnson, "Dogmatism and Attitudes Toward Adoption," *Journal of Marriage and the Family,* Vol. 31, No. 4, November, 1969 pp. 788-792.

4. Dembroski's Adoption Attitude Scale was partially adapted from the interview schedule devised for Kirk's doctoral research. See H.D. Kirk, "Community Sentiments

in Relation to Child Adoption," unpublished Ph.D. Dissertation, Cornell University, 1953, Appendix I.

5. Benson Jaffee and David Fanshel, *How They Fared in Adoption,* New York, 1970.

6. Simon Dinitz, Russel R. Dynes, and Alfred C. Clarke, "Preference for Male and Female Children: Traditional or Affectional?" *Marriage and Family Living,* XVI, No. 2 (1954), 123-130.

7. Michael Bohman, *Adopted Children and Their Families,* Stockholm, 1970.

Part II

A Critique of Institutional Arrangements

Chapter 6

Gresham's Law in the Adoption Services

In this century it was the new helping profession of social work which gave adoptive kinship its distinctive contemporary character. Legal adoption had existed in parts of North America since the middle of the nineteenth century,[1] but only with the rise of professionalized social services came systematic standards for the protection of children in adoption. Inherent in these standards has been the view that optimal human development requires a secure family environment. Accordingly, the placement of children for adoption was organized around the selection of the best possible parents for any particular child. That was the ideal, but it was also the claim of the social casework-centered agencies for having the primary responsibility in the arrangement of adoptions between previously unrelated adults and children. This primary responsibility meant that other professions which had hitherto often acted as go-betweens, particularly lawyers, doctors, and the clergy, would at most become ancillary to social work's sought monopoly of service.[2]

Given the adoption agencies' goal of providing a secure family environment for the children who became their wards, the following question becomes pertinent and even crucial: what did the social work professionals do to help make the adoptive parent-child relationship secure, cohesive, and dynamically stable? In Shared Fate terms, what was social work doing to set the adopters' minds toward the difficult task of risk-taking in a framework of loving acknowledgment-of-difference? Actually, with few exceptions, agencies did little toward that end. Typically, adopters were selected, given institutional sanctions for their new status, and left to their own devices.

I have called this chapter "Gresham's Law." Named for Sir Thomas Gresham, sixteenth century English merchant and financier, this early law of economics states that a debased currency tends to replace in circulation the superior currency, as people begin to hoard more valuable assets (such as gold and silver) against devalued paper or base metals. Here I use Gresham's Law as an analogy for the situation of coping behavior on the part of adoptive parents, who, in the absence of correct professional guidance, are likely to replace A/D means of coping with less sound R/D patterns.

As we saw in the first part of this book, adopters have typically veered between R/D and A/D poles, whether they were principally oriented in one

71

direction or the other. Thus even the group who were more generally inclined toward acknowledgment tended to mix the opposite mode of coping into their daily activities. It is not difficult to see why this should have been so. Such adoptive parents had not been given guidelines to their long-term conduct in the adoptive relationship. Those who toyed with A/D would as likely as not slip into R/D at another time. They did not understand what these actions implied for the wellbeing of their relationship with their child. Whatever they did was intuitive and impromptu.

To return to the analogy of Gresham's Law: unless we were to understand that giving up some immediate pleasure or gratification would serve our interests over the long haul, what would motivate us to curb our immediate gratification in favor of long-term rewards? The adopters did not understand the connection between modes of coping behavior and the wished-for reward of having a relationship of loving trust with their adopted children. The means to their long-term interests thus being ambiguous if not quite obscure, they can hardly be blamed for putting their emphasis where they felt rewarded and secure in the immediacy. Rejection-of-difference meant that they could wear the mantle of their longed-for status as parents pure and simple. And so, this status fashioned out of ignorance of the part they might have played by a consistently loving acknowledgment-of-difference, they made out as comfortably as they could in the here and now. Rejection-of-difference is the "bad money," because it cannot in the long run pay off as well; it will drive out the "good money" of acknowledgment-of-difference if these actions are sporadic, half-hearted, or contradictory, rather than part of a way of life in the family. But an A/D oriented way of coping, consistently and lovingly carried out, would have required awareness on the part of adoptive parents that this was for their own and the child's good. It would have required that they were willing to take risks for the future, so that their child, experiencing their loving openness, could reward them with increasing trust.

How could adopters be helped to the awareness of the need for risk-taking? In the first place, they needed to be given knowledge about the realities of adoptive kinship and what these would demand of them. The social psychologist L.S. Cottrell, Jr.[3] has observed that among the conditions needed for successful adjustment to a future role is clarity of role definition. He suggests that a person's ability to adjust well to the demands of a new role depends in large measure on how clearly the expected behaviors appropriate to the new role have been defined. Let me therefore ask: How well had the parental role been defined for the people who were to carry out its tasks in the context of adoptive kinship? To answer, it is necessary to look at social work and the behavior of its practitioners in mediating adoptions.

Social Work in Adoption

Social work provided adopters with two behavior prescriptions. One of these prescriptions had to do with their picture of themselves; the other had to do with their behavior toward their child. Prescription 1 was meant for the involuntarily childless or those unable to bear more children. Such people must, the prescription suggested, come to accept emotionally their physical limitation, i.e., they must admit to themselves without self-pity their atypical parental position. Prescription 2 bade the adopters tell their child at an early age that he was adopted — thus to admit to him his atypical position in family and society.

One might say that these prescriptions appear quite in line with the acknowledgment-of-difference pattern of coping. The first prescription made the parents acknowledge the difference of their own situation, while the second made for consistent acknowledgment with the child's situation. Thus social work, in my view, quite correctly assessed the adoptive situation as far as the separate prescriptions were concerned. What social work failed to see was that the two prescriptions had to be interdependent if they were to be useful to the wellbeing of the adoptive relationship. To prescribe the two behaviors without regard for their interrelationship was as if a physician had seen the necessity of precribing two drugs for his patient, without considering the effect they would have *in combination*. Adoptive clients were not shown why prescription 1 is helpful — even necessary — for the successful implementation of prescription 2. Further, while in broad outline the direction of the expected behavior for adoptive parenthood had been indicated by social work, the manner in which the tasks were to be approached and carried out, and indeed the full rationale for carrying them out, was never supplied.

The prescription that the adopters should see themselves as atypical parents was ambiguous. They did not see it as part of a meaningful plan for the evolving adoptive relationship. That this is not just a facile assumption can be demonstrated by information derived from the 1961 study of 283 adoptive parents in Los Angeles, Washington, D.C., and New York City, where husbands and wives were given one form to fill out jointly, and then identical forms which they filled out separately in different rooms. Three questions from the separate forms for husbands and wives are relevant to the issue of the prescription that they see themselves as atypical parents. Question 8 read as follows: "Do you feel that adoptive parents have some satisfactions which other parents do not have?" Table 6.1 shows that of 283 couples giving

Table 6.1

Do you feel that adoptive parents have some satisfactions which other parents do not have?

	Per Cent Saying "Yes"	
	H	W
N.Y.C.	67	68
D.C.	82	77
L.A.	73	81
All	73	73

answers, 73 per cent of the husbands and the same proportion of wives said "yes"; they felt that adoptive parents have special satisfactions. Thus, in terms of a very benign differentiation between adoptive and natural parenthood, almost three quarters of our respondents were ready to think of themselves as atypical.

My next question read: "And now what about other parents — do you feel that they have some satisfactions which adoptive parents do not have?" Now 53 per cent of the husbands and 54 per cent of the wives said "yes"; they agreed that adoptive parents miss some satisfactions that other parents do have (Table 6.2).

Table 6.2

And now what about other parents — do you feel that they have some satisfactions which adoptive parents do not have?

	Per Cent Saying "Yes"	
	H	W
N.Y.C.	50	45
D.C.	56	69
L.A.	58	52
All	53	54

Now we see a considerable drop among the couples in their readiness to acknowledge to themselves that they are different. Whereas previously nearly 75 per cent of husbands and wives reported thinking of themselves as different in having special satisfactions as adopters, now only just above half of the group acknowledge that biological parents have satisfactions that adopters do not have.

The next question in my index of parental role definition asked: "Some authorities believe that adoptive parents *need* to have some abilities in addition to those needed by good parents generally. Other authorities disagree, saying that adoptive parents *do not need* additional abilities. You are an experienced authority; what is your opinion?" This was really my most pointed question of role definition. Here 39 per cent of the husbands and 34 per cent of the wives said "yes"; they believed adoptive parents needed additional abilities (Table 6.3).

Here we note that as the issue has become increasingly problematic, as the definition of the parental role moves from satisfactions to deprivations to needed skills, there is greater and greater reluctance to acknowledge the atypical nature of one's position. These adopters had not been given indications of how or why they might consider themselves as atypical parents, so

Table 6.3

Some authorities believe that adoptive parents *need* to have some abilities in addition to those needed by good parents generally. Other authorities disagree, saying that adoptive parents *do not need* additional abilities. You are an experienced authority; what is your opinion?

Per Cent Saying: "Adoptive parents *need* additional abilities"

	H	W
N.Y.C.	39	35
D.C.	38	32
L.A.	40	35
All	39	34

that the prescription had remained ambiguous for them. They were therefore bewildered and their tendency was to cope by means of rejection-of-difference.

Let us now look at the way in which the adopters in the 1961 study dealt with the "telling" prescription. It will be helpful in understanding the data that follow if we remember that more than half of these adopters' children were over five years old at the time their adoptive parents replied to our questionnaire. These data derive from the joint form filled out by husband and wife together.

Question 11 on the joint form asked the respondents whether they had told their children that they had been adopted. Seventy-two per cent answered "yes." In question 13, I asked: "During the past year, have you talked with one or more of your adopted children about adoption, and if so, how often?" Respondents could check one of the following answers:

— We've not talked about it;
— We may have talked about it once or twice;
— We have talked about it occasionally;
— We have talked about it quite often.

Sixty-three per cent report that they talked about adoption occasionally or quite often. But in question 12 we also asked: "Have you talked with your children about the difference between birth and adoption?" To this question 51 per cent answered "yes."

Thus we see that as the issue becomes progressively more specific, the number of adopters who reported having instituted the prescription fell progressively, from 72, to 63, to 51 per cent. The reader who speculates that this was because the children were too young to be told of adoption in more specific ways, may wish to know the ages of the children who were reported to have asked specific questions about their natural parents. Of 68 couples who reported that their children asked specific questions such as the name of the natural mother, or where she lives, 13 per cent were under four years old at the time they asked, 32 per cent were four but under six, 32 per cent were six but under eight, 18 per cent were eight but under 12, and 4 per cent were over 12 when the matter first came up. Thus, as recalled by these parents, two thirds of the children asked first when they were between four and eight.

So, when it came to the prescription that the child must be told of the adoption, we find that the adopters were hesitant to carry it out fully. We can readily understand why that was so: not only did they not know when to start telling, or how far to go into it, but they did not know what the effects on the child were going to be. Below are some illustrative statements from adoptive mothers responding to the following question from the 1961 questionnaire: "If there are other experiences which you found or still find rather difficult or hard, please name these experiences":

> "The actual explaining of adoption, even in simplest terms will be difficult."
> "We anticipate upset on the part of our eldest child when he fully understands what adoption means.. But we may be wrong."
> "Telling the child the truth about her biological parents. Sometimes I think it pays to tell a white lie."

And what are the results of the adopters' hesitation? McWhinnie[4] reported that in her sample of 58 Scottish adult adoptees the majority had been eager but unable to communicate with adoptive parents. The parents waited for the children to ask and the children waited for the parents to explain.

There is, then, little question that adopters tended to accept the "telling" prescription in principle, as a norm of conduct, but also that they followed it rather mechanistically, like a ritual that had little or no vital meaning for them. We have here what Williams has called a "cultural fiction":

> A cultural fiction exists whenever there is a cultural description, explanation, or normative prescription that is both *generally accepted as a norm* and is *typically followed* in conduct but is at the same time markedly at variance with the subjective conceptions or inclinations of participants in the pattern or with certain objective scientific knowledges.[5]

In the case of the mechanistic handling of the "telling" prescription, there was a cultural fiction for two reasons, and these reasons are interdependent.

1. As we already saw, the adopters had not known, and therefore could not appreciate the long-term implications and values for them and their child that flow from a feeling-based and consistent pattern of acknowledgment-of-difference, in which "telling" is a part.

2. Since they had not known or appreciated the long-term benefits, they gave themselves to the short-run satisfactions of "forgetting" that they were substitute parents in a culture in which parenthood is typically defined as linking biological and social elements. In other words, lacking correct objective guidelines concerning the "telling" norm, they carried out what they thought necessary; meanwhile this overt acceptance of the adoption was undermined by their subjective inclinations to see themselves simply as parents.

From the point of view of the adopters' own long-range goals for the relationship with their child, as well as from the point of view of the social worker, what was needed was a consistent pattern of loving acknowledgment-of-difference. In the absence of truly reliable data on the relationship between parental behavior and the development of adopted persons, I must rely on impressions gained from knowledge of hundreds of adoptive families in well over a decade of studies. Almost always I saw much love, but also considerable confusion and denial on the part of adoptive parents. The picture that has emerged of young and older adult adoptees in recent years suggests that many of these intended beneficiaries of the adoption arrangement have experienced a great deal of bewilderment and self-doubt. It is troublesome to think that so much professional effort had been expended on regulating and controlling the legal and administrative procedures that lead to adoption, and that so little concern was shown for the internal and continuing process in adoptive kinship. It is a question that belongs to social structure: why was it that the organizational arrangements that were set up to aid adoptive family life neglected precisely the central matter of its dynamics?

Let me suggest that the answer has to be sought in three sources of professional organization: (1) in a "common sense" ideology of adoption workers, who tended to share their clients' values that led to rejection-of-difference; (2) in patterns of agency practice which, while intended to help the new families, also aided and abetted the adopters' orientation toward rejection-of-difference; (3) in the professional training given at that time to most social work personnel, especially to those in casework. That training had a strong psychodynamic, usually Freudian, slant.

(1) Concerning the ideological outlook of social work staff in the adoption agencies, I have previously shown (*Shared Fate,* 148-149) that the professionals typically supported their adoptive parent clients' leaning toward R/D modes of accommodation. That observation was based on research reporting by Brenner,[6] and clinical writings by Thunen,[7] both social work professionals.

Whatever may have been typical among agencies and workers, their outlook was by no means uniform. At the time of my daughter Francie's legal adoption in 1952, the court decree arrived in the mail. I recall opening it and, seeing my daughter's former name on the document, I immediately called the agency on the phone. The worker who had placed the baby wanted to know what the problem was: had she understood me correctly that I wanted to destroy the document? Her voice rose and she told me in no uncertain terms that I had absolutely no right to tamper with this record of my child's adoption. If I didn't like to look at it I should put it away into a safety deposit box at the bank to keep it there until my daughter came of age. Then it should be hers, since it dealt with her past and her life! Contrast my experience with that of an adoptive mother whose letter came to me from Great Britain in 1967.

> I am interested in your reactions to the legal document. I had a contrary experience. We were told by the adoption agency to please destroy the letter which described the status and attainments of our child's natural parents and to make up a suitable story as to his need for adoption. This I refused to do, not telling the agency so, however, for some quite dim and then unexplained reason I felt it would be wrong, perhaps wrong to destroy part of the process of his acquisition. I don't know. Essentially it was that he was adopted, this was part of his history, part of him. . . . I doubt if I could have put all this so clearly before reading *Shared Fate*.

What is remarkable about this letter, besides the benighted advice this mother was given, is the fact of her own much better sense in going against an R/D oriented agency, following through intuitively with an acknowledgment oriented way of coping.

(2) In *Shared Fate* (pp. 152-153) I showed in tabular form the agency practice patterns to which I attributed support and legitimation for the adopters' tendencies toward coping by rejection-of-difference. That attribution is as firm today as it was in the early nineteen sixties; nothing has been brought to my attention since then that would suggest otherwise. However unwittingly, the agencies were for decades committed to professionalized practices which sanctioned their clients' false consciousness. But to say "unwittingly" does not excuse their errors, especially errors which became formalized and thus resistant to change. No less a spokesman for the adoption field than Joseph H. Reid, long-time director of the Child Welfare League of America, counseled against such formalization of agency practice errors when in 1955 he said:

> Every area of adoption practice is being exposed to scrutiny. Obviously grave deficiencies exist in many aspects of social agency practice. . . . But again, to me, the obstacles are not the things that we should center upon. They should be identified. They should be exposed. They should be corrected. But they should not become beloved obstacles, obstacles that prevent us from examining what we have to examine carefully. . . .[8]

Still, such counsel was easier given than followed. Adoption practice might be "exposed to scrutiny," but in the absence of any operational criteria of sound practice, the readiness to make corrections proved to be ineffective.

Professional claims to the contrary, there simply were no reliable corrective mechanisms, and there certainly was no reliable knowledge about adoptive kinship to which corrective mechanisms might have been addressed. What is more, some of the agencies' practices were given high-level cultural sanctions, so that what had once been a usage justified by the thinking of a group of colleagues now became thoroughly institutionalized. Note for instance this observation of mine from the early nineteen sixties concerning one of the parental coping patterns and the agency practice supporting it (*Shared Fate*, p. 153):

Often adopters seek to simulate the biological family's spacing of arrival of children.	It appears to be common practice of child-placing agencies to insist that a "suitable" period elapse before an application for an additional child can be accepted.

At the time I wrote *Shared Fate* I had not noticed this passage in a 1953 U.N. study of adoption:

> The general experience is that. . . it is better for the adopted child to be younger than the other children and preferably of the opposite sex to the one nearest in age to him.[9]

Clearly, the U.N. study merely stated what appeared common practice. But now that common practice pattern was given sanction by a high-level international body. Such events would tend to give the ordinary professional pattern an aura of transcendental immutability, not exactly the stuff to be questioned or corrected.

(3) The training of most professional social workers, especially in case work, was for a number of decades principally informed by psychodynamic theories of personality. In 1954 I joined the staff at the McGill University School of Social Work to help in making the curriculum more sociological. I do not think that I was prepared for the overwhelming influence of psychiatric medical models along which social workers were being prepared for their tasks. For a number of years I taught material on kinship and on formal organization to first-year students who had not yet been strongly influenced in the direction of the psychiatric models. By the time they were in second year, I found students in my research seminars to have a kind of trained incapacity for thinking along lines of social structure. Psychodynamic theory had taken over.

Let me give an example: a few years ago, a colleague who had taught with me at the School of Social Work went to a Far Eastern university for his sabbatical year. He himself had been trained as a clinician first, and then had obtained a doctorate in social psychology. We corresponded during his stay abroad. One of his letters recounts his meeting with a former casework student who had come from this poverty-stricken area to McGill and later returned to Asia to work. How did this former student approach her casework? She asked these miserable people, who were in need of the most elementary of human creature comforts, how they felt about their poverty, how they understood the misery of their existence. My colleague's response was disgust — not so much with the young woman, who blindly applied the misplaced psychodynamic model, but with the training patterns that had made this possible. Thus, what the psychodynamic model does when it is the principal way of viewing human problems and issues is to cover over the raw and unpalatable aspects of the ordinary world. Of course there are nasty and similarly problematic issues in the *inner* world of human life, but once one can state the mother-child interaction problems in esoteric terms of oedipal dynamics, the events have become esoteric and transcendental, far removed from commonly understood modes of intervention and helping.

What relevance does such an anecdote have for an understanding of social work activities in adoption during the nineteen forties, fifties and sixties? The psychodynamic model stood in the way of the workers' understanding of quite ordinary human experiences, translating them into esoteric, transcendental terms. I am fortunate that I need not assert this merely; I have a powerful witness with me in court. He is Dr. Povl Toussieng,[10] a psychiatrist formerly on the staff of the Menninger Clinic in Topeka, Kansas. Almost two decades ago, Dr. Toussieng saw two papers I had just delivered at sociological conferences, both dealing with my studies on adoptive relationships. I had not met Dr. Toussieng at the time when, on December 30, 1958 he wrote me a long and thoughtful letter concerning my papers. He indicated that he had seen many of the events and issues my paper described — his observations had been in clinical rather than social research settings — but that he interpreted them differently. His interpretations were of course informed by his professional orientation as a psychoanalytic psychiatrist. For instance:

> In my own material I have also had to raise a serious question about the "I chose you" story which adoptive parents are encouraged to tell their children. In a number of children who did become disturbed, this seems to have had the meaning to the child that the adoptive parents "robbed" them from the natural parents. In all these cases, there was a serious barrier, psychologically speaking, between the adoptive parents and the child, and it may be that this is a secondary rationalization. However, judging from the treatment of some adopted children here at Southard School, the robbery fantasy in adopted children really in itself represents a serious handicap in the relationship between the adoptive parents and children.

As a matter of fact, I also had experience with the robbery fantasy in my family. When Peter was five years old he made use of it in the course of dinner; without any apparent connection he said, turning to me: "You stole me." At the time I was defensive and replied that I had not taken him away, but that he had come to us by quite proper means — an agency had arranged for him to have us as his parents. But a year or so later, I came to realize that he had not been accusing me but trying to understand his very difficult position as an adopted child. I had to think about a real situation — an every-day situation about mothers and children who ordinarily are *not* separated as this little boy had been — rather than wonder what the psychodynamic forces in Peter were that led to the fantasy.

Three years after his letter to me, Dr. Toussieng published an article which stirred considerable controversy in child welfare circles. This article, "Thoughts Regarding the Etiology of Psychological Difficulties in Adopted Children"[11] came close upon an earlier paper by another psychiatrist, Dr. Marshall D. Schechter,[12] who had pioneered the view that adopted children suffer from special problems *as adoptees*. Both papers based their interpretations on psychodynamic theory. In his summary Dr. Toussieng, in 1962, said:

> Children who have been adopted at an early age and/or who have not been exposed to psychological traumatization before adoption seem to be more prone to emotional disturbances and personality disorders than nonadopted children. It is hard to explain these difficulties merely on the basis of the children's awareness of being adopted. *It seems much more feasible to think of an unconscious and unresolved aversion toward parenthood in one or both adoptive parents, particularly the mother, as the original cause of the child's disturbance.*" (My emphasis.)

I said above that I wanted to bring Dr. Toussieng "into court" as my witness to the contention that social workers in adoption were long exposed to and influenced by psychodynamic theories of personality as a way of understanding adoption. But Dr. Toussieng is more than a good witness. He is one of those rare professionals who says publicly that he was wrong when this becomes evident to him. In his letter to me of December 1958, he had indicated his belief that "the parent role of an adoptive parent is really not so different from the role of a natural parent." But in a paper published in 1971 he said:

> Initially, both Schechter and I were interested mostly in any internal psychodynamic problems that, for example, might prevent the parents from assuming their parental roles, or might arise in the child after he, at a certain developmental level, discovered that he was adopted. . . .
> The trouble with this approach, however, is that the same psychodynamic conflict may be observed in nonadoptive family members. . . . *Without meaning to, I and my colleagues in various professions who pursued this road fell into the trap of viewing the adoptive situation as essentially the same as the nonadoptive one, because we viewed it from the standpoint of internal psychodynamic conflicts. Thus we ignored that the requirements of belonging to each other as adoptive family members are different in every way from those requirements in a biologic family.* . . .

In my previous paper[13] I found that the ties between parents and children in the disturbed adoptive families seen in a psychiatric setting appeared to be quite tenuous. At that time I ascribed this to various psychodynamic conflicts in the family members involved. Subsequently I found that this way of looking at things made the approach to helping such families cumbersome if not insurmountably difficult. . . .

Beginning to accept the situation of the adoptive family as inherently different has changed my focus from the internal psychopathology in individual family members to the degree of anxiety that is attached to the family members' ties with each other in the adoptive families. . . . The child may come to view his ties to his parents as much more tentative and fragile than they appear to the professional observer.

Thus the lack of a biologic tie becomes the source of an inordinate amount of anxiety. It leads the three persons involved to see their mutual ties as being in constant jeopardy, because they have not come to accept that their situation is different from, and should not and cannot be compared with, a biologic family situation. (My emphases.)[14]

I am glad to have this opportunity to let my readers appreciate the force of the psychodynamic mode of thought that so obscured the immediate and ordinary circumstances in adoptive kinship relations. But I am also glad to think that my own work helped redirect Dr. Toussieng's thinking. In that paper of 1971 just quoted, he also said: "[Kirk's] research findings stress that adoptive parents who acknowledge the difference inherent in their situation have more empathic and ideational communication with their children about their adoption, and that such families show greater dynamic stability."

In this chapter I have tried to make understandable why the adoptive parent clients of social work agencies so typically engaged in R/D oriented coping in spite of the agencies' concern with the new families' long-term welfare. I have tried to show that there was in fact a kind of latent cooperation between clients and agencies in this rejection-of-difference. However unintended and probably unrecognized this cooperation was, it proved effective: many adoptive parents, considering themselves to have been selected as fit for adoptive parenthood, seem to have felt no need for any further special skills or attitudes. Preferring to feel comfortable in contexts they knew well, i.e., rejecting any substantial difference between their current families and those they knew from their own childhood, they unwittingly isolated their children in a no-man's land of genealogical bewilderment.

In tracing myth and reality in institutional arrangements, we shall find that some myths are benign if neutral, and some may be helpful in keeping human society a going concern. But some myths are destructive, especially if they mislead the adherents to feel safe where there are dangers, or to rely on conventional wisdom when innovative behavior is called for. Let us go on to explore why the adoption services did not recognize that their practice patterns tended to undermine the very goals of security, cohesiveness, and dynamic stability which they so earnestly sought for the adoptive families they helped to constitute.

NOTES

1. The first adoption law of English-speaking North America was enacted in Massachusetts in 1851.

2. Note the following remarks by Joseph H. Reid, then Director, Child Welfare League of America, as reported in a U.S. Children's Bureau publication, *Protecting Children in Adoption,* 1955, p. 27.

One of the reasons that social workers are very strongly in favor of social agency adoptions as such is that adoption is not something that can be done by one discipline; the geneticist, psychiatrist, the pediatrician, the obstetrician, the attorney, and many other disciplines, are needed in some adoption cases. And the average person, the average doctor or lawyer working alone is not in a position to call upon these disciplines. . . .

3. L.S. Cottrell, Jr., "The Adjustment of the Individual to His Age and Sex Roles," *American Sociological Review,* 7 (1942), pp. 617-620.

4. A.M. McWhinnie, unpublished Ph.D. dissertation, Edinburgh University, 1958.

A.M. McWhinnie, *Adopted Children: How They Grow Up,* Routledge and Kegan Paul, 1967.

5. R.M. Williams Jr., *American Society,* 1951, p. 366.

6. R. Brenner, *A Follow-Up Study of Adoptive Families,* Child Adoption Research Committee, New York, 1951.

7. M. Thunen, "Ending Contact with Adoptive Parents: The Group Meeting," *Child Welfare,* XXXVII, No. 2 (1958), pp. 10-11.

8. J.H. Reid in United States Children's Bureau *op. cit.,* p. 27.

9. United Nations, *Study on the Adoption of Children,* 1953, p. 16.

10. Dr. Toussieng is currently a member of the faculty of the Department of Psychiatry and Behavioral Sciences, University of Oklahoma. He is also co-author, with A.E. Moriarty, of *Adolescent Coping* (1976).

11. P.W. Toussieng, "Thoughts Regarding the Etiology of Psychological Difficulties in Adopted Children," *Child Welfare,* February 1962.

12. M.D. Schechter, "Observations on Adopted Children," *Archives of General Psychiatry,* Vol. 3 (July 1960), pp. 21-32.

13. See Note 11, above.

14. P.W. Toussieng, "Realizing the Potential in Adoptions," *Child Welfare,* Vol. I, No. 6, (June 1971), pp. 322-327.

Chapter 7

Professional License, Mandate, and Myopia

The leading child welfare organizations became, during the decade of the nineteen fifties, increasingly enamored with the *mechanics* of professional child-placing. It seems to have been their view that, given optimal professional judgment in the selection of the right adopters for a child needing adoption, the future wellbeing of the child in the new family would be secured. Thus in 1956 the head of the U.S. Children's Bureau, Dr. Martha M. Eliot, and her colleague, Dr. Katherine Bain, proposed as much in a paper presented to the American Academy of Pediatrics. They said: "Much of our legal machinery . . . is concerned with the process of legalizing the status of the child, of finishing the job and tying the knot, *and not with the core of the problem — the placement of a child for adoption.*[1] If the legal machinery had previously eclipsed the question of how adoptive parents would relate themselves to their adopted children, now it was the new professionalized adoption agencies which were responsible for a similar goal displacement. It seems strange that this should have happened with a group of people whose intellectual set was human relationships, and it seems proper to inquire how it could have happened.

In discussing the characteristics of occupations, Everett Hughes has drawn attention to the factors of "license" and "mandate." An occupational license, he says, consists of the "right to deviate in some measure from some common modes of behavior." Usually, when professionals

> . . . individually exercise a license to do things others do not do, . . . collectively they presume to tell society what is good and right for it in a broad and crucial aspect of life. Indeed they set the very terms of thinking about it. When such a presumption is granted as legitimate, a profession in the full sense has come into being.[2]

The process of professionalization implies more than having a body of knowledge and skills, controlled by an ethic that is administered by a group of colleagues. The concepts of license and mandate link professionalized occupations to questions of the common good. Whence derives the license to do what others do not, cannot, or may not do? What is the nature and the extent of the mandate that the professional group — here the adoption agency — claims, and by which it seeks to define the meaning of the public interest?

In the older professions, the professionals gather "guilty knowledge" through entry into the private domains of the body (by physicians and surgeons), of social and economic actions (by lawyers), and those of conduct and feelings (by psychiatry and the clergy). Thus the possession of "guilty knowledge" can be regarded as an index of relatively high professional status, prestige, and power. In contrast with the older professions; school teaching and social work with the poor have much lower status; perhaps in part because these activities carry with them little of the burdens of such "guilty knowledge." Once social work entered on the service to unmarried mothers, once it investigated the motives of sterile people who sought parenthood, it dealt with issues that are fraught with the very stuff of guilty knowledge. Moreover, in shifting human beings by social and legal contrivances from one set of forebears to a new kinship system, social workers were in fact manipulating one of the last strongholds of ascribed and thus sacred relations left in an otherwise achievement-oriented and secularized society. The fact that adopters as well as social workers have referred to the role of social work in adoption as "playing God," suggests a tacit recognition of this particular "guilty knowledge" that derives from interference with an ascribed position in social life. Doctors, lawyers, and priests deal with more or less awe-inspiring matters: death, the law, and God. In adoption, social work had likewise found an awe-inspiring medium of action. This has been made the more important because the sectors of society that came to the adoption agency as parent-applicants typically represented the middle and upper middle classes.

The professional claims of social work in adoption were most forcibly made by two organizations, one governmental and the other private. The United States Children's Bureau has been active in this undertaking over many decades, and so has the Child Welfare League of America. The League's National Conference on Adoption in January 1955, which resulted in a two-volume work edited by Michael Schapiro,[3] was a watershed in the codification of adoption practice in North America. Later that year, the U.S. Children's Bureau followed suit with its own conference. The report of the latter contains quotations from a statement by Joseph H. Reid, the long-time director of the Child Welfare League. His view was that the professional activities of the adoption worker were given particular legitimation by the fact that adoption is an institutionalized practice:

> Adoption, because of its implications to at least four groups — the natural parents, the child, the adoptive parents, and society as a whole — goes beyond the interest of simply two people making a private arrangement. Rather, it is something with which society as a whole has a right to be concerned, and around which appropriate social institutions have to be established.[4]

As noted, the spokesmen for the professional point of view in adoption arrangements saw the core of the problem to lie in child placement rather than in statutory provisions. It was for these professional activities that the adoption agencies and their lobbies sought license and mandate, and for which it was claimed there could and should be specialized professional preparation. This view was voiced by no less an authority than the Hon. Justine Wise Polier, Judge of the Domestic Relations Court of New York City:

> . . . there is a growing recognition that just as we require by law preparation and proof of qualification for the practice of law, medicine, dentistry, or even the underwriting of insurance, there is a duty to require proof of ability before any person or agency outside the immediate membership of a child's family, shall be entrusted to determine the future life of a child through adoptive placement.[5]

Who would want to disagree with the view that finding families for children through adoption was an activity that ought to have been secured by very special knowledge and skills? Drs. Eliot and Bain affirmed it when they said: "But even though we know that our knowledge is incomplete, we do have a well-developed body of practices that has been acquired through the experience of social workers, aided in many cases by psychiatrists and social scientists, and one that has as a rule given good results."[6]

But what preparation should adoption workers have possessed to implement this body of practices? What proof of qualification should they have been able to show? The answer to this question has to be inferred from the papers and articles that dealt with the three principal areas of professional activity in the adoption agencies: (1) work with parents wanting or needing to surrender children for adoption, (2) the selection of adopters from among the applicants, and (3) the testing of infants to ascertain their suitability for adoptive placement. The first two of these sensitive psychological activities required, it was believed, knowledge of and skill in the use of psychodynamic theory, which was to enable caseworkers to identify the unconscious needs and motives of their clients. The more professionalized the agencies, the more they seem to have relied on psychodynamic theory as guides to working with unwed mothers and applicants for adoptive parenthood. Caseworkers who specialized in dealing with pregnant women depended on psychodynamic theory to help such women "work through" feelings engendered by their plight. Such "working through" was believed to facilitate a decision which would be in the woman's and her child's best interest; it seems to have generally favored the child's surrender when the child was healthy and of Caucasian background. For workers who specialized in the selection of applicants for adoptive parenthood, psychodynamic theory became the principal tool for identifying the clients' deeper motives, quality of marital relations, and emotional maturity. The assumption was that psychodynamic theory gave the workers clues to their clients' personality structure.

Claim of Competence No. 1:
Helping the Unwed Mother Decide the Future of her Child

Because the majority of relinquishing parents who, during the past decade, placed children through adoption agencies were young unmarried women, I will here refer to them as "unmarried mothers." And because the majority of applicants for adoptive parenthood were married couples, I will subsequently refer to them in these terms.

Leontine Young's book *Out of Wedlock*[7] came to be a mainstay of the psychodynamically oriented work with illegitimately pregnant women and unmarried mothers. Here is how Young portrayed the unwed mother's needs and motives:

> One thing is clear. The baby is not desired for himself but as a symbol, as a means to an end. Precisely what he symbolizes and for what end he is to be used can be discovered at least in part from the girl's attitude toward him and what she does with him. Obviously, he must serve some extremely important purpose for her, and *while she would be consciously unaware of what that purpose is or even that it exists, her actions again delineate its outline.* He is the focal point of her unconscious fantasy; she must seek to force him to fulfill that purpose for which he was conceived. . . . *An unmarried mother who is bound hand and foot by the iron bonds of her own neurotic needs has little freedom for concern for the needs of the infant she has to bear.*
>
> Why does a girl have to bear a baby at such a cost to herself? The answer can only be sought in her past life, her home and her childhood. Like every human being she responds dynamically to her particular life situation. *The question is what particular combination of factors and circumstances produces that psychological development which finds its expression in an out-of-wedlock child.*[8]

Here we can see the psychodynamically-based diagnosis leading almost directly to the conclusion that it is best for the unmarried mother to relinquish her baby: having been conceived as a result of immature motives, the baby is not really desired for himself. Naturally then, he ought to be given to people who are mature and who want him for himself! (The identification of such persons among the myriads of people wanting to be adoptive parents is the other task of social work in adoption. At this point, however, we must stay with the professional activity of helping the unwed mother to make the decision that is best for her and the child.) Two years prior to the appearance of Young's book, a psychiatric social worker on the staff of one of New York's elite agencies had written:

> On a clinical basis it has been found that giving the baby up for adoption is the most positive solution for the majority of unmarried mothers and makes possible greater opportunity for her future development. Therefore, it is understandable that social workers have been oriented toward the achievement of this goal with the client, and with

the reality and time pressures involved, to the accomplishment of this as quickly as possible. Thus the client's ambivalence and resistance to coming to a decision about adoption have often been viewed by the worker with anxiety.[9]

In the same paper, Sarah Evan also noted that "more has been written, primarily by psychoanalysts, about the psychodynamics of the pregnancy. [It] has been viewed as a fantasy fulfillment of oedipal and pre-oedipal strivings or as a neurotic solution to problems such as loss of a loved person, or anxieties about one's sexuality." No wonder then that the unwed mother was seen as immature, and that the optimal solution for her and the child was seen to be the surrender of her child.

One of the psychoanalysts who had written about the dynamics of the unwed mother's pregnancy was Dr. Ner Littner. In a paper dated 1955 he reported on a study of unwed mother clients of a Chicago agency:

> It is [the] strong relationship, that is built up throughout the pregnancy, that allows the caseworker to be so effective after the delivery, in helping the unmarried mother with her emotional difficulties. And it is the lack of this relationship, and the resulting restoration of the usual defenses against being helped, that make it extremely difficult for the unmarried mother to be referred to, or treated by, any other therapist.
> *In view of the fact that the large majority of the unmarried mothers that we have seen, were far better off emotionally (as were their babies), when the latter were given in adoption as soon after birth as possible, then the desire of the unmarried mother to give her baby to the caseworker's agency, can be a very healthy step forward for both, and thus well justifies the relative concentration of casework service.*[10]

Let me now look more carefully at psychodynamic theory as a tool which served caseworkers in this helping service. Psychodynamic theories of personality utilize life history information to make the social and psychic behavior of a person understandable. In that sense such theories may be helpful as a source of insight in therapy, but they cannot predict what a particular person's experiences or behaviors will be in the future. In the professional services of the adoption agency, considerations of the future welfare of its clients are important. What will happen to the unwed mother after she has surrendered her child? Will the casework help she has received remain a source of support for the rest of her life? Here, as in the selection of adopters, the social worker needs indications of the clients' future capabilities to make proper decisions with an eye to the clients' long-term welfare. But if, professional beliefs to the contrary, the theory tool used is in that sense ineffective, what will the social worker use instead? I suspect that the worker will tend to fall back on the guidance of diffuse and unreliable sources of information, such as personal insights and intuition. But insights and intuition are not open to critical examination. Biases derived from personal fortunes, social class position, or professional aspirations may therefore be mistaken for more sound and reliable directives. Having to determine the relative maturity of the client without specific and objective criteria for defining "maturity," the worker is therefore liable to draw on her or his own social class or profession-derived model of proper adulthood. Such models would appear to have become avenues to labelling clients as "mature" or "immature" and this in turn seems to have served the agency's readiness to receive the unwed mother's surrender of her child. There is socio-linguistic evidence of the use of such labelling in the literature of the nineteen fifties, for many of the social work documents refer to unwed pregnant women as "girls." My examples derive from a publication of the United States Children's Bureau:

— What happens when an unmarried *girl* suspects she is pregnant?
— The unmarried *girl* must face her own inner feelings as well as the outward reactions of society.
— Our immediate concern here is with those *girls* who turn to individuals for help.
— We know that one of the first concerns of many unmarried pregnant *girls* is medical care.[11]

Evidently what is implied here is that children are not mature enough to be raising other children. Thus the pressure for surrendering the out-of-wedlock child is justified by the very terminology employed. Inherent in such linguistic usage was the belief that illegitimacy resulted principally from the sexual activity of juveniles. This myth was exploded by Clark Vincent, whose researches were reported from the mid-nineteen fifties to the early sixties.[12] Referring to a steep rise in the illegitimacy rate in the United States during the nineteen forties and fifties, he said:

Contrary to popular opinion, the illegitimacy rate increased least among the women aged between fifteen and nineteen (108 per cent), and most among the women aged between twenty-five and twenty-nine (453 per cent) during the twenty year period of 1938 to 1957.[13]

However unwarranted, the use of the "child" label in reference to unmarried pregnant women or mothers served to justify the license and mandate which social work in adoption had claimed. Children, too immature to raise the children they bore, must be helped to make the right decisions for *their* children's futures. This need for help on the part of the unwed woman implies her dependency. This secondary labelling of the birthmother as dependent was graphically illustrated in an issue of the *National Parent-Teacher* journal.[14] The article was written by Lucile Kennedy, who was then Chief of the Division of Child Welfare, California State Department of Welfare. Its title page showed a social worker seated at her desk, smiling at a somber woman standing before her in a supplicant position.

WHY DO WE NEED

Adoption

Agencies?

Lucile Kennedy
*Chief, Division of Child Welfare
California Department of Social Welfare*

This article, published in a journal directed to one of the largest publics in the United States, illustrates how social work organizations lobbied for the license and mandate to carry on the work of the adoption services.

Claim of Competence No. 2:
The Selection of Adopters

The agencies' standards for the selection of applicants for adoptive parenthood hinged on the numbers that applied. When the quantity of applications was much higher than the number of available children, the standards were high and rigid. When the number of applications waned, the standards were relaxed. But during the nineteen fifties, there was generally a glut of applications, so that Joseph Reid, then director of the Child Welfare League of America could say in 1955:

> . . . [One] premise on which adoption practice rests is the fact that it is a child-centered program, not an adult-centered one. And this is an important distinction. *Adoption agencies exist to find the best opportunity for a child; not necessarily to find children for adults.* . . .
> Children who come out of the tragedy of illegitimate birth do have the advantage of having at least ten people who want to adopt them. And from the group, certainly regardless of what standards we agree upon, there ought to be one family that perhaps is a little better suited to care for that child than nine others.[15]

So the agencies existed for the sake of the children — to find for each available child the one best family out of ten applications.

Selecting the best possible adoptive parent for the child is second only to understanding the child himself and evaluating the desirability of adoption for him. Perhaps the two processes are actually of equal importance since they are inextricably linked. *A great deal of material exists in the literature and in workshop reports about every phase of this selection* as it relates to the child, the adoptive applicants, and the community of which they are a part.[16]

With these words, Schapiro introduced the chapter "Adoptive Parents" in the volume on agency practices as they were reported in the Child Welfare League's study of 270 adoption agencies. In answer to the question as to the eligibility requirements which these agencies set out for adoptive applicants, 245 of the responses mentioned physical health and 244 of them said they required evidence of emotional health. Schapiro comments as follows:

The most common requirement, physical health, is easily understood. In choosing parents for a child, an agency has the responsibility for protecting the child against loss of his adoptive parents, exposure to disease, etc. While it may be more difficult to determine emotional health, there is very little disagreement that the child must be protected against neglect and emotional conflict. *However, emotional health is a broad concept and defining the elements that make up this broad concept is a more difficult task.*[17]

Then, quoting a paper by Florence Brown,[18] Schapiro continues:

A definition of emotional health might include: "the personal adjustment of each of the prospective parents, their relationship to each other, their relationship to their own parents and siblings, their deeper, as well as expressed motives in seeking a child, their attitude toward childlessness and toward infertility; their ability to accept an adopted child; and their understanding of children and their need."

Once again we see psychodynamic ideas and assumptions operating as underpinnings of the adoption worker's expertise in the selection of adopters. As in the case of the unwed mother and her child, one must question the validity of the ideas as well as the reliability of the judgments made by the workers. It is perhaps worth repeating that psychodynamic theory, however useful it may be for purposes of insight-giving during therapy, cannot predict a person's future behavior. Thus the theory is quite useless for telling the social caseworker how a particular applicant for adoptive parenthood will act *as parent* in the changing circumstances of the family cycle years later. So much for the validity of the theory as applied to parent-selection in adoption. Concerning the workers' reliability in making decisions about particular applicants, some well-designed and executed research information is available.

In 1959 the Child Welfare League published the result of a study conducted by Donald Brieland, a psychologist, who had tested the view that social workers can make reliable judgments concerning adoptive applicants. One reviewer[19] of the results of the Brieland study summed it up succinctly and, I think, fairly:

> One agency's initial interviews with five couples seeking to adopt were taped and sent to agencies around the country; the purpose was to determine the amount of agreement among professional caseworkers about the desirability of these couples. Each of the interviews was approximately an hour and a half in length; and caseworkers were asked to indicate not only if they felt the couple should be accepted for further study, but also how they would rank the couples in relation to each other. Twenty-eight agencies in thirteen states cooperated, with 184 worker-judges taking part. It was decided that the "correct" judgment would be defined as that reached by the majority of caseworkers. Three couples were accepted and two rejected by the consensus.
>
> The agreement between the caseworkers ranged from 89.13 per cent for Couple A to 61.41 per cent for Couple D. However, as the author of the study himself noted, the agreement, while statistically significant, was of little practical value. For example, while seventy-five caseworkers put Couple B first of the five, thirty-six rejected Couple B outright. In many agencies, moreover, there was an even split between the social workers as to whether to accept or reject a given couple. Workers wrote comments on sections of the interviews, and the range of reaction to specific statements illuminates the problem better than statistics. At the close of the interview the husband in Couple B remarked:
>
> > "Well, we're not perfectionists on this thing and if it's possible for us to get a child, we'd sure be very happy to have one. I mean if through your examining and cross-examining you feel that it isn't our time right now, that's up to you folks. We're not going to come down here swinging an axe at you."
>
> While some social workers interpreted this remark as showing healthy objectivity, others thought it revealed a deep fear of rejection, while still others felt it showed a clear desire to be rejected. The hard fact seems to be that an adoptive couple's chance of acceptance by an agency is determined not so much by objectively discoverable merits as potential parents as by luck — luck in being interviewed by a congenial agency staff member.[20]

At the end of his concluding chapter, Dr. Brieland himself says: "Reliability in judgments is not a problem unique to social work. Most research on the problem has concerned psychiatry and clinical psychology.[21] The results show trends similar to the data herein reported."

Claim of Competence No. 3:
The Testing and Evaluation of the Child for Adoption

The adoption agencies also had to make decisions concerning the infants who had been surrendered. There psychodynamic theory could manifestly be of little help: human beings still quite unformed psychologically would have to be assessed differently. Therefore special infant tests were used which were thought to be effective in identifying liabilities in physical and mental makeup. Here again the agencies were acclaimed as singularly capable of bringing together all the needed skills. In *Shared Fate* (pp. 22-23), I quoted a number of claims made for the efficacy of infant testing in the leaflets intended for adopters during the nineteen fifties. Two of these sources are worth repeating here:

> An agency. . . takes time to study the child, to make as sure as possible that adopting parents will not have some unknown grief ahead of them, like a child's mind that never develops. Between foster mother, the agency's nurse, social worker, doctor, and psychiatrist, the agency gets to know him [the child] very well. By the time a baby is three months old, it can know a great deal about him — his mind, his body, his emotions. It can gauge which kind of family he needs. When he is younger than that, it can't be so sure. That's why many agencies will not place babies under three months old.[22]
> You want to know something about his heritage, his physical and mental development, his emotional stability, and above all, you want to know his potentialities.[23]

But what were the facts about infant tests? As early as 1941, Professor Woodworth's monograph had categorically assigned them very limited utility:

> Intelligence testing in the first few years of the child's life encounters. . . difficulty. We can put the infant through certain tests and determine whether his sensorimotor development is proceeding at the average rate, or how much accelerated or retarded he is in the development appropriate to his age. But we are not sure that the function we are measuring is the same as is later measured by the intelligence tests. Apparently it is not the same, since *the infant tests do not enable us to make any close prediction of his IQ as it will be at the age of six years or later.*[24]

If the predictive power of these tests had been called into question early on, the work of other investigators reinforced Woodworth's warnings. Thus in 1957 Richard Wittenborn[25] provided further evidence of the tests' shortcomings. He reported follow-up work on children who had been tested by the Yale Infant Examination. In one study two groups of adopted children were retested — one of these a group of 114 five-year-olds and the other a group of 81 seven- to nine-year-olds. Within the limitations of his subjects and his methods, Wittenborn showed that predictive utility could not be claimed for the Yale Infant Examination.

Nevertheless infant testing persisted for many years after the Woodworth report, and even after Wittenborn's book had appeared. Perhaps coincidentally — it was in that same year, 1957 — Joseph Reid, head of the Child Welfare League, defended the agencies' use of the tests. Apparently in reply to criticisms from outside the adoption field, he said that the practice of testing had been forced on the agencies in the process of recruiting adopters. The outside world expected agencies to guarantee to the adopters that "the child was without physical, emotional, or mental defects. . . ."[26]

Whence the Myopia?

I have tried to show that certain esoteric claims of competence staked by social work in adoption tended to be spurious. Since I am not imputing charlatanry to the adoption lobbies or their constituents, how is their myopia — the inability to see their errors — to be explained? Were they simply badly informed? Did their professional personnel not know the scientific research findings? I suspect such simplistic explanations are not sufficient; there were staffs that were highly trained, conscientious, and intelligent. But clearly their intentions were better than their awareness of their methodological shortcomings. I believe that we must look to the structural conditions under which adoption work was carried out if we want to understand the myopia which we have observed.

As noted, professionalization of an occupation requires legitimation for the special prerogatives sought. Such legitimation is given for claims of special competence, claims in which scientific principles, theories, and methods are invoked. Noting the errors of omission or commission of an occupation ought properly to be the task of its members. Social work spokesmen for the adoption field were not unaware of or insensitive to this rule of professional conduct. But it is a rule easier acknowledged than put into practice. Thus Professor Hughes has observed that:

> . . . We are faced with. . . [the problems] of defining what a failure or mistake is in any given line of work or in a given work operation. This leads to still another, which turns out to be the significant one for the social drama of work: who has the right to say what a mistake or a failure is? The findings on this point are fairly clear; a colleague-group (the people who consider themselves subject to the same work risks) will stubbornly defend its own right to define mistakes, and to say in the given case whether one has been made.[27]

This is undoubtedly true, for social work practitioners no less than for those in medicine and law. But there are circumstances which insulate the professionals from awareness of their mistakes. One of these circumstances is demographic, the other organizational. The urban, white-collar middle class from which the great bulk of adopters were typically drawn has also been highly mobile socially and geographically. The adoptive parents could therefore be expected to move during the child-rearing years from the city where the adoptions were made. Thus, if and when they might have consulted their agency in matters of their children's development or behavior, they were not in the vicinity to do so. It is not common for such migrants to consult an adoption agency in another metropolis, for the social worker's expertise is linked to the files about the adopters and their child. There is a second factor, this one organizational, that I think has tended to shield the adoption agency from readily becoming aware of its errors. It is the wall of prestigious professionals which the adoption lobbies, i.e., the U.S. Children's Bureau and the Child Welfare League, built around the agencies. With this kind of defense perimeter around them, the agencies were less prone than they might otherwise have been to see and hear the evidence of their mistakes at work.

Finally, let me recall here that the adoption agency has for some years been on the decline as an organization of social power and prestige. There are simply too few adoptable infants available to make the adoption worker an important intermediary. But the ideas and actions of the adoption agencies and lobbies of a generation ago have left their mark upon the institution of adoption. Legislatures and courts have for decades been exposed to social work's claims of special competence. While these claims centered around the interests of children which social work sought to protect, they required the cooperation of the polity. Adoption was to disappear as a vital statistic,[28] adoptive families were to become officially indistinguishable from the families of the mainstream. And this in turn required that the old records of the child's antecedents, ancestry and birth records, would have to disappear publicly too. So they were sealed by way of legislation, with new amended birth certificates issued. The intent was clearly to protect children from being stigmatized and families from being disturbed by outsiders. But it was to be made a closed issue for all time, not just for the child-rearing years. Thus alongside the myth of special professional competence, there came into being the myth of adoptive kinship as a firm, well-constructed institution.

NOTES

1. Katherine Bain, M.D. and Martha M. Eliot, M.D., "Adoption as a National Problem," *Pediatrics,* Vol. 20, No. 2 (1957), p. 366 (emphasis added).

2. Everett C. Hughes, "The Study of Occupations," in Merton *et al.,*(eds.) *Sociology Today* (1959), p. 447.

3. Michael Schapiro (ed.), *A Study of Adoption Practice,* 1955.

4. Joseph H. Reid, in *Protecting Children in Adoption,* U.S. Children's Bureau — Report of a Conference (1955), p. 26.

5. Hon. Justine Wise Polier, "Adoption and the Law," in *Pediatrics, op. cit.,* p. 374.

6. K. Bain and M.M. Eliot, *op. cit.*, p. 369.

7. Leontine Young, *Out of Wedlock*, 1959.

8. *Ibid.*, pp. 38, 39 (emphasis added).

9. Sarah Evan, "The Unmarried Mother's Indecision About Her Baby as a Mechanism of Defense," paper given under the auspices of the National Association on Service to Unmarried Parents at the National Conference of Social Work, Philadelphia, Pa. May 23, 1957 (mimeo).

10. Ner Littner, M.D., "The Natural Parents," in Schapiro (ed.), *op. cit.*, Vol. II, p. 32 (emphasis added).

11. United States Children's Bureau, *Protecting Children in Adoption, op. cit.*, (1955), pp. 8-11. (emphasis added).

12. Clark, E. Vincent, *Unmarried Mothers*, 1961.

13. *Ibid.*, p. 1.

14. Lucile Kennedy, "Why do we Need Adoption Agencies?" *National Parent Teacher*, April 1957.

15. Joseph H. Reid, in *Protecting Children in Adoption, op. cit.*, p. 26 (emphasis added).

16. Michael Schapiro, *op. cit.*, Vol. I, p. 67 (emphasis added).

17. *Ibid.*, p. 75 (emphasis added).

18. Florence Brown, "What Do We Seek in Adoptive Parents," *Social Casework*, April 1951.

19. Rael Jean Isaac, "Children Who Need Adoption," *The Atlantic Monthly*, November 1963.

20. Donald Brieland, Ph.D., "An Experimental Study of the Selection of Adoptive Parents at Intake," Child Welfare League of America, May 1959, p. 60.

21. A part of Brieland's footnote reads:

It is also of interest that two psychiatrists who heard one of the tapes in the present study gave very different characterizations of the same couple. One recommended acceptance and the other rejection. Differences were also shown among psychologists who heard the tapes as staff members of participating agencies.

22. From *How to Adopt a Child in Louisiana*, Louisiana Department of Public Welfare, 1950.

23. From "So You Want to Adopt a Child," Oklahoma State Department of Social Welfare, 1951.

24. R.S. Woodworth, *Heredity and Environment*, Social Science Research Council, Bulletin #47, 1941, p. 38 (emphasis added).

25. J. Richard Wittenborn, *The Placement of Adoptive Children*, 1957.

26. Joseph H. Reid, *op. cit.*, p. 27.

27. Everett C. Hughes, "Mistakes at Work," *The Canadian Journal of Economics and Political Science*, Vol. 17, No. 3 (August 1951), pp. 322-325, quoted in H.M. Vollmer and D.L. Mills, *Professionalization*, 1966.

28. Professor Jonassohn's experience is a case in point. During 1962-63 he had begun to make inquiries into the ways in which adoptions were reported statistically. Finding that the usual demographic measure of *rates* was almost nonexistent for adoptions, he prepared a paper "On the Use and Construction of Adoption Rates." When he submitted that paper for publication to a demography journal it was rejected

with the following observation: "adoption is not a vital statistic." Kurt Jonassohn's paper was subsequently published in the *Journal of Marriage and the Family*, November, 1965.

Chapter 8

Legal Contradictions, Precarious Institution

William Graham Sumner, that intrepid pioneer of American sociology, did some very useful thinking about human institutions. In *Folkways* (1907) he distinguished what he called "crescive" from "enacted" institutions, noting that the former had arisen long ago out of customs (folkways) and unwritten rules (mores). These he considered to be sturdier social structures than the more recently enacted institutions which are "products of rational invention and intention." Sumner held that "pure enacted institutions which are strong. . . are hard to find [because] it is too difficult to invent and create an institution, for a purpose, out of nothing." Let us now inspect the modern enacted adoptive kinship institution against the legal baseline of consanguineal kinship which is "crescive" in Sumner's sense. Our baseline will be statutory provisions in Canadian jurisdictions, as these affect kin relationships. In the course of thinking about some of the legal arrangements that now constitute adoptive kinship we will find that not all is well with the institution. There are major contradictions in the legal arrangements of adoptive kinship.

Unlike Sumner, I am not proposing that crescive institutions are in the order of things sturdy, while enacted institutions are necessarily more precarious. Nor do I wish to suggest that the social arrangements of some institutions are internally fully consistent, that there are no serious discrepancies between the purpose ascribed to the institution and its actual workings. All institutions possess some such contradictions. When I speak here of adoptive kinship as a precarious institution, I am speaking in relative terms. However contradictory many aspects of contemporary mainstream kinship may be, adoptive kinship is more so. But beyond the matter of degrees of precariousness, the contradictions built into adoptive kinship by enactment call into question the nature of the institution itself.

The contradictions between consanguineal and adoptive kinship arise because the latter has been billed as something that it cannot be or become. Adoptive kinship is not and cannot be the equivalent of blood relationship. This assertion may sound preposterous, but I think that the reader will not find it so as we move through the information gathered here. Let me begin with a definition by Professor Eugene Weinstein which appears in the *International Encyclopedia of the Social Sciences:* "Adoption is the institutional practice through which an individual belonging by birth to one kinship group acquires new kinship ties that are socially defined as equivalent to the congenital ties."[1] Given that Weinstein is one of the few sociologists of note who have written on the subject of adoption, and considering the nature of the work in which his definition has appeared, that definition is fully established and official. One may assume that it represents the view of those who wield the authority to regulate adoptive kinship through law.

Earlier I began to analyze the adoptive family in a new perspective, namely that of kinship as institution; now I would like to enlarge that perspective with an emphasis on law. *Shared Fate* was written in an interpersonal relationship context, not an institutional one. Technically speaking, it was more social psychology than structural sociology. And that perspective did not greatly alter for me until 1967, when an event in my private life forced me to look carefully at the institutional underpinnings of adoptive kinship.

It was the beginning of a new school year. Francie and I were driving along the New York Thruway when she turned the conversation to the family at home. She would be away during all of the next term; perhaps she was storing up images for a time when we would be missed. I too had been thinking along similar lines. Francie was our first child; when she was not quite two we adopted Peter, who was about the same age. Not surprisingly, Peter and Francie soon developed ways very similar to those observed in twins. They had a language only they could understand and they came to be all but inseparable. When Debbie and later Bill arrived in our family, Francie and Peter retained a special closeness which the younger ones did not breach for some time. Now, that day in early September 1967, Francie spoke of her feelings for members of the family. When she came to Peter she turned to me and said with a little laugh, "Say Dad, what would you and Mom do if some day Peter and I wanted to marry?" It was a bombshell of a question. At the next turn-off I drove to a little restaurant where we could sip tea and talk. Of course I was disturbed. What *would* I do if two of my children wanted to marry each other? I couldn't recall that the question had ever crossed my mind before, but that day on the road I met it head-on.

"Francie," I said, "I don't really know whether it is legally possible. Perhaps it is, since you and Peter are not related by blood. But why don't we think about the possible effects of such a step? Let's first suppose you had our approval and went ahead to marry. What would be your relationships to Ruth, or me, or to Debbie and Bill? It would be strange, to say the least, to have one's children now married to each other, and for your brother and sister to have that funny sense that their siblings were simultaneously in-laws. But that's just the beginning. Let's suppose things didn't work out between Peter and you in marriage. It isn't inconceivable. More than a quarter of all marriages fail and end in divorce. What would you do if it happened to you and Peter? Could you just go back to being brother and sister? I doubt it. And wouldn't it be a deeply upsetting event for all of us in the family?" Francie was very thoughtful; she let me know that she was glad I had spoken as I did. It was quite an interlude for both of us. We were silent a long time, each with our own thoughts, as we drove into New England. I remember saying to myself how fortunate it was for me that I could think sociologically. Without that frame of reference, Francie's question would have remained merely upsetting.

When I returned home several days later, I made it my business to check whether it was technically possible for adoptive siblings to marry. The legal statutes I consulted were not very helpful: adoption was defined as the equivalent of consanguineous relationships. Nothing was said there about permissible lines of consanguinity in marriage or about incest. I checked some of my library holdings and came up with one useful note. In her interesting work, *Child Adoption in the Modern World*, (1952) Margaret Kornitzer had this to say about the legal statuses produced by adoption in England under the Adoption Act of 1950:

> The Act lays down that adopter and adopted come within the prohibited degrees of consanguinity and may not marry each other. This was not so under the older law, but as the Lord Chancellor observed on the point, "Surely it is undesirable that [the adoptive father] should be placed in the position where he could even contemplate marriage with that child. . . . I would throw out for consideration whether the corollary of what we are doing ought not to be that the boy and the girl (two adopted children) become brother and sister in the ordinary way, so that the natural home life which happens in a normal family should take place in this family."
>
> But as the law now stands there is nothing against the marriage of adoptive brothers and sisters, or others related through adoption, and, although for some of the purposes of the law adoptive brothers and sisters are regarded as brothers or sisters of the whole or half blood, consanguinity is not affected. Some other countries regard the matter differently; the Australian state of Victoria, for instance, where the law with respect to marriage within the degrees of consanguinity or affinity apply both to adoptive and natural relatives, creates a wide field of taboo.
>
> As to relationships outside of marriage, although an adopter may not marry an adopted child, there is nothing to forbid their sleeping together. The question of incest between adopters and adopted was not forgotten when the law was framed, but the law is not anxious to add to the list of criminal offenses.
>
> The common-sense aspect of this was admirably put by Lord Amulree, a doctor: "I do not see how, by making a person into a relative in legal fashion by a stroke of the pen, you necessarily bring about the effect which is required. One may say that if a family adopts a child then that child should be regarded, even from a consanguinity point of view as part of the family. Unfortunately it is difficult to confine such matters within any legal terms."[2]

The passage was an eye-opener. As so often happens, apparently by chance but actually because one has now been cued to the significance of a particular event, I noticed some weeks later in a magazine article a reference to the American sculptor Jo Davidson (1883-1952) who, after his wife's death, is said to have married his adopted daughter. It had happened on this continent, only three decades or so before. It might be possible here, now. I found that a disturbing possibility, not only in terms of Francie's inquiry, but even more in terms of the larger question about adoption: was this *kinship* in the sense that we all attach to the term?

As I began to think along these lines, I asked myself more systematic questions about kinship as such. I asked what values and rules of conduct regulate and set limits a) in the nuclear family of parents and children, and b) in the extended family of grandparents, uncles and aunts, cousins, and other relatives. My question was, what ultimately determined whether one really belonged to one's nuclear family, and similarly what determined whether one really belonged to one's extended family? Undoubtedly the main line of demarcation for the nuclear family is sex. Only the marriage partners in the nuclear family have legitimate sexual access to each other. Parents may not cohabit with their children, or siblings with each other. It is the prohibition of incest that thus defines, that identifies, who is truly a member of the nuclear family. Paradoxically, it is the normative ordering of what may *not* be done that determines one's legitimate membership in the nuclear family. Similarly, I began to think about membership in the extended family. Though the question of consanguinity for purposes of marriage is still at issue there (in some jurisdictions first cousins may not marry), legitimate sexual access is not the principal defining factor. What counts in the extended family, what defines rights of membership there is the connection between descent and inheritance, i.e., who has non-testamentary rights to the property of a deceased relative. If I wanted further to investigate the true position of the adopted as members in their nuclear families of adoption as well as their position in their adoptive parents' extended families, I would have to go to the statutes. In the former case, I would have to inspect the legal provisions for the regulation of permissible degrees of consanguinity in marriage, as well as laws pertaining to incest. In the case of membership in the extended family, I needed to review the legislation that pertains to intestate[3] inheritance rights.

During the latter years of the nineteen sixties I was preoccupied with other issues, personal and academic, so that the question of investigating the institutional bases of adoptive kinship had receded for me. Finally, in September 1971, it came back very strongly into my awareness. During the summer of that year I received an invitation to participate in the first International Conference on Adoption and Foster Care in Milan, Italy. The preparation of my paper[4] brought me back to data and issues that had faded into the background. What stood out for me, during the three days of presentations and discussions, was the range of conceptions and legal arrangements in the different countries of the delegates. Here were the Italian conference organizers, deeply concerned for thousands of children languishing in orphanages, because blood relationship was considered so important in Italy that adoption was made all but impossible. And here were delegates from North America, who complaind that the laws there gave adult adoptees no rights of access to information about their origins. When after the conference I spent some days in Israel, I found that the young nation's adoption legislation had ingeniously combined a regard for the adoptive family's needs for privacy during the child-rearing years and the desire of adopted adults for information about their origins. In this context of comparative adoption laws and regulations, I was made conscious again of the contradictions that inhere in the conception of modern adoption as the equivalent of consanguineal kinship.

During 1972 I had an opportunity to investigate the matter further. A senior student wished to write his honors paper on some question in the sociology of law. I suggested that he look into the possibility of researching Canadian statutes either directly or indirectly pertaining to adoptive kinship and its participants. Steve Pierce eventually produced a respectable piece of research[5] which, though only suggestive, could serve as a jumping-off place for studies in the institutionalization of adoption.

Adoptive Kinship in the Nuclear Family

Pierce states the purpose of his paper as an attempt to learn "whether the artificial ties established by adoption are indeed socially defined as equivalent to the congenital ties." Then he asks about law as an institutional arrangement, what one ought to expect of legal order in society. "Laws," he notes, following Evan,[6] "regulate social interaction, thus minimizing overt and covert conflict." And drawing on the work of Parsons,[7] he adds that "normative consistency may be assumed to be one of the most important criteria of effectiveness of a system of law. This [implies] not subjecting the same individuals to contradictory rules." Thus the study of laws involving marriage, if these were shown to be contradictory to laws regulating adoption, might show up weaknesses in the institutionalization of adoptive kinship.

Pierce goes on to inspect the Revised Statutes[8] of the ten provinces of Canada, hoping to shed some light on the question whether there the adoptive relationship is defined as the equivalent of the consanguine. First he read the provincial acts pertaining to marriage to determine whether there were provisions that referred to permissible degrees of consanguinity applicable to adoptive as to biological kin. While the liberal construction by a court might lead to an interpretation of some of these statutes, whereby adoptive kin would be included in certain prohibited degrees of consanguinity for purposes of marriage, none of the statutes had unambiguous provisions of this sort:

> There is no mention of adoptive relationships in those acts which deal specifically with marriage. Any restrictions that are present are those of

affinity and consanguinity, which do not appear to apply to the adopted and other biologically unrelated members of the adoptive family. The restrictions seem however to apply to the relationships between the adopted and other members of their natural or biological kin.

Incest is a federal offence, dealt with under the Criminal Code of Canada rather than the provincial statutes.

Section 150 of the Criminal Code states that "everyone commits incest who, knowing that another person is *by blood relationship* his or her parent, child, brother, sister, grandparent or grandchild, as the case may be, has sexual intercourse with that person (emphasis added). There is no mention of an adoptive situation. Section 153... states: "Every male person who has illicit sexual intercourse with his step-daughter, foster daughter or female ward, ... is guilty of an indictable offence and is liable to imprisonment for two years." This section may thus apply to the situation of adoption. If it does, a male may *marry* his step-daughter, foster daughter, or female ward since the provision concerns itself solely with 'illicit sexual intercourse'. . . . If the relationships dealt with by Section 153 implied incest, they would have been included in Section 150. From this, then, it would seem that if a father had 'illicit sexual intercourse' with his adopted daughter, he would be guilty of an indictable offence, but not incest. . . . However, section 153 of the Criminal Code. . . does not take into consideration that a female can have illicit sexual intercourse with her step-son, foster son, or male ward.

In examining the various provincial acts pertaining to adoption, one finds both differences and similarities between the provinces. . . but the broad procedural outlines are essentially similar. . . . The general effect of an adoption, as well as the intent behind these effects, is the termination of rights and duties between the natural parents and the child, and the substitution of an equivalent relationship between the child and the adoptive parents. With reference to the five provinces which include within their adoption statutes provisions for incestuous relationships, these statutes are not internally consistent.

Thus the provisions that refer to the shift in rights and duties from natural kin to adoptive family could be interpreted as bringing the adopted child within the prohibited degrees. There is, however, another provision which says that the termination of the relationship between kin and adopted person does not apply for purpose of laws relating to incest, *i.e.* does not remove a person from a blood relationship. By this provision, the adopted child is still to be considered within the prohibited degrees of consanguinity with respect to his or her natural kin. . . . In the rest of the provinces of Canada in whose statutes the above provision is not given, there is even more ambiguity regarding the adoptee's relationships to both natural and adoptive family. There legislation has completely overlooked the problem of whether the prohibition against inter-marriage between certain family members does apply to members of an adoptive family as well.

In his attempt to see whether the situation he had identified in the Canadian provincial and federal statutes applied also to jurisdictions in the United States, Pierce found a paper by Professor W.J. Wadlington of the University of Virginia Law School. Pierce says that Wadlington "is concerned about the same legal problems that were found to exist, by means of this study, in Canada." From this article, Pierce learned that:

> In the United States a number of cases have been brought before state courts in which [these] courts have had to determine whether the adoptive relationship falls within the laws relating to incest and the prohibited degrees of marriage. By briefly looking at these cases the. . . ambiguity [that exists] in the legal system in this regard becomes evident. Generally, neither criminal incest laws nor provisions defining capacity to marry. . . make any specific mention of adoptive relationships. Wadlington states:
>
>> Thus far the decisions have been uniform in their refusal to consider the adopted child as a 'relation' within the prohibitions of the statutes, usually on the rationale that they apply only to persons related by consanguinity or affinity.[9]

Usually United States statutes regarding this matter are phrased in terms of consanguinity and affinity:

> An adoptive parent and his adopted child are not related by blood or marriage, at least where the child is not a stepchild; in the absence of a statute making it incest for an adoptive parent to marry his adopted child, the marriage will not be held incestuous.[10]

In [the case of] *State of Mississippi v. Lee,*[11] 1944 . . . a man was charged with having incestuous relations with his adopted daughter. In Mississippi, the statute explaining the requirements of marriage forbade the marriage of a father with his daughter or step-daughter. The question then arose as to whether an adopted daughter is a daughter within the meaning of the statutes, in their criminal aspect. [The court found]. . . the word 'daughter'. . . to mean "an immediate female descendant and not an adopted daughter, a stepdaughter or a daughter-in-law." The decision was that "an adopted child is not a 'daughter' within an incest statute forbidding sexual relations between persons within the degree within which marriages are declared to be incestuous and void, the marriage law providing that a father shall not marry his 'daughter.'" . . . One salutary though limited result of *State v. Lee*, according to Wadlington, was the Mississippi legislature's subsequent enactment of the provision that an adoptive father can neither marry nor have intercourse with his adopted daughter. However, it seems that the adoptive mother and adopted son apparently may. . . .

In Ohio a similar case occurred and the same decision was reached *(State v. Youst).*[12] The court stated that "the relationship was not actually one of father and daughter, or mother and daughter, but that of adopted daughter, and the fact that she was an adopted daughter could not by the wildest stretch of the imagination constitute her the natural daughter of the accused.". . . With these cases in mind, Wadlington reaches this conclusion:

> In view of the current decisions adhering to the rules of strict construction, there seems little hope that the problems will be alleviated until corrective legislation has been enacted.[13]

And on the basis of what he has noted he proposes that:

> If the adopted child is to be fully integrated into the adopter's family (and this seems to be the prevalent desire as expressed in most adoption statutes), then he should be treated no differently from the natural-born child under such marriage statutes. Though the eugenic basis for prohibition may not exist, the social factor is equally important for the adopted child. . . . The suggested form for amendment of the statutes governing capacity to marry would be a statement that for such purposes an adopted child should be considered exactly as a child related by consanguinity.[14]

Here I leave Steve Pierce's inquiry and ask whether such judgments as those of the Mississippi and Ohio courts are perhaps archaic events of the past and whether, in spite of contradictory laws, current interpretations would not be less strictly constructed and thus more enlightened. The answer to this question came to me some time ago through Professor Cyril Means of the New York Law School. He furnished me with information on a case that occurred in the State of New York in 1975. I shall quote the information as it was given in the *New York Times* of May 2, 1975:

> Following a landmark court decision, Lleuwana Bagnardi, 22, of Watervliet, N.Y. is now the wife instead of the daughter of Frank Bagnardi, 50. She was adopted in 1966 by Mr. Bagnardi, a railroad employee, and his wife. Two years later the couple were separated, and their divorce in 1973 gave Mr. Bagnardi custody of Lleuwana and the Bagnardis' own four minor children, who still live at home.
>
> Mr. Bagnardi filed a court suit last summer after he and Lleuwana were refused a marriage license in Troy. State Supreme Court Judge William R. Murray ruled last month that state laws on "incestuous and void" marriages apply only to blood relatives. This week Mr. and Mrs. Bagnardi announced that they were married April 8 before two witnesses in Watervliet's Presbyterian church.

Although neither Steve Pierce nor I have come across similar decisions made in Canadian jurisdictions, a late nineteen seventies proposal before the Senate has been meant to reform the law so that closely related persons could marry without bothering Parliament. It applied specifically to couples from Quebec, and included uncles and nieces wanting to wed as well as a man and woman related by adoption. The latter case required federal intervention because the Adoption Act of Quebec gives persons adopted into the same family but not related by blood the status of a true sibling. Thus here is a law which seeks to reduce the contradiction between adoptive and consanguineal kinship, but which has been successfully challenged by appeal to the higher authority of Parliament.

These quite recent events, both in Canada and the United States, provide evidence for the contention that adoptive kinship in the nuclear family is not the equivalent of consanguineal kinship. If my adopted son could marry his adopted sister, then theirs is not a true brother-sister relationship, since in law true brothers and sisters cannot marry. And if the adopter can marry a person whom he or she has previously adopted, then the previous relationship cannot possibly be regarded as a true parent-child relationship, since the law does not permit parent and child to marry.

In 1953 a study of the United Nations showed inadvertently how little the two types of kinship had in common in terms of permissible lines of consanguinity for purpose of marriage:

> In all countries, even in the case of adoptive legitimation, normal marriage prohibitions laid down by the law, remain valid with regard to the child and his natural family. As regards marriage prohibitions arising out of the adoptive relationship, these vary. There may be no marriage prohibition between adopter and adoptee, but marriage automatically cancels the adoption, as in Denmark and Uruguay.
>
> In some countries, marriage between the adopter and adoptee is prohibited, but if it nevertheless takes place, adoption is cancelled. This is the case in Argentina, Greece, Peru and Switzerland.
>
> Finally the marriage prohibition may not only be absolute, but extend also to other persons than the adoptive parents, for example, in France and the United Kingdom, to other adopted children and to children born to the adopter.
>
> It is the opinion of agencies in general that measures which are designed to assure the normality of the child's relationships are clearly in his interest.[15]

What is not clear from this statement is what was meant by "normality." I suspect that it meant that those measures that make adoption the true equivalent of consanguineal kinship are in the child's interest. Clearly, however, adoptive kinship was not then and is not now that kind of equivalent. If the agencies meant to assure it, they were not successful then or later. The fact is that no one could have been successful in that sense. But one might have thought that the contradiction would have been visible to the professionals of the social work and legal disciplines, seeing that their training has presumably been in critical thinking.

Let us stop a moment and take stock. We have been inquiring into the structural soundness of adoptive kinship as institution. Our first point of reference was the nuclear family, where we took sexual relations as the key issue that defines membership in the unit. There we found that at best, the provisions are ambiguous, and at worst, they allow the adoptive participants to have sexual access where such access is prohibited to persons related by consanguinity. Such a discovery had confirmed our suspicion that this foundation of adoptive kinship in the context of the nuclear family is precarious. Let us turn next to the question of the adopted person's place in the extended family.

Adoptive Kinship in the Extended Family

The question of inheritance was a topic in the 1955 *Study of Adoption Practice:*

> Several agencies raised questions regarding inheritance. Unless there are broader statutes in a state, the adopted child "becomes the issue of the adopting parent," but "he does not become a blood-relation of all the kin of the adopting parent. One adopts a child for himself and not for the other members of the family." Consequently the general law on inheritance is that an adopted child will inherit only from his adoptive parents and he cannot inherit as a collateral heir unless the statute makes such provision. There are many places where he can inherit from his natural parents as well as his adoptive parents.[16]

Nothing could have stated the issue of adoptive kinship with respect to inheritance rights more clearly. "One adopts a child for himself and not for the other members of the family. . . [The child] does not become a blood-relation of all kin of the adopting parent." In other words, the adoptee does not belong to the extended family if gauged by the standard of intestate inheritance rights. We will see that the same applies to insurance benefits.

Steve Pierce's inquiry into provincial legislation in Canada revealed that in the case of eight out of 10 provinces (Quebec and Manitoba apparently being exceptions) it was expressly stated that "in any enactment, conveyance, or bequest the expression 'child' includes the adopted child, unless stated otherwise." The intent then was to treat the adoptee as the natural child of the adopters, a concession apparently limited to the nuclear family. What, however, of the extended kin group? Data on inheritance rights — specifically intestate inheritance, i.e., where the deceased has left no last will and where the rights of inheritance have to be determined on the basis of membership in the family and degrees of relationship to the deceased, such data are currently fragmental. But what is available suggests that the adoptee's rights are *not* the equivalent of those of the descendant of the blood.

In December 1973 an Order in Council established the Royal Commission on Family and Children's Law in British Columbia. A partial report by the Commission deals with inheritance rights in three Canadian provinces — Manitoba, New Brunswick, and Newfoundland:

In *Manitoba*, it is only in the 1974 *Child Welfare Act* (not yet pro-claimed) that the right to continue to inherit from natural parents has been removed. Sec. 96(1) states, "Upon the granting of an adoption order all prior parental ties of the child cease to exist under the law, and the relationship newly constituted by the order is valid for all lawful purposes and has the same effect as if the child had been born to the adopting parent(s)."

In the earlier Act, Sec. 96(2) stated that an adopted child does not lose the right to inherit from his natural parents or kindred, and al-though 96(1) (b) provided "for all purposes. . . as if born to. . . including descendants, ascendants, and kindred," 96(1) (e) & (g) refers to rights and interests which may be limited by an intestacy of or disposition by "any person."

In *New Brunswick*, Sec. 30(3) continues to provide that inheritance rights from natural parents and kindred are retained, while 30(2) states that "a person adopted shall stand in regard to the legal descendants, *but to no other kindred*, of the adopting parent in the same position as if he had been born to the adopting parent in lawful wedlock." (Empha-sis added.)

Newfoundland also continues the rights of inheritance from natural parents and kindred (sec. 21(3), while 21(1) states that an adopted person, upon the intestacy of an adopting parent, shall stand, in regard to the legal descendants *but to no other kindred* of the adopting parent, in the same position "as if born to." When the adoptee dies intestate (21(2)) property received by gift or inheritance from the natural parents shall be distributed "as if no act of adoption had taken place."[18]

The British Columbia Commission also sought information about practices outside Canada. In the memorandum concerning inheritance rights of adopted persons is this note about Great Britain:

> In a letter of August 23, 1974 to the Commission, Jane Rowe, Director of the Association of British Adoption Agencies, states, "I have been making enquiries for you about inheritance rights in Scotland and find that since 1964 the position in Scotland is the same as in England — the adopted child inherits from the adopters only and is considered in law as the adopters' child. Before that date adoptees did not automatically inherit from adopted parents but could inherit from biological par-ents. . . ."

Clearly, the different jurisdictions about which we learned here have in dif-ferent ways and to different degrees sought to make the situation of adoptive kinship more closely equivalent to the situation of consanguineal kinship in terms of inheritance. But there is evidently some official recognition that this is at best a slow process and perhaps in reality not entirely feasible. Thus in 1972 the United States Children's Bureau, Office of Child Development, Department of Health, Education, and Welfare, published a four-page pamphlet entitled "Statements Regarding Insurance Policies and Wills — Directed to Adoptive Parents." It was a statement originally prepared by Mr. Richard B. Barker, lawyer and founder of the Barker Foundation, a voluntary adoption agency in Washington, D.C. Here is his counsel to adopters in its entirety:

Insurance Policies

These suggestions and those that follow concerning wills are not intended to substitute for the professional advice of your insurance agent or attorney but only to bring the problem to your attention.

Insurance policies are phrased in technical language. However, it is believed that if you read your policies carefully, you can spot certain *dangers which if allowed to remain might cut off the adopted child from being a beneficiary.* Examine the terms of the policy itself for phrases which would limit the payment of the proceeds only to a "child or children born of the marriage of said assured and said wife." Note particularly the beneficiary provisions of the policy for words or phrases such as "issue," "born to," "born of," "child or children of the marriage of the insured and his wife," "child or children born of the marriage of the insured and his wife," "heirs," "heirs at law," "next of kin," or "descendants." In some states even the words "child or children" may cause your adopted children to have no claim, unless the policy clearly states that the term "child or children" includes a legally adopted child. Words fixing beneficiary rights on the basis of family relations such as "husband," "wife," "family," "child," should be avoided unless the policy has an express provision showing the family relationship includes that existing between the adoptive father or mother and their adopted child.

Beneficiary provisions can be changed as often as necessary. Therefore, if your examination of the policy reveals certain doubtful words or phrases, consult your insurance representative or contact the insurance company and make the necessary changes. *The best way to make sure that each adopted child will receive the benefits, is to have the beneficiary provisions of the policy state the interest of the child by name.* For example, it can be provided that the policy proceeds "shall be payable to Jane Doe, my wife, if living; otherwise in equal shares to John Doe, my son, and Mary Doe, my daughter." Another proper designation would be "to my wife, if living, otherwise to my children, including adopted children, in equal shares." If your family includes one or more natural children and one or more adopted children, particular care should be taken so that all the children can receive the benefits. The precise wording is not important but care must be taken to avoid general language which might be so phrased as to raise a question of whether or not you intended to include your adopted child.

Unless you are absolutely certain that your policies apply to adopted children, we strongly urge that you write to your company (retaining a carbon) advising it that you have adopted children and request confirmation or endorsement that the policy applies to adopted children.

Wills

What we have said above applies with respect to insurance policies but the same words and interpretation are equally applicable to the drafting of wills. In this connection attention is called to the fact that there are two types of inheritance laws. There is the so-called "from" law and the so-called "from and through" law. An illustration gives the best possible explanation of these two types of inheritance laws. "A and B have a daughter C who married D, and C and D adopt X. C and D are killed in an automobile accident. A and B die leaving a will which provides that they are leaving their property to their children and such words as "their heirs, descendants, etc." Under a "from" law, X would not inherit from his grandparents, A and B. Under a "from and through" law, X would inherit from A and B.

The Barker Foundation was instrumental in getting Maryland, the District of Columbia and Virginia to enact "from and through" laws but many other jursidictions have not so modernized their laws and it is the law of the residence of decedent which controls.

Mr. Barker's advice to adoptive parents and grandparents are further evidence of the lacunae and contradictions in the legal provisions as they affect the adopted. Given the facts of the precariousness of adoptive kinship as institution, Professor Wadlington's call for corrective legislation appears applicable. But even if all the sex-related and property-related questions were eventually to be equitably answered, so as to create truly equivalent positions for the adoptee and the natal child *within the family,* it would still not give the adopted the same place as that given to other members of the society. There are additional legal constraints which have the effect of making the adopted, who were to have been the primary beneficiaries of the institution, into victims.

I have sought to shed light on contradictions and strains which make the institutional arrangements of adoption precarious. Of course it would have been desirable had fuller and more recent data been available. It is my hope that with adequate funding, the Pierce study can be replicated and extended to jurisdictions in the United States, and that it will be possible to undertake systematic research into laws regulating intestate inheritance on this continent. In the meantime the admittedly fragmentary picture is sufficient to indicate serious disabilities for the constituents as a result of the precarious condition of the institution.

NOTES

1. Eugene A. Weinstein, "Adoption," *International Encyclopedia of the Social Sciences,* The Macmillan Co. and the Free Press, 1968.
2. Margaret Kornitzer, *Child Adoption in the Modern World,* 1952, pp. 143-4.
3. By "intestate" is meant the state of being without a last will and testament.

"Intestate inheritance" refers to the rights of direct descendants of the blood to the property of a deceased who has not left a last will or testament.

4. H. David Kirk, " 'Shared Fate' as Theory of Adoptive Relationships and as Theory of Human Community," paper for the World Conference of Adoption and Foster Placement, Milan, Italy, September 16-19, 1971. Published in *Proceedings* of the Conference, 1972.

5. Steve Pierce, "Law, Marriage and Family — A Socio-Legal Enquiry Into the Institutionalization of Adoptive Relationships in Canada," unpublished Honors paper, Department of Sociology, University of Waterloo, 1972.

6. William M. Evan, "Some Approaches to the Sociology of Law," in *Law and Sociology*, 1962, p. 6.

7. Talcott Parsons, "The Law and Social Control," in Evan (ed.), *Law and Sociology*, pp. 58-61.

8. Pierce notes: "Each province publishes what is called the "Revised Statutes" of that province. In these publications the various acts of the provinces are collected and brought up-to-date as far as revocations, amendments and additions are concerned. . . . The following are the dates for the Revised Statutes used in this study:

Newfoundland	1952
Nova Scotia	1967
Prince Edward Island	1951
New Brunswick	1952
Quebec	1964
Ontario	1970
Manitoba	1970
Saskatchewan	1965
Alberta	1955
British Columbia	1960"

9. Walter J. Wadlington III, "The Adopted Child and Intra-Family Marriage Prohibitions," *Virginia Law Review* 49 (1963), p. 485.

10. "Incest," American Jurisprudence, 2d, 41, 516.

11. 196 Miss. 311, 17, So. 2d 277 (1944), 151 *American Law Reports,* 1143-1146.

12. 74 Ohio App. 381-383, 59 N.E. 2d 167 (1943).

13. W. J. Wadlington III, *op. cit.,* p. 488.

14. *Ibid.,* pp. 489, 490.

15. United Nations, Department of Social Affairs, *Study on Adoption of Children,* 1953, p. 90.

16. M. Schapiro, *A Study of Adoption Practice,* Child Welfare League of America, 1955, p. 102.

17. Schapiro quoted this from S.O. Bates, "Change of Names, Legitimation and Adoption," *Tennessee Law Review,* June 1946.

18. Apparently, a working paper.

Chapter 9

Stepchildren and Other Beneficiaries as Victims

Let us now examine certain consequences of precariously institutionalized kinship in adoption, with particular reference to the categories of people most dependent on it. Although I do not wish to imply that the institution of adoptive kinship does not yield useful and helpful results, our concern here must be with problematic consequences. Furthermore, I want to draw attention to so-called "latent dysfunctional" consequences, i.e. those which were most probably unintended and which have remained generally unrecognized as problematic.

Stepchildren at Risk

I begin the analysis with the circumstances of the stepchild who is being adopted by a stepparent. It is typically a situation which follows divorce and remarriage, with a new spouse adopting the child or children born of the former union. Although no mention has been made so far in this book of stepparent adoption, this chapter opens with it because in the context one is able to see very clearly the link between institution and persons. Remarkably little has been written about stepparenthood, and even less about stepparent adoptions. A recent book by Maddox[1] lays bare some of the issues I wish to discuss here. Maddox makes clear how little the matter of adoption by stepparents has been taken into serious consideration by the legal and social work functionaries of the institution. Apparently it was thought that the institutional arrangements of child protection were applicable largely to those adoptions in which no relative of the child was involved in the new family constellation.

In stepparent adoption, the intention is of course that the child should benefit from the new circumstances. In North America the presumption of law and social administration appears to be that what should be, will be. As Maddox notes, it is not a view universally shared:

> In Britain the prevailing view is that to encourage stepparent adoption is bad social policy. The Houghton Committee on adoption law reform in 1972 came down strongly against the practice. The committee's basic argument was that adoption is an irrevocable legal act that cuts a legitimate child off not only from one of its legitimate biological parents

but from an entire half of his family. It wipes out kinship links with brothers, cousins, grandparents, and aunts. For the many stepparents with stepchildren by divorce, the Houghton Committee felt that in most cases guardianship was a better solution. If stepparents were embarrassed by the difference in surname, the name could be legally changed. Any uncertainty about inheritance could be eliminated by providing for the stepchild in a will. With a stepparent as a guardian, a stepchild would retain the option of reverting to his real father's name later in life if he wanted.

Behind these objections lay serious doubts about the motives behind stepchild adoption. The mother may urge adoption as a way of forcing the stepfather to demonstrate his commitment to her and her children. Or the couple together may be trying to take revenge on the ex-husband, by obliterating his tie to the children.[2]

The Houghton Committee's views were given legal form and sanction in the Children Act of 1975. That law "accepts guardianship as the preferred alternative for many stepparents wanting a legal form of relationship with their stepchildren, except that it is now called custodianship. It means that the legal custody of the child is transferred to the stepparent, but that the child keeps his original family name and ties."[3] Having pointed to a clearly stated view which does not favor automatically granting adoption decrees to stepparents, Maddox proceeds to a somewhat equivocal position:

> Stepparent adoption is yet another example of supposedly enlightened attitudes in conflict. One holds that adoption is desirable because it gives the stepchild the nearest approximation to the secure status of a child living with his two natural parents. The other holds that a child's identity is derived from his real kin, that it is his unique biological and cultural inheritance that should not be taken away. — Which is right I would not presume to say.

Whereupon she turns to the adoption agencies and berates them for not counseling potential stepparent adopters prior to taking the step into adoption. But she also admits that the agencies lack the authority to interview the stepfamily; that authority must come from law and she notes that the State of Connecticut has such a law. In the absence of legal constraints to assure that they avail themselves of counseling, Maddox then calls on would-be adoptive stepparents to examine their consciences (p. 172):

— Do they need the legal status of parents?
— Do they want their relationship to the child to continue beyond marriage?
— Are there relatives who might try to claim the child if the natural parent died?
— Are they ashamed to admit that their spouse has been married before?
— Are they after revenge or social convenience?

It seems to me that Maddox asks pertinent questions, if not always clearly. But she does not realize that the adoption agencies, even if there were a law to require counseling, would seldom be more successful than "conscience" in preventing an ill advised stepparent adoption. Why does Maddox not instead call for legislation like that of Britain's, in which the preferred mode of caring for the stepchild's needs is through guardianship? That arrangement gives the child all the security adoption might, without destroying his or her bonds to an existing birthparent and the line of kin. One need not be a romantic adherent of blood lineage to see the risks which are typically built into stepparent adoptions.

How serious is the issue of stepparent adoptions in quantitative terms? Maddox shows figures indicating that between 1952 and 1971 approximately one half of all adoption decrees were granted to relatives of the child. Of these relative adoptions about one half were made by stepparents. Between 1968 and 1971 at least 40,000 stepchildren were legally adopted in the United States. For Canada as a whole, no figures or estimates are available. However, figures for British Columbia[4] show that while in this province the absolute number of stepparent adoptions had risen from 416 in 1961-62 to 763 a decade later, the proportion of stepparent to other adoptions has been on the increase from 28 per cent in 1961-62 to 46 per cent in 1976-77.

The central issue here is not, however, whether large numbers of stepchildren are at risk as much as the nature of the risk. At issue is the tendency to treat stepparent adoptions as if they were "all in the family" matters, of little concern to society. The Houghton Committee's recommendations to Parliament and Maddox's questions of conscience are strong indications of the risks to which adopted stepchildren are exposed when the practice is relatively unregulated.

The institutional arrangements on behalf of the stepchildren who become legally adopted are then precarious for at least these reasons: (1) There is danger that the child's kin continuity, broken by the adoption, may be broken by yet another divorce of stepparent from birthparent. (2) The moral authority of the courts which have the power to grant adoptions is in most jurisdictions on this continent not reinforced by restrictive legislation, i.e., by legislation that allows stepparent adoptions only sparingly, upon the showing of good and necessary cause. (3) The social work agencies and their umbrella organizations, like the U.S. Children's Bureau and the Child Welfare League, have not spread their protective mantle of professional interest over these adoptions as they have over adoptions between persons without prior blood ties. One aspect which Maddox misses in this connection is this: it appears that very young children adopted by stepparents are not infrequently left in ignorance as to their true status. There are no social workers to insist that the child be told of the adoption. Being thus misled about family and personal identity places the adopted stepchild in adulthood at risk, especially with respect to his or her genetic-medical history.

Before proceeding to an examination of the other principals served by the institution of adoption, let us briefly call to mind the main focus of this chapter. By inspecting risk factors that face clients, we can identify structural strains of the institution. If the institutional structure is precarious, that fact should show up in the risks to which its clientele is subjected. We began with the circumstances of stepparent adoptions. Now we proceed to adopters, birthparents, and other adoptees.

Adoptive Parents at Risk

Although we have previously dealt with the circumstances of the adoptive parents, I must briefly summarize the risks that this group encounters. They are caught in a dilemma of action: how can they follow simultaneously the cultural prescription for all parents to integrate their children into their family, and also to follow the professional prescription to tell the child the fact of adoption, which implies not integrating but differentiating the child? If they deal with the dilemma by "telling" as apparently most of these adopters do, they are next faced by ambiguities: how are they to "tell" without upsetting the child or themselves? Finally, this uncertainty of how to carry out the prescription leads to the uncertainty of outcome: what will their actions ultimately do for their relationship; how can they make sure that their family bonds will be cohesive and stable? For adopters, the institution is precarious then for these reasons: (1) It confronts them with incongruous role obligations. (2) It has neglected to identify and then instruct adopters how to cope with that incongruity in their and their children's lives. (3) It has not provided an understanding of the dangers of denial (R/D) modes of coping, and the long-term rewards which are more likely to accrue to those who will go the more demanding route of consistent and loving acknowledgment-of-difference.

Birthparents at Risk

In 1977, while I was attending as observer a conference of adopted adults and birthparents, I was introduced to one of the delegates. She was a birthmother who some 25 years earlier had surrendered a child for adoption. In the course of our conversation, she offered to help with any subsequent studies I might undertake. That is how, some months later, I wrote to her. I asked whether she would spell out in some detail what she now understands to have been the circumstances leading to the surrender, and if possible to put her story into the context of what she may know or suppose about other unwed parents. Also I explained that by "circumstances which led to the surrender" I meant (a) economic circumstances, (b) circumstances involving her family and friends, (c) conventional and other rules of conduct, and (d) how people, including herself, understood what was implied by notions like "parenthood," "adoption," and "relinquishment." Mrs. "Virginia Fuller's" reply followed roughly the outline I had suggested. I record it here with her permission, as she wrote it:

(a) It is my opinion that in 1950 economic resources were more lacking for an unwed mother than in 1970. Social acceptance of the unwed mother has also helped. Also the general rise in women's employment would contribute. Most unwed mothers then and now lack resources: because of their young age — they are unprepared for work (not qualified) and lack places for child care. Even older married women have difficulty to find adequate child care.

(b) I am not sure what other unwed mothers experienced with their families. I removed myself without their knowledge. I would have been helped by my family. However, the social stigma of unwed mothers in 1950 often placed a family under strain and forced them to send her away. For example, one argument my boyfriend used against marriage before the child was born was the effect upon my family, especially my younger brother and sister. It was a factor in my decision (to place my child for adoption).

(c) My parents would have encouraged my marriage, perhaps have insisted had they known of the child. I was never encouraged by anyone — social worker, agency, lawyer, doctor, or friends to keep the child, but was reinforced in my decision to relinquish.

(d) I have had strong parental feelings dormant all the years. I married and soon had other children, but mourned the loss of that first child and all the days and years of our not knowing each other. Not knowing what had happened to the child was perhaps the hardest of all. When I met her[5] I felt a burden lift. One interesting reaction I had was my motherly protection of her at the expense of my husband, family, and friends. However, I believe as time has passed and meeting her occasionally, I see her in her life with her friends, belonging to them and herself, not the child I relinquished. I see the reality.

Summarizing the factors she considered then, Mrs. Fuller put them in the order of their importance to her at the time:

(1) My boyfriend [father of the child] would not marry me; this was my first choice; his was abortion. (2) I wished to preserve my self image and be free from social stigma, for I was a selfish twenty-year-old girl. (3) I wished to protect my family from community social rejection. (4) I wished to protect the child; this was emphasized by social workers and others I knew then and has been reinforced by books and articles since. [In terms of the child's protection] I wished her to be raised in a family unit in my own religion and I wished her to be free from social stigma.

Then Mrs. Fuller added these poignant lines:

Notice, Mr. Kirk, the order of these choices — the child's welfare last! But then, I was so young; how often I regret that choice. I never thought until I read *The Search for Anna Fisher*[6] that my daughter might wonder and wish to know me. The problem lies in society's failure to make all of us responsible. An unwed mother is encouraged and allowed to believe she can emerge unscathed from the situation and be free from any responsibility to the child. She is told to forget. The adoptive mother is encouraged to believe she is the natural "real" mother. Children do not belong to anyone; they are not extensions of parents — they belong to themselves. "Nice little families" cannot be created by agencies but through diligent, democratic family love and interaction.

So much for Mrs. Fuller's account. What can we extrapolate from her statements for an understanding of the institution? Was she at risk, and in what sense? Let me suggest that for unwed mothers, especially for young ones without occupational security, there has long been an institutional hiatus in the lack of economic resources and adequate child care facilities. Second, without imputing duress from the social services, there was considerable cultural pressure on the unwed mother to forgo carrying out her role of mothering. This cultural pressure was used by the professional services in effecting the surrender of the child. In other words, from the point of view of the unwed mother, the institutional arrangements of adoptive kinship were not powerful enough to devise some mechanism for assuring her long-run as well as short-run interests. Third, the birthparent finds herself in a dilemma of contradictory rules of conduct. One of these is the cultural rule which suggests that a mother must always look after her child, come what may. The other, the professional rule, is that for the sake of her own growth toward maturity as well as the child's future, she must consider surrendering the child for adoption. Thus the institution is normatively precarious in that it does not give reasonably clear guidelines to the birthmother's action for her child. Finally there is the matter of meaning: if she decides to surrender the child, what will this act mean to her in the years to come? Is she still a "mother?" Can she totally forget — can she put the surrender aside, and with it the birth, and the pregnancy? And if she cannot forget the fact of the surrender, how can she make sense of the fact that out there, somewhere, is the child whom she has given life, but about whose life she knows nothing; and more, about whose life she is not supposed to know anything. Thus the institution is precarious for the birthparent in that the "solution" it has evolved carries with it many ambiguous meanings and enigmatic answers; as in Mrs. Fuller's case, it leaves her in limbo, unless by remote chance, she should learn about or meet her birthchild.

Adopted Persons at Risk

In the preceding chapter reference was made to a court decision which allowed the marriage of an adoptive father to his daughter by adoption. What such an event shows is that adoptive kinship within the nuclear family cannot be the equivalent of consanguineal kinship. The institution of adoption is then precarious in that it cannot give to the adoptee an unequivocal place as the child of the adopters. Now I want to show that the adoptee is further at risk by the fact that the act of adoption does not vacate the prohibition against incest with kin of the blood. Professor Cyril Means drew my attention to a case from

1971 which sheds light on the further contradictions in the institution and the liabilities resulting for the adopted. The case is presented here as it appeared in the *New York Post* of September 3, 1971:

> San Diego, California (Associated Press) — A mother and son who became husband and wife have been sentenced to jail for bigamy. Incest charges were dropped after they pleaded guilty to bigamy. They have a 2-year old daughter.
>
> A Superior Court judge, saying "this is a serious crime — a felony," sentenced the mother, Rebecca Slater, 41, to six months in the county jail. Her son, Wyley Kitzmiller, 23, was sentenced to nine months on a county work farm and fined $500. Each also received three years' probation.
>
> Defense attorney George Lerg 2nd told judge William P. Mahedy that Kitzmiller was given up for adoption immediately after his birth in 1948 [and] that his mother didn't see him again until he was nineteen. By then, Lerg said, Kitzmiller, who had taken the name of his adoptive parents, was a grown man and the only mother he'd ever known was his stepmother [sic]. Lerg said Kitzmiller's only crime was "falling in love with a total stranger who happened to be his natural mother."
>
> Although Kitzmiller was unmarried, he could be charged with bigamy under California law, which holds that marrying another man's wife is bigamous. Kitzmiller's mother testified she and her son's father, Michael Slater, 52, were separated but that he would not give her a divorce. They had five other children. She said she and Kitzmiller, a sailor aboard the missile cruiser USS Chicago had eloped in 1969 and were married in Vallejo, California.
>
> Lerg asked the court for leniency, but Judge Mahedy said: "This man lived with his own mother and married her. I don't see any extenuating circumstances. She is his natural mother and this is incest and bigamy."
>
> Charges were filed in the case after Slater contacted police and Naval intelligence less than a year after the marriage and told them about the couple.

If natural parent and child long separated by adoption cannot legally marry, neither can blood brother and sister separated by adoption. Such a case occurred in New England quite recently. The following is quoted from the *Kitchener-Waterloo Record* of June 21, 1979:

> Lawrence, Mass. (AP) — The brother and sister who met and married after growing up in separate adoptive families say they are hopelessly in love and unable to part.
>
> "It's too late for Vicki and I to change our feelings," said David Goddu, 22, who met his natural sister for the first time a few months ago. "We set our minds to do it (separate) but when it comes down to it, we can't do it. How can we stop a relationship that's already started?"
>
> Goddu and his sister, the former Victoria Pittorino, 23, were reunited after the sister spent six years trying to locate him and their parents.

Goddu had been adopted by James and Eileen Goddu of Holyoke and his sister has grown up across the state in Arlington.

The couple was arrested last week after Isabelle Pittorino, Vicki's adoptive mother, signed a complaint charging incest, and a court hearing is scheduled for July. The Pittorino's lawyer says the parents want their daughter home and under a psychiatrist's care.

"We had decided before we got married, we had discussed it, that we would not have children, that Dave would get a vasectomy," the new Mrs. Goddu said in an interview with the Lawrence Eagle-Tribune published Tuesday.

"I found Dave in Holyoke two weeks before Easter," she said. "When we first met we didn't feel we were meeting as brother-sister. How can you have a brother-sister relationship after 23 years? We saw each other as boy-girl.

"It was love at first sight I guess, but I can't say at this time whether it was right or wrong."

The couple blame the state for separating them during childhood.

"If they hadn't split us up we wouldn't be in this mess," Mrs. Goddu said. *"We felt legally the state separated us and put us up for adoption. Legally we were not brother and sister."* (Emphasis added.)

Unusual and bizarre as the Kitzmiller and Goddu cases undoubtedly are, they nevertheless point to the paradoxical situation in which adoptive kinship currently casts the adopted. When Victoria Pittorino Goddu said that she and her brother-husband are victims of the separate adoptions which had taken place, she was undoubtedly correct. She was also emphatically correct when she pointed out that, when she and David had been made members of different families by adoption, they were legally no longer brother and sister. Clearly something is wrong with legislation which leaves this kind of unresolved discrepancy hidden except when it is unearthed by some tragicomic event.

Let us briefly look back to Professor Wadlington's proposal referred to in Chapter 8. He has suggested that legislation should put the adopted into the same position as family members of the blood. That well meant proposal would, however, have one unintended consequence: while it would equalize the adoptee's position, in terms of the prohibition of incest, with those of natal siblings, it would simultaneously add one more social disability to the existing one which will undoubtedly not be vacated. Clearly Wadlington is not proposing for the Kitzmillers and the Goddus to have an open season for incestual marriage, nor is it likely that any legislature or public for that matter would allow intra-family incest prohibitions generally to be taken off the books. So, whichever way we turn, however much we want to see the circumstances of adoptive kinship realistically rather than mythically made into the equivalent of kinship of the blood, we see it is not possible. And we see that in the process of pretending that it is the equivalent, the adopted also are put at genuine risk.

But is that kind of legal discrepancy — the kind we have seen in the Kitz-miller and Goddu cases — not the reason for officially sealed adoption records? In the Kitzmiller case the son had not been searching for his birth-mother, nor she for him. That is not how they found each other. Their sexual attraction occurred precisely because they had not known of the blood relationship they shared. In the case of the Pittorino-Goddu couple, Victoria had been searching for her brother and had been successful. In their case, David's adoptive father is reported to have said: "We were happy for David [when the sister located her brother]. Now we wish it never did happen. I wish the laws were most strict about disclosure of information to adopted chil-dren." As an adoptive father, I have considerable sympathy for Mr. Goddu, Sr. and even for Mrs. Pittorino, Victoria's adoptive mother, who charged the young couple with incest. These adopters must have felt some of the things I felt that day with Francie on the New York Thruway, except that the problem for me remained hypothetical while theirs directly impinged on their lives. Furthermore, they had most probably not subjected their plight to a socio-logical anaylsis, not only because that was likely not their regular mode of thinking, but because they had hardly the time to do so. One day Victoria found a brother and before the families understood what was happening, he had become lover and husband. For these families there had not been a hypo-thetical threat to their internal order; they experienced such a disturbance of all the rules as they knew them that the Pittorinos wanted "their daughter home and under a psychiatrist's care," while Mrs. Goddu said she had been "a nervous wreck and had cried every night for the past week."

Though I have sympathy with these families in their plight, I cannot agree with Mr. Goddu in calling for even stricter laws of disclosure of information "to adopted children." While Victoria Pittorino apparently began searching for her brother when she was 17,[7] an age which may seem child-like to some, she found him when she was legally of age. It is this issue of labelling the adopted as "adopted children" which has, I suspect, contributed to their role handicap as adults. The institution of adoptive kinship has never clarified at which point in life an "adopted child" becomes legally an adult who also happens to be somebody's child by adoption. The following statement by Joseph Reid,[8] former director of the Child Welfare League of America, suggests why the "adopted child" label came to be so firmly affixed to mean "beneficiary":

> Social agencies are placing children in order to find permanent family homes for them. We are not placing children to save an unhappy marriage, to try to prevent a woman from having a psychosis, or for any of the other reasons concerned with fulfilling an adult's desire to have children. Rather, *we are attempting to fulfill the child's right to have parents.*
> Now, in the majority of cases, these two needs do compliment [sic] each other, the adult's need to have children and the child's need to have

parents. But social agencies do reject the concept that a couple has a right to children in and of itself; only if that right goes along with *the needs of the child,* do we favor placing a child with them.

The "needs of the child" — these may have been represented well by the adoption lobby, but at the same time the interests of the adults have been both forgotten and neglected, perhaps precisely because of the "child" label. But if the agencies considered the needs of the parents to be secondary to the interests of the children, why were the professionals not able to see that children, including adopted ones, must be allowed to grow up and make adult choices if they are to become full adult members of society? When a person cannot legally obtain basic documents relating to his or her own life, then that person does not have the basic rights and duties of adults as that term is defined in society.

Let me show you why I speak of "rights and duties" of adulthood. My example is access to medical records. When my children were small and our pediatrician asked about family histories with respect to genetic background, we had to say again and again: "Sorry, we don't know about that; our child is adopted." Again and again the pediatrician would put a line through a page or a segment of our children's medical records. It was our duty to protect our children's health as best we could, but our best was not very good. In the case of adopted persons who marry and have children, this ignorance of their own background can become a serious liability for their offspring. One adoptee, Nancy Sitterly, Coordinator of the Connecticut Adoptees Search and Support Group, is the mother of a little girl born with a neuroblastoma tumor. She says that when she could not tell the doctors any facts of her own genetic history, she knew she was unable to do her parental duty by her child. Mrs. Sitterly's story is a case in point of how adopted persons are placed at risk through the sealing of birth and adoption records in perpetuity, ostensibly to safeguard the integrity of the adoptive family. Somehow the legal and social service benefactors did not consider that families cannot be protected in perpetuity, and that to try to do so would greatly hamper the rights of persons. Though readily available divorce may damage the stability of many families, to shut the door on divorce would limit the rights of adults to the choice of legitimate mates. Thus contemporary divorce laws recognize the rights of the adults as well as the rights of children in divorce. In contrast, adoption laws typically do not recognize the rights of adult adoptees as much as they do the rights of the adopters. There the concern appears overwhelmingly to be directed to the maintenance of the adoptive family.

Of course the contemporary world being what it is, the interests of individuals will be asserted even against stonewalling such as this:

No Divorce for Adopters until the Child is 18? Sir George Baker, President of the Family Division of the High Court, proposed at the annual conference of justices' clerks at Harrogate on 9 May 1975 that there should be a radical change in the divorce laws, so that couples adopting a child would not be able to obtain a divorce until the child reached 18.[9]

Such tactics are acts of desperation and do not succeed because they are too outrageous even for the institutional apparatus of adoption as it now exists. But that apparatus has managed, in almost all North American jurisdictions, to maintain adoption records and original birth records all but inaccessible to the great majority of the adopted of whatever age. Insofar as it has managed to do so, it has also placed the adopted at greater risk than people whose life situations, except for the fact of adoption, are otherwise similar. But the example of medical records is only one in a list of institutional circumstances that threaten the adopted of North America. Some of these points are so ordinary that they have been neglected even by the spokesmen for the rights of adopted adults:

1. At the coming of their first child, adoptive parents have typically been older than birthparents. People who begin life with their children late will also have a shorter time to be parents, for they will die sooner in the child's life.
2. One-child families have been more frequent in adoptive than in biologically formed families, with the result that adopted adults frequently have no brothers or sisters. Aside from the immediate loss in childhood, it means that at the adoptive parents' aging and death there are no close partners to share the work, the grieving, and the loneliness.
3. Contemporary adoption has been most typically practised among urban, middle class people, the very people who have been most socially and geographically mobile. The fact of mobility brings with it lessened opportunity for frequent contacts with the wider family, so that the adopted will have fewer social roots after the parents die.

The common factor among these three points of risk is social isolation. The adopted are subject to greater social isolation than persons reared in the families to whom they are born. But however common, not all three risk factors will regularly affect every adoptee's life. It is much more likely that almost every adoptee will find a type of cultural isolation in that other people do not readily grasp the nature of their situation, or sympathize with it. In *Shared Fate* (pp. 33-34) I quoted a letter from a woman whose small adopted son had died. The undertaker asked: "For parents shall I put 'unknown'?" If such had been the cultural climate experienced by adopters in the nineteen fifties, similar sentiments were in the air two decades later. In 1976 I heard from Florence Fisher, an adoptee and the author of *The Search for Anna Fisher*. She told me the following story. The one member of her adoptive family to whom she felt close was her maternal uncle Abe. When uncle Abe died in 1975, she went to claim the body as next of kin. But the undertaker would not release it, saying that as an *adopted* niece he did not regard her as next of kin! Thus, both in terms of potential social isolation within the adoptive kin group and cultural isolation from unrelated outsiders, the institution of adoptive kinship is precarious, placing the adopted at risk. There is little question as to the benefits adoptive kinship confers on adopted persons *as children;* there is considerable question for them *as adults.*

NOTES

1. Brenda Maddox, *The Half-Parent,* 1975.
2. *Ibid.,* p. 170.
3. *Ibid.,* p. 171.
4. H. Philip Hepworth, *Foster Care and Adoption in Canada,* 1980, Table 49, p. 134.
5. When the daughter was in her early twenties she searched for and found Mrs. Fuller.
6. Florence Fisher, *The Search for Anna Fisher,* 1973.
7. Scotland's adoption law permits adopted persons of 17 and over access to their original birth records.
8. Joseph H. Reid, in U.S. Children's Bureau, *Protecting Children in Adoption,* 1955, p. 26 (emphasis added).
9. Legal note in *Child Adoption,* 81, No. 3, 1975.

Chapter 10

Emerging From Obscurity

A Social Movement of the Adopted

Given the institutional contradictions of adoptive kinship and their consequences for the adopted, what has occurred? Has there been public articulation of the issues? Have attempts been made to look beyond the issues to potential remedies? The answer is that articulation of the issues and presumed remedies came first from a fledgling social movement and then from a number of professionals.

The acknowledged pioneer of the adoptee movement is Jean Paton. In 1954 she published *The Adopted Break Silence,* a report of her study of the experiences and outlook of adopted persons. I was told about this book, sent for it, read and annotated it. Looking at the copy with my notes from the mid-nineteen fifties, I realize that the book troubled me, but more in terms of what I then considered short-comings of sampling and data analysis rather than in terms of the ideas presented. I think now that I was simply taken aback by Paton's attack on the institutional arrangements of adoptive kinship.

Jean Paton went beyond a research project and book financed by herself. Subsequently she organized Orphan Voyage, which was her contribution to the development of an adoptee movement. In that context she instituted Reunion, a voluntary register which was to promote searches and reunions between adopted persons and birthparents. Thus, while her group's ultimate goal was the thorough overhaul of existing administrative and legal arrangements, there was also to be a mechanism to serve more immediate ends.

As so often happens with the beginnings of a social movement, the pioneer was apparently ahead of her time. In spite of concerted efforts at writing and speaking, Jean Paton seems to have reached only a small number of people during the first years of her operation. It may have taken relatively daring souls to join her in the early days. But with the emergence of more and more minority groups calling publicly for equitable opportunities, the day was dawning for a wider membership appeal by adoptee groups. That membership appeal was made possible because the children, adopted during the nineteen forties and fifties, had grown up. When these people reached young adulthood during the late nineteen sixties and early seventies, they had seen blacks and then women form militant social movements that pressed for remedial legislation and other action to alleviate their conditions of deprivation. Faced with these models, the previously hidden and silent adoptee population may well have been more receptive to the messages that pioneers like Jean Paton had been sending for years. Thus when Florence Fisher placed an advertisement in *The New York Times* early in the nineteen seventies asking fellow adoptees to indicate interest in getting acquainted, she was swamped by replies. Evidently the time had come for the adoptee movement. By 1971 ALMA was formed, and other adoptee associations sprang up in various parts of North America. Then two years later there appeared *The Search for Anna Fisher,* which became a kind of rallying post for the movement's advance. Thus almost two decades after Paton's book signalled the entrance of the adoptee as a visible and audible entity, Fisher's book gave notice of the adoptee's coming of age. Their combined efforts brought forth a remarkable movement: not one monolithic association but many local, regional, and national groups with the common aims of mutal aid and institutional reform.

Although the adoptee movement was by no means incapable of stating its case in social science terms, the more detached advocacy of its interests had to await the latter nineteen sixties and seventies. It was then that establishment professionals published works in which the adopted rather than adoptive parents were the principal actors, and where finally also the birthparents were given major billing. The first two of the studies to be cited in this chapter were oriented around the adoptee. Since they were conducted in Scotland, the investigators were able to approximate representative samples; Scotland has for half a century given adopted persons of 17 and over access to their original birthrecords. Thus McWhinnie,[1] seeking "to find out how adoption was experienced by the person ultimately most concerned. . .," interviewed what she believed to be "a representative group of 58 adult persons, aged 18 and over, who had been adopted as children."Her case history study actually involved 52 adoptees as well as six persons fostered but not legally adopted. Her interests were those of the social worker wanting more reliable facts to guide the selection of adoptive applicants and the placement of children in adoptive homes. In general, McWhinnie's in-depth work with these Scottish adoptees confirmed what I had learned from my survey data and personal observations:

> [The] question of discussing adoption within the adoptive family showed a lack of communication between the world of adults and that of children. . . and . . . with regard to. . . telling the child of his or her adoption, the present study [shows]. . . that this is a problem for adoptive parents (p. 265).
> . . . [Generally] the adopted and fostered children in this series wanted on the whole to have factual information about their biological parents and about why and how they had been placed for adoption. *Inadequate, incomplete or varying information here led to difficulties* (p. 263, emphasis added).

McWhinnie also concludes that these adults for the most part viewed their adoptive parents as their "real" parents (p. 264).

Unlike the foregoing general inquiry into the experiences of the adopted, Triseliotis'[2] focus was "to identify the general circumstances of adopted adults who seek information about their origins; to establish the reasons for their search, their motivation, their needs and objectives and also to what use they put the information gained." For this endeavor, Triseliotis sampled "70 adoptees who applied or called at Register House in Edinburgh asking to be supplied with information from their original birth entries." (p. 11)

As in McWhinnie's study, Triseliotis learned from these adoptees that "there was a general reluctance among adoptive parents to reveal or share information about the child's original genealogy and also how he came to be adopted." (p. 156) But as Jane Rowe pointedly notes in the foreword to the book, ". . . a need to seek original parents [as against impersonal information] was often associated with lack of satisfying relationships within the adoptive family." (p. ix) Triseliotis' concluding comment (p. 166) sums up the theoretical and normative thrust of his work:

> The self-perception of all of us is partly based on what our parents and ancestors have been, going back many generations. Adoptees, too, wish to base themselves not only on their adoptive parents, but also on what their original parents and forebears have been, going back many generations. It is the writer's view, based on his findings, that no person should be cut off from his origins.

In reading Triseliotis' study, I had a strong experience of *déjà vu:* I had seen and heard very similar matters raised by my children as they sought clarity about their birth status. In 1958 Peter had borrowed a children's book on archeology from the library. He sat absorbed over its pictures and stories of early humans and announced: "Some day *I'll* be an ancestor!" As I have so often done during the early years of my children's lives, I misunderstood Peter's interest here and promptly got for him several books on the same subject. I don't think he ever looked at them, certainly not with me. But it took me a while to weave Peter's interest in ancestry into the larger adoption issue. That event occurred when he was eight. Two years later, Americans went to the polls to elect a president. As we watched a televised debate between candidates John Kennedy and Richard Nixon, Peter informed us that some day he too would like to go into politics. Since he had American citizenship by birth, he could even run for the office of President. Why would he want to do that, someone asked. The explanation Peter gave remains etched in my memory: had we not all seen how the candidates became well known in the course of the campaign? Had we not read the stories of their beginnings, when and where they were born, the kind of families they had lived in, and what had happened to them during the years of their growing up? "So, if I were to run for the office of President," said Peter, "the newspapers, radio, and TV would carry the story of my life. They'd tell that I'd been adopted and when, and they'd also tell when and where I was born. Surely my first mother would read or hear about me and recognize that this candidate was her son. Then she could try and get in touch with me."

Both McWhinnie and Triseliotis had called for changes in the adoption laws of England and Wales, changes that came into being with the *Children Act* of 1975. No similar laws have been passed in North America, though there have been a number of commissions of inquiry and bills before legislatures. The question of why change occurred in Great Britain and not on this continent will be raised in the next chapter. Here our attention must remain with the movement advocating reform. The adoptee movement was not unaffected by the studies I have cited. Such findings by more detached investigators into the issues of adoptive kinship where bound to give support to people who had so recently emerged from obscurity. I judge that the new "scientific" literature gave further impetus to the development and proliferation of adoptee associations. Now these groups had more than their own intuitive and existential rationale for the drive for reform of the institution. Now they could combine their emotional appeals with reasoning based on considerable scholarship.

Social movements must appeal to a sense of fairness among larger publics that could potentially support their cause. They must therefore seek outside support through growing public sympathy with and understanding of what the movement considers the plight of its members. Instrumental in such public education and propaganda are the very labels or names which the associations in a movement assume. In the case of the adoptee movement, the names of the associations are remarkably revealing of the interests, goals, and outlook of the membership:

Adoptees' Liberty Movement Association ("ALMA" — multiple locations, U.S.A.)
Adoption Forum of Philadelphia
Adoption Identity Movement of Michigan
Adoptees Journey (Texas)
Adoptees in Search (Maryland)
The Family Tree (Texas)
Liberal Education for Adoptive Families (Minnesota)
Link (Minnesota)
Parent Finders (multiple locations, Canada)
Orphan Voyage (multiple locations, U.S.A.)
Triadoption League for Justice (California)
Yesterday's Children (Illinois)

The clues in these names speak for themselves; they are concerned with liberty, identity, linkage, and the rights to find one's own way as adults, as *yesterday's* children. In the sense that these names proclaim what the adoptee movement seeks, they speak of a minority group's grievances and aspirations. But some of them, like Paton's Orphan Voyage or the Canadian Parent Finders, seem to this observer ill chosen to create sympathy from the outside. If, as in Triseliotis' book, the adopted typically think of their adoptive parents as the "real" parents, then they do not think of themselves "orphans" and they do not need more "parents." It is difficult enough for people on the outside to recognize the issue of adoptive kinship as one involving deprivation. What many people, including professionals, think instead is that, since as children many adoptees had opportunities they might not have had save through adoption, therefore they must be privileged. Thus to some outsiders the often strident demands for reform of the institution appear as rank ingratitude, somewhat like biting the hands that fed the adopted. What the adoptee movement must project if it wants to make a more thoroughgoing impact on wider publics, and specifically on those who must make decisions in legislation and administration, is the contradictions inherent in the institution itself. Victimization related to minority status cannot be dealt with unless that issue is understood and addressed. I myself came rather late to understand the fact that the interpersonal tensions experienced in adoptive families — the parents' tendency toward rejection-of-difference and the consequent isolation of their children — have their roots in the contradictions of the professional and legal arrangements that make up the institution. When such impersonal aspects are really understood, then there can be more understanding and sympathy with the persons who are most centrally and lastingly affected by the institution.

Once more I want to recall some of the events that alerted me to the identity needs of the adopted, needs that make institutional reform vital and necessary. During the early summer of 1961, just after I left California and the study of adoptive parent groups, I taught summer school at Allegheny College, in the small city of Meadville, Pennsylvania. One of my courses was the sociology of the family. During the spring, while still associated with Whittier College in California, I had given a series of five public lectures entitled "Parent-Child Relations in Adoption." In these lectures I tried to summarize the work of the previous decade, culminating in the formulation of the Shared Fate theory. It seemed a fitting ending to my two years of concentrated research in California. The lectures were issued in mimeographed form, and I brought several sets with me to Allegheny for my course on the family.

One morning, about a month after I had arrived at the college, I was sitting at my desk reading when I heard steps outside my office. Someone walked the length of the corridor, slowed down in the vicinity of my room, then passed by and returned the same way. This happened three or four times; I began to wonder what was going on. Just then there was a soft knock, and one of my students asked if she might disturb me. For a moment she stood awkwardly in the door. Then she began to speak of my lectures, which she felt had clarified much in her own life. She wondered whether she might borrow a set to take home to her mother over the weekend. She wished for her mother to read them, in the hope that this would enable them to talk more intimately and more realistically about her adoption than they had done. I gave her an extra set, and she left. When on the coming Monday she returned them, nothing more was said. Two weeks later the course ended, and I returned to Montreal.

There I found a letter forwarded to me from Allegheny College. My student wrote to tell me that she and her mother had had a number of good and frank talks, and that now she had even felt free to broach the possibility of locating her birthparents. She had written also to her father (her adoptive parents were divorced) to tell him that she hoped to search for knowledge of her biological roots. At year's end I had a card telling me of her graduation and new job. Some months later came news of her marriage. But what interested me most was a note scribbled on the annoucement to the effect that she had been able to obtain some facts about her biological past, though she had not yet located her birthparents. Now she knew at least something about the people from whom she had come, and could more confidently look forward to having children of her own.

A decade later I had an even more remarkable reminder of the adoptee's urge to come to grips with the undiscovered past. A colleague who is also an adoptive father confided in me that his daughter, who was 18, had no known history. She was a foundling, discovered as a tiny infant on a doorstep in a large U.S. city with a sizable Puerto Rican population. The daughter was a beautiful woman with dark hair and olive complexion, but also given to dark moods which seemed to be connected with her unrequited wish to know about her history. Her adoptive parents had told her that she was a foundling and might well have a Puerto Rican ancestry, but she was not satisfied with that explanation, and her parents knew it.

One summer her adoptive father was asked to give a series of lectures at the University in San Juan. His daughter was unable to accompany him, owing to her own school term. While in Puerto Rico, the father made contact with a private girls' school whose principal was looking for an English-speaking playground assistant for the summer months. He encouraged his daughter to apply, and she was offered the job.

During those weeks she mingled with local people, made friends, visited their homes, and took trips to coastal and inland cities on the island; she saw and experienced more of Puerto Rico than most tourists would. She came home a very different person. When a member of her family remarked that she seemed much more content, she is reported to have said: "Well, it's Puerto Rico. There I was immediately accepted, there my looks didn't stand out, there people didn't ask me about my background the way they do here so often. It just feels good to have discovered such a place."

Open Records and the Question of "Contracts"

When Alex Hailey's *Roots* appeared in 1976, it became a literary sensation overnight. But the adoptee movement was already well aware of the fact that

Americans generally yearn for roots. Can anyone imagine de Tocqueville, in his journey to the America of the last century, discussing such an idea? Americans then exuded optimism about the present and future and could afford to shed their links with the past. But now they were likely to say with John Dos Passos that "a sense of continuity with generations gone before can stretch like a lifetime across the scary present."[3]

When the adopted seek information about their forbears, but not contact with them, such a quest seems more readily understood by outsiders and supported by the authorities. Such concerns do not seriously rock the institutional boat. The more threatening challenge to institutional adoptive kinship has come with the pressure for open records on demand to any adoptee over a certain age. Institutional representatives in North America have generally balked at this proposal, ostensibly because it would mean going back on a contract with the birthparents — a supposedly firm assurance of permanent anonymity. It is arguable whether such "contractual" arrangements are binding on persons who, like the adoptee, were not party to the contract. But there the adoptee associations cannot simply plead for equity, seeing that one party's gain may well be another's loss. Here more thorough information on the current life circumstances and outloook of birthparents is called for.

The requirement for information on the current condition of people who years ago surrendered children for adoption brings us to the work by Sorosky, Baran, and Pannor.[4] McWhinnie and Triseliotis both conducted their inquiries in Scotland, where adoptees could at age 17 readily obtain their original records of birth. Scanty though the information on such records may be, it is basic to knowledge of one's original identity. In contrast, Sorosky, Baran, and Pannor did their work in a North American setting which, because it precludes by law even such scanty background information, has immensely enlarged the entire issue of the adoptee's identity quest. Thus the issue is here doubly complicated for the researcher: on the one hand the persons with whom the research concerns itself are institutionally hidden; on the other hand the very mystery has heightened the necessity for knowledge that is all but unobtainable. Here is what Sorosky, Baran, and Pannor say in describing the goals and interests underlying their study plan:

> . . . Despite the sealed record, a number of searches and successful reunions of adoptees and birth parents . . . have taken place. We felt it important to explore the causes and effects of these reunions and to understand the attitudes of birth parents, adoptive parents, and adoptees.
>
> This is the first research study that has investigated the feelings and attitudes of birth parents years after they have relinquished their children for adoption. In this regard, we have challenged the traditional concept of adoption which severs the ties between the adoptee and his/her birth family. (p. 14)

In many respects the findings of this study overlap with and support those of the work by McWhinnie and Triseliotis. But there are in the American study previously unavailable and poignant insights into the lives and feelings of birthparents. Especially important for my understanding were excerpts from letters written by them. In the following paragraph the authors have summarized what they learned from these letters:

> Even in the letters that pleaded for secrecy and indicated no desire for contact, there was still the intensity of feeling and the need to describe the pain, still carried within. Two areas, in particular, stand out as causing most unwed mothers continued pain: (1) there was the concern that the child would not understand the reason for the relinquishment and grow up feeling rejected and abandoned; (2) there was a worry that the child would think poorly of them and never know what they had done with the rest of their lives. Even if the birth parents had become comfortable with the decision because there were no viable alternatives, they nevertheless felt loss, pain, mourning, and a continuing sense of caring for that long vanished child. In some cases a reunion would be accepted, in others it would be pursued, and still others it would be discouraged or refused. In all situations the intensity of feeling and involvement is clearly there. (p. 72)

In thus opening up the circumstances of the birthparent and showing her life in the larger drama of adoptive kinship, Sorosky, Baran, and Pannor have done yeoman service. Their proposals for changes in the institutional arrangements of adoption, which I quote in Chapter 11, are thoughtful and merit careful consideration. What I found disappointing was the dearth of methodological information in a study report that had set itself so critical a policy task. But the beginning it has made is substantial and it complements the knowledge gained from the work of its Scottish predecessors. All three underscore what the Shared Fate data and theory suggested, namely that the social psychology of adoptive relationships is one of mutual deprivation. In *Shared Fate* I noted that an awareness of their own and their child's deprivations could serve adoptive parents in strengthening the parent-child bonds and so the solidarity of their family. Perhaps, with the insights provided in the pioneering studies by McWhinnie, Triseliotis, and the Sorosky, Baran, Pannor team, it will now be possible to enlarge the scope of the Shared Fate theory by including the birthparents in the empathic and communicative network that is made possible by acknowlegement-of-differnce. If that were done institutionally, it would make the birthparent also emerge from obscurity. At present the birthparents' obsurity is part and parcel of the anonymity which was supposedly guaranteed by the agency's "contract" with the surrendering birthparent.

This "contract" is the major stumbling block to the reform called for by the adoptee movement. Some spokesmen for the adoption professionals have claimed that this "contract" is sacrosanct, that the birthparents depend on it to protect the new lives which the surrender of their children afforded them. But there are now birthparents who maintain that the "contract" is a two-edged sword: it has not only cut them off from a once difficult past, but it has also made them invisible in society at large. In that sense the "contract" is also an order to disappear. The literature of the adoption professionals of the past several decades suggests that this disappearance of the birthparent was regarded as necessary to the adoptive parent's sense of entitlement and in creating firm boundaries around the adoptive parent-child relationship. That was the message given to adoptive parents and the public when the adoption lobby fought against "independent adoptions," i.e. third-party arrangements not involving a licensed agency. Only the latter, the message said, was able to effect adoptive placements that could guarantee both the anonymity of the birthparent and the separate integrity of the adoptive family. For the birthparent it was thus a two-sided message: it protected her and it also warned her to stay away, to disappear from the scene.

Because of the adoptee movement's agitation for open records, the question of the inviolability of the "contract" has become increasingly important. Since there has seldom if ever been such a contract in writing, since it is a mental construct that derives from the culture of the social work agency, it is reasonable that one should ask what birthparents currently understand by the "contract." In 1976-77 the Children's Home Society of California conducted a survey[5] of adoptive parents, birthparents, and adoptees through a questionnaire sent mainly to former clients. The study, appropriately called "The Changing Face of Adoption," asked the former clients how they now saw their adoption-based experiences. Among the people who were located and who responded there were 104 birthparents. Of that number, 103 were women, and of these birthmothers 96 were single at the time of the surrender of their child to the agency. Eighty-five of these birthparents answered the following question, here especially pertinent: "Do you feel the agency made a 'contract' with you never to reveal your identity?" Sixty-two per cent of the birthparents said they believed there had been a contract, while 38 per cent thought there had not. That seems interesting from the point of view of a cultural message:

Table 10.1

A comparison of the responses by the year the child was placed shows:

Year Child Placed	Birthparents Who Thought There Was A "Contract"	Birthparents Who Thought There Was No "Contract"
1967-1976	15	17
1957-1966	21	9
1947-1956	12	2
1937-1946	4	2
1927-1936	1	1
1917-1926	0	1
	53	32

almost two thirds of these birthparents had apparently got the message that they should or at least would disappear, by contract! But now let me make a breakdown of their replies by the decades during which these birthparents surrendered their children for adoption. Table 10.1 shows this breakdown as it appeared in the research report of the Children's Home Society of California.[6] To simplify inspection, and highlight what the data tell us in the context of the present discussion, I have slightly modified this table. Because California's legislation restricting access to adoptees' records stems from the year 1927, I have in the modified table omitted the one birthparent who belonged to the decade 1917-1926. And because there were only eight birthparents belonging to the two decades 1927-1946, I have created a combined category 1927-1956.

Table 10.2

	Year Child Placed		
	1927-1956 N= (22)	1957-1966 (30)	1967-1976 (32)
Per cent of birthparents who thought there was a "contract"	77%	70%	47%
Per cent of birthparents who thought there was no "contract"	23%	30%	53%

Thus in Table 10.2 we can compare the responses of birthparents who relinquished their children between 1927 and 1956 with those who surrendered between 1957 and 1966, and compare them with the birthparents who gave up their children during the decade of 1967-1976.

Table 10.2 shows that the 1957-1966 birthparents were only slightly less likely (70% as against 77%) than their predecessors to say that they had assumed that there was indeed an anonymity "contract." On the other hand, the 1967-76 group was considerably less inclined to hold such a "contract" view. Now only 47% as against the previous 70% said that they considered the arrangement for anonymity to be contractually binding.

In drawing on these data, we must bear in mind that the samples of people who answered the Children's Home Society questionnaire were entirely self-selected. Such samples cannot therefore be regarded as representative of the same categories of people in the population at large. However, in spite of the limitations imposed by the nature of the data, considering that these are the only such quantitive data available, I shall take the California birthparents' responses as a straw in the wind of change. It may be that those people who had surrendered children during the past decades will, in this newer climate, be less anxious or willing to remain in hiding, readier to be sought out. In any case, the adopted have now emerged from an institutionally created obscurity. They are claiming opportunities that challenge the institutional structure of adoptive kinship as it now exists. That is a fact with which everyone must now reckon: adopters and birthparents, the social services and the legal establishment. But no pressures emanating from a social movement or from the writings of learned advocates can guarantee the desired change. In the remaining chapters we will inquire into the forces that currently appear to obstruct, and other forces that may yet facilitate, institutional reform.

NOTES

1. A.M. McWhinnie, *Adopted Children: How They Grow Up,* 1967, p. 30.
2. J. Triseliotis, *In Search of Origins,* 1973, p. 2.
3. John Dos Passos quoted in Richard Hofstadter, *The American Political Tradition,* 1959.
4. A.D. Sorosky, A. Baran, and R. Pannor, *The Adoption Triangle,* 1978.
5. Report of Research Project "The Changing Face of Adoption," Children's Home Society of California, March 1977.
6. *Ibid.,* p. 14.

Chapter 11

Barriers to Institutional Reform

While we are principally concerned with the chances for reform of the institution of adoption in North America, Great Britain's journey along the same road is instructive, illuminating the very different picture on this continent.

In 1927, Parliament enacted the first adoption statutes in England's history. That act produced adoption law for England and Wales with parallel legislation for Scotland coming by 1930. The early thinking behind this British legislative program can be gleaned from an official government publication of 1954.[1] Then came a 1970 working paper[2] containing provisional proposals from the Committee on the Adoption of Children appointed by the Secretary of State for the Home Department and the Secretary of State for Scotland. This working paper was somewhat later supported by a statistical handbook[3] of data on adoption in Great Britain. In 1972 the preceding studies were placed into a framework of legislative proposals known as the Houghton Report.[4]

In terms of the institutional reforms around which the adoptee movement was then organizing in North America, the 1970 working paper and the subsequent Houghton Report of 1972 are important base-line documents. Thus the working paper proposed for legislative and popular consideration that "in England and Wales access to original birth records should only be granted by permission of a court."[5] But since Scotland's legislation had from the beginning made provision for adult adoptees to gain access to the original records of their birth, and since Triseliotis' research was currently looking into the experiences of Scottish adoptees, the Houghton Report was more flexible in its 1972 recommendation than in its 1970 proposition. The 1972 Houghton Report recommended that "an adopted person aged 18 or over should be entitled to a copy of his original birth certificate."[6] Not surprisingly, that recommendation became part of the law of the land through the Children Act of 1975.[7]

Thus in the course of less than half a century Britain's parliament legislated first a sealed records law and then enacted a liberal reform, allowing access to birth records. It should be noted, however, that the 1975 act also requires at least one meeting with a counselor for all adoptees seeking birth records where the adoption was completed before the enactment of the law. This provision seems to have been written into the act to assuage those most anxious about the possible consequences of the open records portion of the act. That the concern has not abated among professionals can be seen in articles of the Journal of the Association of British Adoption and Fostering Agencies.[8]

In Canada, Marcus (1979) has summarized[9] the provincial and territorial provisions as they existed in this country in the fall of 1978. Her rendition shows that in all but one[10] of the Canadian jurisdictions it is relatively easy for adult[11] adoptees to obtain non-identifying information concerning their backgrounds. However, in none of them is it possible to obtain identifying information[12] without going to great lengths to show "cause," and then it is very unlikely that it will be granted. Still, the Canadian adoption scene does exhibit some changes. Thus a Royal Commmission sitting in British Columbia had in 1974 considered[13] the establishment of a reunion register, but in the end such a measure was not recommended. Marcus reported succinctly on the recent decision of Ontario to establish such a register, and then comments as follows on its limitations:

> In 1976, the Ontario Committee on Record Disclosure, set up by the provincial government, recommended that Ontario adopt the reunion registry concept, with a mediation board to handle special cases. In 1978, after a long and often heated debate, Ontario legislators passed, by a narrow 37-36 vote, a bill for establishment of a three-party disclosure registry. The legislation gives adopting parents power of veto over disclosure, but it is a step forward. Some proviso is expected in handling the consent of adopting parents in cases where they are elderly or infirm. Adult adoptees, who are free to make their own decisions in other areas of life, are not likely to be satisfied with any consent apron strings attached to this type of legislation; nor are birth parents who wish to experience the healing of reunion contact. Nevertheless, the Ontario legislation is a hard-won breakthrough.[14]

My own view is perhaps less charitable than Marcus'. I suspect that state-operated register mechanisms stipulating that three parties must be in agreement before a reunion can be effected constitute means to hinder rather than advance the program of institutional reform. There are of course a number of registry systems devised and administered by associations of the adoptee movement.[15] For this as for other search questions, Marcus' book shows itself very informative and useful.

Let us now proceed to the adoption picture in the United States. With five times the number of jurisdictions as exist in Canada, the American pattern is accordingly as complicated and confusing, if not more so. Marcus notes that Alabama was the only American jurisdiction which at the time of her writing (1978) allowed "access to both the original birth certificate and the court decrees. Original birth certificates only are available to adult adoptees in Kansas and Florida, while Virginia and South Dakota statues limit inspection by an adult adoptee to the relevant court records."[16]

This chapter is not intended as a survey of the adoption law conditions in North America. It is only to indicate briefly the enormous range, variability, and inconsistency in the overall pattern. One of the most useful publications on the current state of U.S. adoption legislation is one by Joseph D. Harrington. It is not only an enormously helpful paper in demonstrating the current heterogeneity among American legal provisions, but it provides extensive references to other review articles. Harrington makes clear that for all the differentiation among the American legal provisions, there is also a central secrecy aspect that is quite uniformly applied everywhere:

> The preceding survey shows that the two principles of anonymity of the birth parents and confidentiality of court adoption proceedings, which have been an integral part of adoption in this country since the 1930s, have not been abandoned, despite legislative efforts to do so. Even the three states — Minnesota, Connecticut, and North Dakota — whose legislatures have permitted adoptees to learn the identity of their birth parents have done so only on condition that the birth parents consent. In other words, the birth parent's anonymity is perpetual unless they agree to end it. Likewise, while some agency adoption files have been viewed by adoptees, no state has permitted court adoption proceedings to be opened. Thus, to date, all attempts to give adoptees access on demand to the most crucial information about their origins have failed.[17]

In a second article,[18] Harrington surveys the manner in which the courts in several United States jurisdictions have interpreted the laws, in particular when confronted with moves by adult adoptees to gain access to identifying information about their past. He notes that in the absence of adequate procedural guidelines, judges have been forced to decide each case on its own merits. Yet he sees hope for the development of a more rational procedural line, citing the Mills case,[19] in which the state of New Jersey specifically asked the judge to provide guidelines to be followed in the future.

I am less hopeful than Harrington about the reformability of North American adoption laws, based on experience where such attempts have been made. We have already seen the requirements for the register as developed by the Province of Ontario. When there is a stipulation that birthparents as well as adoptive parents have to consent to activate an adoptee's search, then the procedure will in many instances make that search either long delayed or impracticable. Another "model reform law" is that of Connecticut, enacted in 1977. In his first paper, Harrington discusses that law in some detail:

> Until recently, Connecticut was an "open records" state. As such, an adult adoptee had the right to obtain a copy of his or her original birth certificate. In 1975, however, a law was passed requiring that a court order be secured before the original birth certificate could be seen. Yet it is not entirely clear how this law was interpreted and how birth certificates were treated. For example, the Child Welfare League survey found that two Connecticut state agencies, each citing the 1975 law,

disagreed as to whether a court order was needed to see these documents.

Then Connecticut passed another law which took effect on October 1, 1977. It provides for the release of the birth parents' identities provided they consent or various other conditions are met. The current law also provides for the outright release by the courts of specified items of nonidentifying information.

The law goes into considerable detail in defining "nonidentifying information," a term used widely but not always in the same sense. The list of nonidentifying data in the Connecticut law is something of a model:

(a) age of genetic parents in years, not dates of birth, at birth of such adopted person;

(b) heritage of genetic parent or parents, which shall include
(1) nationality
(2) ethnic background and
(3) race

(c) education, which shall be number of years of school completed by the genetic parent or parents at the time of birth of such adopted person;

(d) general physical appearance of the genetic parent or parents at the time of birth of such adopted person in terms of height, weight, colour of hair, eyes, skin and other information of similar nature;

(e) talents, hobbies and special interests of the genetic parent or parents;

(f) existence of any other child or children born to either genetic parent prior to birth of such adopted person;

(g) reasons for child being placed for adoption or for genetic parental rights being terminated or for genetic parents being removed as guardians or for genetic parental rights to custody being removed;

(h) religion of genetic parent or parents;

(i) field of occupation of genetic parent or parents in general terms;

(j) health history of genetic parent or parents and blood relatives on a standardized form provided by the Department [of Children and Youth Services];

(k) manner in which plans for such adopted person's future were made by genetic parent or parents, and

(l) relationship between the genetic parents.

The Connecticut statute also provides for an appeal by the adoptee to a review board if he or she feels that any of this information is being withheld by the court. The Adoption Records Review Board, established under the act, consists of the probate court administrator and five persons appointed by him or her: an adult adoptee; an adoptive parent; and one representative from the Department of Children and Youth Services, from a child placement agency, and from the Department of Health.

The statute allows the court to grant identifying information to an adoptee who petitions the court, provided the genetic parents can be located and their consent obtained. If the genetic parent or parents are deceased or cannot be located, a "guardian" is appointed by the court, at the expense of the adoptee, to decide whether or not to give consent in the name of the genetic parent or parents. If the adoptive parents are alive, they are to be notified of the filing of a petition for disclosure of the identity of the natural parents, but their consent is not required to release the information. Finally, if the petition is denied and the adoptee is dissatisfied with the decision, he may appeal to the Adoptions Records Review Board.

I have quoted Harrington's careful exposition in full because I am of the opinion that this law is less helpful than it pretends to be. Complexity is no sure sign of utility; and the complex provisions of the Connecticut law become problematic for adoptees because the adoption agencies have been made responsible for the investigating and reporting that is called for. Social workers are not trained as detectives; such work is alien to the main thrust of the agencies' interests and time commitments. An "Adoptees Search and Support Group" in Connecticut has reproduced a letter from a member who availed herself of the services offered under the Connecticut law. One aspect of that letter concerns the cost of the service,[20] but more interesting from our point of view is the question of its effectiveness: after the agency "searched" for seven months, the woman herself, assisted by the coordinator from the Adoptees Search and Support Group, located the birthmother after an hour's research in the public library. Of course no anecdote can serve as evidence of a law's inadequacy; however, it can alert us to questions. For instance: can such a law assist those most anxious for reform of the institution? If not, then is it at least not a roadblock in the way of reform? My hunch is that laws like that enacted in Connecticut may in fact obstruct institutional reform, but not necessarily by intention. I surmise that on this continent much of social structure, including the structure of legislative and judicial arrangements, is inhospitable to the reform aspirations emanating from the adoptee movement.

A cogent analysis of the obstacles to institutional reform in the U.S. has been provided by Chang.[21] Overall, he appears not optimistic for genuine change such as that in Great Britain; he finds that claims for open records on constitutional grounds have so far failed and will probably continue to fail. Chang suggests that little is to be expected from either legislatures or the courts in bringing about any thoroughgoing reform of the institution of adoptive kinship.

Why, on this continent, where experience with legal adoption dates back 130 years, have adopted persons been given less freedom than those in Great Britain with an adoption law history of only half a century? Why legal adoption came to Britain when it did is discussed in considerable detail by Benet (1976).[22] Let me try to explain the difference between the legislative directions of Britain and this continent with reference to the structure of our respective societies.

For all the influx of other cultures and peoples into the British Isles in recent decades, Great Britain has retained to a considerable degree a sense of its own way of life, of its history and tradition, much as Orwell[23] described it in his famous essay "England, Your England." In contrast, there has been in North America (perhaps less in Canada than the United States) an enormous heterogeneity of values, standards, interests, and lifestyles to the point of anomie, of lack of a common center. In that circumstance the family becomes whatever people want to make it, but certainly no longer the kind of value center that it is when institutional authority and controls give it fixed and recognizable boundaries. Calhoun's monumental *Social History of the American Family*[24] has shown the family system of the United States (except possibly of the early South) less and less able to marshal authority and control over its members. Increasingly the family has become a democratically administered "voluntary association" rather than a centrally organized and run kinship institution. If the family in Britain was, institutionally speaking, no stronger, it may not have mattered there, since British society as a whole was relatively integrated. In Britain there may have been less need than on this continent for a *model* of the family as the nostalgic picture painted it (perhaps falsely): with solid boundaries, reciprocal loyalties, predictable places for its members.

It is not surprising that with the weakening of institutional kinship — the decrease in parental (certainly paternal) power, the enthronement of children's rights — there has come a nostalgic concern with stability and loyalty to traditional values of home and family. I am reminded of a phrase from the *Tao Te Ching* by Laotzu:

> When people lost sight of the way to live
> Came codes of love and honesty. . . .
> When differences weakened family ties
> Came benevolent fathers and dutiful sons. . . .[25]

As the family has moved from institution to association, from socially controlled relationship to increasingly individualistic companionship, all manner of problems have been laid at the door of the vanishing family institution: child abandonment and abuse, delinquency, desertion and divorce. Naturally, no one could devise a system which, in the settings of secular social life, could buttress the erosion of the traditional family. But in one secular family type, moral authority and social control *could* be asserted: that type was the family by adoption. Because it was artificially put together and legitimated by state contrivance, its center of authority and control had to shift from the family unit itself to the institutional apparatus of legislature, court, and social agency. The adoptive parents thus became dependent for their domestic sovereignty on the protection granted by these institutional offices. The mechanisms used for this protection were the sealed record of adoption and the anonymity "contract" with the birthparent.

Adoptive kinship, having been grafted onto the mainstream family system and intended to simulate it in all ways, became thus a kind of symbolic bulwark against the progressive weakening of the family *as institution*. While this was intended for the benefit of adoptees and adopters alike, it has become increasingly apparent that the adopted — partially at least bene-ficiaries of the arrangement — have grievances, chiefly relating to their inability as adults to command the same freedom of information as that given to other adults in this society.

It is clear from the several public hearings held in California, British Columbia, and Ontario in recent years, that some adoptive parents have been powerful voices against change. In spite of the fact that there are adoptive parents who would welcome more equitable legislation, there is evidently much fear among adopters that their families might be reduced to little more than "18 years of babysitting." The fact is that raising a family, whether of children born to us or adopted, amounts to babysitting, or rather a kind of custodial care. No one can guarantee to parents their children's eventual loyalty. That's the gamble taken by all of us who rear children.

Perhaps the adoptive family and the legislation that brought it into being represent the last possibility on this continent for an assertion of institutional authority and control in family matters. In that sense, the legislative and judicial apparatus may be quite rational in their motive for resistance to change. But the fact is that even if they never give way, the secularization of society will continue apace, and will further weaken the family as an institu-tional arrangement. Thus, stonewalling adoptive kinship will not save the mainstream family. It may be, however, that the opposite is true: namely, that a drastically changing pattern of adoptive kinship can come to serve the wellbeing of the mainstream family.

NOTES

1. British Home Office/Scottish Home Department, *Report of the Departmental Committee on the Adoption of Children*, 1954 (reprinted 1967).

2. Departmental Committee on the Adoption of Children, *Adoption of Children*, 1970.

3. Eleanor Grey and Ronald M. Blunden, *A Survey of Adoption in Great Britain*, 1971.

4. *Report of the Departmental Committee on the Adoption of Children*, Home Office/Scottish Education Department, 1972.

5. *Adoption of Children*, Her Majesty's Stationery Office, 1970, p. 86. It is interest-ing to note the Committee's reminder of the paper's limits and intents: "This working paper is published for comment and criticism only — it does not represent the unanimous or final views of the Committee." The reasoning behind this disclaimer is illustrated in this quotation from the paper:

In regard to the right of a child to have access to the original entry relating to his birth, *we considered first the position in England and Wales where such access is only possible if a court makes an order to that effect. We understand that applications to courts for such orders are few and that the number of orders actually granted is very small indeed. We are conscious that many adopted persons, particularly in their teens, have a psychological need to know as much as possible about their origins in order to establish their own identity. This need can largely be met by background information of the type referred to in paragraph 15, but there are some who feel a need to know the actual names of their parents.* In many cases knowledge of the names would not make it easy to trace the natural parents, but in others e.g. where the natural parent was, or had since become, a prominent personality without change of name an immediate approach to them would be possible. *On balance we consider that courts should be left with the responsibility to decide, after taking advice in relation to the natural parents' circumstances where this is practicable, and the adopted person's needs, whether access to the original birth record should be granted on application by the adopted person after his 18th birthday.* Whether, in Scotland, the existing right of access to original birth records should be withdrawn is a more difficult question which the committee will consider further when the results of the current research are available. (Emphasis added.)

6. The change was explained in these words:

. . . We suggested in our working paper that there should be no change in the position in England and Wales, but we proposed to reconsider the position in Scotland in the light of research being undertaken there. The results of this research have now been made available to us and we summarise it in the following paragraph. . . .

. . . *Two out of every five who sought. . . information had lost one or both adoptive parents by death, separation or divorce before they reached the age of 16, and in one-third of all the applications it was the death of an adoptive parent that triggered off the search for information about the natural parents.* . . . *Although 42 adopted persons, or 60 per cent of the sample, sought to trace their natural parents, only four succeeded in doing so, although seven others were able to contact blood relations. The Deputy Registrar General for Scotland said that he could not recall any complaint made by natural relatives who had been traced through the Registrar General's records.* The fear of being traced may therefore have been unduly magnified, particularly as all the indications are that the climate of opinion is changing and mothers are becoming less concerned to conceal the fact that they have had an illegitimate child. Research into the views of a sample of adoptive parents revealed that 63 per cent considered that their adoptive children should be allowed free access to their original records.

While we consider that an adult adopted person should have an automatic right to a copy of his original birth certificate, we do not consider it desirable that he should automatically be granted access to the court records of the adoption proceedings as is at present the case in Scotland. (pp. 84-86, emphases added.)

7. *Children Act 1975,* Chapter 72, Her Majesty's Stationery Office, pp. 17-18.

Amendments of Adoption Act 1958
26. — (1) In section 20 of the 1958 Act, in subsection (5), after the word "except"

there are inserted the words "in accordance with section 20A of this Act or".

(2) The following section is inserted in the 1958 Act after section 20: —

20A. — (1) Subject to subsections (4) and (6) of this section the Registrar General shall on an application made in the prescribed manner by an adopted person a record of whose birth is kept by the Registrar General and who has attained the age of 18 years supply to that person on payment of the prescribed fee (if any) such information as is necessary to enable that person to obtain a certified copy of the record of his birth.

(2) On an application made in the prescribed manner by an adopted person under the age of 18 years a record of whose birth is kept by the Registrar General and who is intending to be married in England or Wales, and on payment of the prescribed fee (if any), *the Registrar General shall inform the applicant whether or not it appears from information contained in the registers of live births or other records that the applicant and the person whom he intends to marry may be within the prohibited degrees of relationship for the purposes of the Marriage Act 1949.* (Emphasis added.)

8. Alfred Leeding, "Access to birth records," *Adoption and Fostering,* 89, No. 3, 1977 and Cyril Day, "Access to birth records: General Register Office Study," *Adoption and Fostering,* 98, No. 4, 1979.

9. Clare Marcus, *Adopted?,* 1979, Appendix 1, pp. 85-93.

10. It appears that New Brunswick is more restrictive than the other jurisdictions in this country (p. 87).

11. As that term "adult" is defined in the several jurisdictions.

12. "Identifying information" apparently includes adoption decrees that carry the name of the birthmother.

13. The following notice from Great Britain concerning the British Columbia register thinking is of interest:

ADOPTION REGISTER IN BRITISH COLUMBIA

A controversial proposal for an adoption register in British Columbia, whereby natural parents and adopted persons might contact one another, was raised during a regional conference of the Child Welfare League of America in Vancouver in June 1975. Public hearings on the matter had generated emotion and hostility, and a number of objections had been raised, one by a woman who had given up her child for adoption 18 years before and who said that any form of register would put her through the 'emotional wringer' again. *She said that if a register were set up she would feel compelled to put her name on it to make sure that her natural son, if he also registered, would not receive the ultimate rejection.* — *The Province,* Vancouver, 11 June 1975. (Emphasis added.)

in *Child Adoption,* 82, No. 4, 1975

14. C. Marcus, *Op. Cit.,* pp. 77-78.

15. Association registers include those of Parent Finders ("Reunion Registry"), Orphan Voyage ("Reunion File"), Yesterday's Children (National Adoption Registry"), ALMA'S ("International Reunion Registry"), and Jigsaw International ("Contact Register").

16. C. Marcus, *Op. Cit.* p. 80.

17. Joseph D. Harrington, "Legislative Reform Moves Slowly", *Public Welfare,* Vol. 37, No., 3, Summer 1979, pp. 49-57.

18. Joseph D. Harrington, "The Courts Contend with Sealed Adoption Records."
Public Welfare, Vol. 38, No. 2, Spring 1980.

19. *Mills vs. Atlantic City Department of Vital Statistics* 372A. 2d 646 (Superior
Court of New Jersey, Chancery Division) 1977.

20.

	$35.00	Initial interview
	$35.00	To sign document in which I legally request that the agency search for my birthmother, and to get nonidentifying information
	$35.00	To the Probate Court for court hearing to legally authorize the search
	$35.00	To the social worker (legally required to appear at court hearing)
	$35.00	To discuss how the social worker would make the contact with my birthmother
	$97.50	7 hours of actual searching — telephone calls and trip to library
	$15.00	Typing fee for report on the "investigation" of my case
	$15.00	Searching for my file at the agency to provide nonidentifying information and to prepare for the search

Total Cost $302.50

Currently, I am trying to obtain a copy of my original birth certificate. I have been told
this will be an added cost of $35.00 from the Probate Court. It hardly seems fair
considering there is only a cost of $2.00 to the non-adoptee for his birth certificate.

21. Jeffrey C. Chang, "A Step Towards Resolving the Adoption Records Controversy: The Adoption Agency as the Key to Unlocking Sealed Identies," *Univerisity
of California (Davis) Law Review,* Vol. 12, No. 2, Summer 1979.

22. Mary Kathleen Benet, *The Politics of Adoption,* 1976, p. 72.

23. George Orwell, "England, Your England," Part I of "The Lion and the
Unicorn," in *Collected Essays, Journalism and Letters* (1968), Vol. II, pp. 56-78.

24. Arthur W. Calhoun, *A Social History of the American Family,* 3 vv., 1918,
1945.

25. Witter Bynner, *The Way of Life According to Laotzu: An American Version,*
1944.

Chapter 12

Opportunities in Unexpected Places

Enter Child Welfare

Anyone left unconvinced by the preceding chapter of legislative reticence to institute genuine change should inspect a listing of 19 states and their bills concerned with the "right to know."[1] Published in 1979, this list shows a remarkable lack of uniformity and consistency, both within the legislative approach and in the outcome of bills passed between 1976 and 1979. Whatever the future may hold for reform through legislative action, for the time being the outlook in North America does not appear hopeful. I propose therefore to look in other directions for structural opportunities at least potentially more hospitable to reform of the institution — particularly the child welfare and adoption agency system.

This proposition, that the child welfare apparatus might become an effective agent for the reform of adoption, may on the face of it seem preposterous. My analysis[2] had left me in little doubt of the professionals' strong involvement with false definitions of adoptive kinship as institution, and faulty theories of intervention for work with unwed parents and childless adoptive applicants. One might well question why I would assume the apparently antithetical position of looking to the professionals as potentially serving the adoptee movement's reform cause. To make this apparent contradiction understandable, I must take the reader briefly through some of the salient writings by social work professionals. But before I deal with journal articles it is appropriate to look at a work which represents the adoption lobby itself, emanating from the Child Welfare League of America. In July 1976 the League issued a research report entitled *The Sealed Adoption Record Controversy — Report of a Survey of Agency Policy, Practice and Opinions.*[3] From a Canadian point of view, the survey results are disappointing because of the low participation of Canadian agencies in the study.[4] The information is nevertheless of great importance for all areas of North America.

In its summary of the findings the research report says:

> Assurances of anonymity to both the adoptive and the biological parents are almost universal among agencies responding to this survey questionnaire. Some beginning indications of hedging are seen, how-

ever, in the expressed discomfort of several respondents with the term "guarantee," the mention of advising all concerned at the time of the adoption that the guarantee cannot be absolute, the occasional question to biological parents of whether they would desire contact with the relinquished child at some future date, and the acceptance of waivers of anonymity for the case record. Policies regarding anonymity have usually been intact for the agency's entire history in adoptions, though they are seldom written down, and most agencies say they are satisfied with their policy.... Nearly all of the agencies perceive their state laws as requiring a court order for access to the information contained in the court adoption records and the original birth certificate.... Two thirds of the agencies report that their adoption records are also sealed by law, *though there was greater disagreement within states regarding this. Even where agencies agreed that their records were sealed, there was considerable disagreement on what information was affected.*

I have emphasized the last two sentences to draw attention to the problem of ambiguity and lack of uniformity which exists in the law as reflected by these agencies. But what is even more disconcerting is the fact of disagreement on what information was technically sealed in their records. That surely should long ago have been a matter for governmental directives or voluntary standard-setting. To continue with the findings:

> Over 3,000 adult adoptees returned to these agencies during 1975. The range was from none to over 200. The agencies report that only two-fifths of the returning adoptees wish to locate or learn the identity of their biological family. The others wish only non-identifying information. This figure is likely to be an underestimate of the number who *would* request identifying information if it were available. . . . Most agencies will give non-identifying information and provide counseling to the returning adoptee. Only one agency, however, said that it gives the name of the biological parent to the adoptee on request, and only about a fourth of the agencies conducted at least one "search" for biological parents in 1975. They averaged 6.3 searches each. In total, these agencies undertook 246 searches in 1975, half of which resulted in an actual meeting ("reunion") between the adoptee and the biological family. Nearly all of the reunions were judged successful for all parties involved. The agencies are about evenly divided on whether or not they are satisfied with their policy regarding returning adult adoptees.

Here, then, the reader sees that there is considerable variability among the agencies concerning the sealed records controversy. What we do not know from such a survey is what discussions and thoughts are played out behind the scenes. But there is in this research report also an indication of such "latent" forces: The Child Welfare League's questionnaire asked about the degree of satisfaction among agency personnel, with respect to their organizations' policies on record confidentiality and reunions. The report says:

Satisfaction did seem to be related. . . to the amount of activity at the agency regarding returning adult adoptees: the less activity (fewer returning adoptees, fewer or no searches, etc.) the greater the satisfaction. . . . There was greater satisfaction with the agency's policies and practices where the biological mother's rights are held paramount, where the controversy is not expected to affect agency practice, where non-identifying information is expected to be sufficient for the returning adult adoptees, and where continued guarantees of confidentiality are supported. (pp. 27-28)

My interpretation is that while there was considerable variation of practice among the agencies with respect to the sealed records controversy, workers were happier with a state of affairs in which the institutional boat was not being rocked. In other words, while there is change taking place, these professionals, like most human beings, would prefer to move in accustomed rounds.

Let us now look at other literature which deals with the sealed adoption record controversy. Like the League's research data, that literature appears to lean in two opposite directions: there is evident understanding of the issues which the adoptee movement has raised, but there is also concern expressed for the institution as the profession of social work and the law had conceived and created it. While some writers represent mainly the one side and others mainly the opposite, there is nevertheless an indication of a shift toward those who speak for a more open policy. My evidence is impressionistic; it derives from two journal symposia devoted to the issue of sealed records. The September 1978 issue of *Family Process* had a four-author section entitled "The Family and Child Placement Practices." It contained Opening Comments by Braulio Montalvo, and articles by Fernando Colón ("Family Ties and Child Placement"), Roberta G. Andrews ("Adoption: Legal Resolution or Legal Fraud?"), and the team of Pannor, Baran, and Sorosky ("Birth Parents Who Relinquished Babies for Adoption Revisited"). Colón's article is highly empathic with the point of view of the adoptee movement. It is an elegant and convincing exposition of the problems of bonds and connectedness in the process of identity formation. Andrew's paper is also highly competent, but her point of view is that of the clinically oriented administrator who is concerned with the human beings under her care as well as the ailing institutional structure. Her paper is essentially a warning that if the adoptee movement were to have its way, legal adoption would become a legal fraud. It is a real problem which cannot be made to disappear by denying its existence. The institutional issue must be confronted, especially by those who want to reform present practices. The Pannor, Baran, and Sorosky article appears comparatively neutral, in that it describes the present circumstances and outlook of a group of birthparents. But the very fact that these three authors have in other publications been known to take a very partisan position toward open records makes the neutrality of this article suspect. Will not the reader be inclined to class their paper together with that of Colón's and see the symposium as having a two-to-one ratio of contributions on the side of open records for the adopted? That may not have been what the editors of *Family Process* wanted to convey, but it is the message that seemed for me written between the lines.

My second piece of impressionistic evidence is based on the Summer 1979 issue of *Public Welfare* .The entire issue is really a symposium of nine articles and one book review, all joined by the theme "Adoption: Who Has the Right to Know?" While several of the articles are principally descriptive, the overwhelming impression from the sequence of papers is that the issue as a whole is partisan on the side of open records for the adopted. But besides a number of articles that are friendly to reform and others that are strongly partisan for the point of view of the adoptee movement, there are two which speak forcefully against it. One of these is by Roberta Andrews, the other is a paper by Richard Zeilinger. The appearance of these two symposia toward the end of the nineteen seventies with the adoptee movement ferment does not seem coincidence or chance. Why would both symposia be weighted toward an understanding (if not approval) of institutional reform?

Now I must return to my main theme that the child welfare system offers a more hospitable opportunity for the reform of the institution of adoptive kinship than the legislative apparatus. I am not unaware of innovative steps taken in some individual courts. I recall especially a paper by Judge Norman B. Ackley which is as provocative as it is brief.[5] But given the heterogeneity of legal systems and courts in North America, it seems highly unlikey that more than a localized improvement in jurisdiction is to be expected in the foreseeable future. On the other hand, where there are some 60 different state and provincial jurisdictional domains in North America, the social welfare domain and especially the child welfare domain represent far more homogeneity in outlook and method. Still, what of my critique of that outlook and that method when it came to the work of the adoption agencies? Had I not seen the psychodynamic approach as partially at least responsible for major errors in professional activities in adoption? I have no intention of altering these judgments, but I wish to suggest that there is a structure of common professional sensibilities, ideas, and organizational links that could make the welfare apparatus into a pioneer of concerted efforts at reform. Furthermore, an organization with the experience and stature of the Child Welfare League, even more than a government body, can bridge regional and national differences by setting common standards of professional action. If that central organization were to take the lead in rethinking the cultural definitions of adoptive kinship, then legislative and judicial officials would most likely follow in their wake, stimulating the possibility of reform.

Chang's article[6] closes on a similar note; he also expresses the view that "the inability of most legislatures and courts to depart from decades of sealed records policies requires adoption agencies to take the lead in this difficult area." However, he also thinks that individual agencies can effect the breakthrough to institutional reform because of clinical contact with all the participants in the adoption drama. So he relies on counseling to bridge unbridgeable differences. I believe that the direction he charts is generally correct, but do not concur in the choice of arbiter. If the individual agency is left to its own devices in working out a policy toward the sealed record and the anonymity "contract," only more confusion can result. But if under the leadership of the Child Welfare League, for instance, a set of new standards could be worked out to guide the agencies, then there is at least the possibility that the institution of adoptive kinship can be rationally and humanely reformed. Nevertheless, Andrews' warning must be kept in mind if a poorly constructed institutional framework is not to be replaced by a vacuum. Similarly, I think the conservative views of Richard Zeilinger's paper[7] must be carefully considered before agencies move randomly into opening their records or instituting reunions. While I do not agree with him that legislative restrictions against sealed records of birth automatically limit access to the agency records, it is an issue that ought to be faced by a recognized standard-setting organization like the League. When that is done, there opens up the possibility of an alternative legal system to that of the state, namely the legal system of the professional organizations.

A view of administrative codes created and used by private organizations can greatly assist us in an analysis of adoption law reform. In his scholarly treatise *Organization Theory* (1976), William M. Evan has included a chapter entitled "Public and Private Legal Systems," which is pertinent to the question of child welfare organizations as instrumental in bringing about adoption law reform:

> Virtually all legal scholars and many political scientists view law as being inextricably interwoven with the state, and the state, having a monopoly of coercion, is identified as the sanctioning agent of law. Accordingly, phenomena analytically similar to law that do not fall within the framework of the state have been either largely neglected or else conceptualized in unrelated terms. And the sanctioning power pervasively exercised by organizations less inclusive than the state has been inadequately explored. With its stress on the sovereign state as the source of positive law, analytical jurisprudence has played a dominant role in the articulation of this conception of law.
>
> Certain scholars, however, have departed from the prevailing view of law; two are especially noteworthy. Ehrlich, one of the earliest students of the sociology of law, conceived of law as consisting primarily of rules by which persons in society order their conduct and only secondarily of "norms for decisions" developed by the courts and of legislation enacted by the state. These rules or "facts of the law," as he called them, are developed by various "social associations" — families, clans, religious organizations, corporations, labor unions, employer associations,

political parties, social clubs, and so on. It is the "inner order of the
[social] associations" that is the "basic form of law." Similarly, Weber's
view of law includes a "legal order" that falls outside the province of the
state.[8]

With this introduction to the problem, Evan approaches certain matters
specific to the sociology of law, such as typologies of legal systems, but these
issues do not concern us here. What does concern us is his development of
"interrelationships between public and private legal systems," for it is in that
nexus that we have been asking about structures potentially hospitable to
reform of adoptive kinship:

> The relationship between public and private legal system has usually
> been conceived of and examined in terms of the role of pressure groups
> in the legislative process, or in terms of the government's regulation of
> private organizations, especially business organizations. It also has long
> been observed that public legal systems confer on private legal systems
> rights, duties, privileges, and immunities through the process of grant-
> ing a charter of incorporation, license, permit, franchise, and so on.
> Several modes of interrelationship, however, have been neglected.
>   First is the increasing tendency for the norms of private legal systems
> to be judicially recognized, as, for example, in a medical malpractice suit
> in which the code of ethics of the American Medical Association is
> invoked, in a suit involving the internal relations of a trade union in
> which the union's constitutional provisions are accorded legal status by
> the court, or in a suit by a student against a college or university in which
> the institution's disciplinary rules are judicially recognized. Such
> judicial recognition, particularly under a system of common law, results
> in precedents, that is, in the growth of new legal norms guiding judicial
> decision making. The adoption, as it were, of the norms of private legal
> systems by public legal systems is functionally equivalent to the con-
> ferral of rights on private legal systems.
>   *A second interrelationship is the diffusion of norms in letter or spirit
> from private to public systems. Although such diffusion is prob-
> ably less common than judicial recognition of the norms of private legal
> systems, this is an important source of growth of the norms of public
> legal systems.*[9]

It is clear that Evan's first mode of interrelationship — the judicial recognition
of the private legal system by the public one — includes the case of licensing of
adoption agencies by the state or province in which they operate. It is his
second mode that is so pertinent to the present inquiry. I have proposed that
the child welfare apparatus might, through the considered application of its
legal system, become the mainspring of institutional reform of adoptive
kinship, influencing the state's legal system in that direction also. But my
proposition is not founded on optimism; it does not imply that the private
legal system of the child welfare organizations would readily influence the

public system of adoption law. In fact I think that the private legal system would have an uphill fight. Once again Evan's work is instructive:

> Private legal systems are obviously not all of equal importance as sources of new legal norms and organs in public legal systems. Those rooted in certain institutional spheres have greater effect on public legal systems than others with different institutional bases. For example, the legal systems of the trade associations, professional associations, and trade unions, because of their links with economic institutions, presumably have more effect on public legal systems than the legal systems of, say, educational, familial, or recreational organizations.[10]

Although the legal system of any organization labelled "welfare" would undoubtedly have less influence on the state system than one labelled "defence," or "energy," there is reason to believe that the child welfare apparatus stands a chance of winning the fight for reform. My reason is based on the history of past endeavors by that group of organizations. During the nineteen fifties, it was very active in lobbying powerful professional associations, notably those in the fields of medicine and law. Such lobbying had the objective of securing for the adoption agencies a monopoly of child placing powers, eliminating from that activity physicians and lawyers acting as independent intermediaries. Although that "independent market" was never entirely controlled, the child welfare lobby was, on the whole, remarkably successful both in gaining the cooperation of the professional associations and the licensing authority of the state. As I sought to show in Chapter 7, the demand for a monopoly of practice was based in part at least on erroneous claims of special competence. But right or wrong, the claim was accepted as correct, and the lobby was in the main able to establish professional hegemony. Whatever the causes of that success, such a history leaves no doubt that the same lobby could, if it saw fit to do so, concentrate its attention on the reform of the arrangements and rules that make up the institution of adoptive kinship.

Obviously it is not within my capacity as sociologist to prophesy the future. Nonetheless, it seems reasonable to see both the professional commitment of child welfare agencies and their long-term self interest as likely motivating forces in the direction of reform. That the professional commitment to human well-being had produced a shift in the direction of reform seems evident from the Child Welfare League's 1976 research report discussed earlier in this chapter. Similarly, such a shift appears visible in the professional literature as shown in the two symposia of articles discussed above. Note also that British and North American social work writings have lately emphasized the importance of the agencies to institute more "post-adoption support" activities. Thus Picton[11] suggests continuing education of adoptive parents and the availability of counseling. Both moves, I gather, would be in the long-term interest of the agencies' maintenance of professional staff in a time of reduced demand[12] for child-placing. Thompson[13] goes even further. Writing in the official journal of the Canadian Association of Social Workers, she suggests that agencies act as intermediaries in meeting the search-oriented needs of adoptees and birthparents. Furthermore, her proposal is based on the interpretation of data from an indigenous Canadian study[14] conducted by the agency on whose staff she serves.

Reform Begins at Home

At this point it may be well to remind ourselves about the context of "institutional reform." In Part II of this book we began to inspect first the adoption agency's operation as part of the institutional context of adoptive kinship. Thereupon we made a critical incursion into the realm of adoption law. In both areas, the administrative and the legal, we saw a number of severe contradictions. These constitute what C. Wright Mills[15] called "public issues of social structure" and also "crises in institutional arrangements." Such issues or crises tend to have their counterparts in "personal troubles of milieu." The troubles of the adopted are, as we saw, made up of a number of structurally given role handicaps. One of these consists of the restriction of rights of access to the records of birth and adoption. Thus while reform of the institution calls for a thorough rethinking and restructuring of legal and administrative definitions and practices, the issue of the sealed records and of the "contract" of anonymity lends special urgency to the task.

The necessity for reform of the sealed records regulations within the child welfare system is illustrated by the following story. The reader will recall the young woman described in Chapter 10, whose status as a foundling had been deeply troublesome to her. It was known to her parents that she was found in an area of the city inhabited by Puerto Ricans, so she had begun to think of herself as of Puerto Rican ancestry. After a summer of work and travel in Puerto Rico she felt encouraged at having discovered the country of her roots. Subsequently I had further contact with her father, who is a scholar in one of our universities, and who knows my interest in the complexities of adoptive kinship. He imparted this additional piece of information to me.

Not long ago, his daughter expressed a wish to travel to the city where she had been found, to see the location where she had been left. Her dad made a telephone call to the agency which had placed her in her adoptive home, and spoke to the supervising social worker. She pointed out that records from that long ago were in a storage vault, but promised to call back when the file had been located. Two or three weeks later my colleague received a long distance call from the agency. Yes, the file had been recovered, and there was a record of the address where the infant had been found. Unfortunately the agency could not reveal this information as it was considered confidential. However, the agency's staff would be happy to have the young woman make an appointment to see one of the workers acquainted with her case. Then she could avail herself of the opportunity of counseling.

My colleague asked me, what did these people think they were up to? Since when was a city street address considered confidential information? Whom or what could it possibly identify, after all these years? What was more, the offer of counseling seemed to him not so much helpful as an affront. He told the social worker that he wished he had never contacted them. The matter rested there.

One day the daughter applied for a passport and had to produce a birth certificate. She went to her family's safety deposit box at the bank where her personal documents were kept. There, to her utter amazement, she discovered that the certificate gave the presumed date of her birth, the names of her adoptive father and mother, and an address in the very district of the city where she had been found — an address that the agency had been unprepared to divulge, ostensibly because of the rule of confidentiality! Lest it be assumed that these events took place in some out-of-the-way place and in connection with an agency of dubious standing, let the reader be assured that the opposite is true. These events should therefore not be passed off as incidental. While they do not imply malfeasance or acts of bad faith, they illustrate the kind of misfeasance and arbitrary use of professional power that a badly patterned system of rules and regulations readily invites. Once the goals and means of an equitable institution of adoptive kinship are newly thought out, the child welfare organizations can in combination redesign the administrative legal system best suited to protect its participants.

Some parameters for reconsidering the ends and means of the institution will be introduced in our next and final chapter. Here I must limit discussion to the question of agency records, those instruments of professional policy around which much of the present controversy rages. Adoptees who consult agencies for information about their past frequently find that the records contain only scanty data. Thus Triseliotis[16] notes:

> The outcome of the search left many adoptees with mixed feelings. Those who were looking for additional information. . . would have liked more detailed particulars. They were surprised to find the paucity of the official records which often did not go beyond what they already knew.

How late the implications of lack of uniformity and paucity were recognized within the profession can be seen in this note from an article entitled "Keeping Records," which appeared in the British journal *Adoption and Fostering* in 1977:

> As a preparation for future counselling, we would place special emphasis upon collecting and recording relevant material and on re-examining the content of interviews with various parties. *It will be necessary for the social worker to keep in mind the possibility that recorded material may be used for counselling in the future.*

Thus the need for record-keeping was discovered very late in the day when professionals realized that they might be called upon some day to produce information from them.

That records were not always kept well or guarded safely was demonstrated to me in 1959 when I had to check back on my 1956 sample to collect information on the non-respondents. One of the participating agencies had not long before moved its offices within the same city, not more than five or six blocks from its previous location. When I asked for data on the original sample, it was discovered to everyone's dismay that almost exactly one third of the record folders were missing. The explanation given was that they may have been lost in transit. It seemed a scandalously loose handling of an adoption agency's valued tools of trade. That they were so regarded by its spokesmen is readily evident: Schapiro, summarizing the state of the art in his book *A Study of Adoption Practice,* Volume I, 1956 speaks about the advantages of agency as against independent adoption. He lists eight "unique contributions of the agency staff, plus the continuing program, which *is* the agency." The third of these eight points refers to agency records: "*Only an agency prepares, preserves, and makes available the record of the whole transaction*" (p. 110; emphasis added). If records are basic to the agencies' expertise, what rules should govern them? Schapiro's discussion of the advantages of agencies over non-agency placements does not go into any criteria for preparing records, or means or duration of preserving them, or indeed to whom such records would be made available.

The state of preparation and preservation of records was studied during the mid-nineteen seventies in Great Britain. In an article entitled "Finding Adoption Records," Margaret Kornitzer, former editor of the journal *Adoption and Fostering* (formerly *Child Adoption*) reported as follows:

> By the end of November 1976 we had received enough answers to our questionnaire to local authorities to issue an interim list showing where the adoption records of some 50 authorities are held, with details as to how complete these are. The officers making the returns have quite often found it impossible to give a full or exact picture of what records they have, or whether some have over the years been lost or destroyed, or perhaps, in some cases, strayed. This is not surprising when there have been changes of address as a result of re-organisation, and seemingly in some cases somebody or other has taken decisions that have resulted in the destruction of records, not always, we suggest, after the statutory 25 years have elapsed. Understandable, perhaps, when it was thought that the past and origins of adopted people were buried forever in the dust of oblivion, but to be regretted now that people in search of those origins have not only the legal right to certain basic information, but a reasonable expectation that their counsellors will be able to supplement this with further details to turn the past into flesh and blood again. . . .
>
> One slightly alarming fact that has come to light is that in some cases where one authority borrows a file from another authority, the file is not returned but remains with the borrower, which could make the task of tracing it far more difficult than need be. Could we make the suggestion that files as such should not be exported from the archives of the auth-

ority that rightly lodges them? Instead, suitable extracts or photostats only should be sent, and those always in a way to assure maximum confidentiality. We are not very sure that confidentiality within the local authority itself or between local authorities, is fully respected in some places, when there is transit of vital files.[18]

While there is no research evidence available for North American agencies to document the state of preparation, preservation, and utilization of their records, all hearsay reports suggest that similarly "slightly alarming" conditions obtain on this continent. My own experience with one agency's lapse is not reassuring. Clearly reform of the institution would have to begin at home if the child welfare field were to be the first real force for reform in North America. It could do no better than to begin with that basic legal requirement of good and reliable information: "the record of the whole transaction."

NOTES

1.

SIGNIFICANT STATE BILLS CONCERNING THE "RIGHT TO KNOW," 1976-79

STATE	APPROACH	STATUS
California	access on demand	pending
Connecticut	access with consent	enacted 1977
District of Columbia	access with consent	defeated 1979
Indiana	access on demand	shelved
Lousiana	access only for compelling reasons	enacted 1978
Maryland	multiple	withdrawn in favor of study resolution
Massachusetts	multiple	pending
Michigan	access with consent	pending
Minnesota	access with consent	enacted 1977
Missouri	access on demand	defeated 1979
Nebraska	access on demand	pending
New Mexico	access with consent	defeated 1979
North Dakota	access with consent	enacted 1979
Oklahoma	access with consent	defeated 1979
Oregon	access with consent (2 similar bills)	shelved; pending
Pennsylvania	limiting of access	defeated 1978
Tennessee	access with consent	pending
Virginia	limiting of access	enacted 1976-77
Washington	access with consent	pending

This listing appears in the article previously cited: Joseph D. Harrington, "Legislative Reform Moves Slowly," *Public Welfare,* Volume 37 No. 3, Summer 1979, p. 51.

2. See Chapters 6 and 7.

3. Written by Mary Ann Jones and prepared with the assistance of Renee Neuman and Karen Brown. Research Center, Child Welfare League of America, Inc., 67 Irving Place, New York, N.Y. 10003 (mimeo).

4. Out of a total of 203 agencies in the United States and Canada to which the League's researchers had addressed questionnaires in April 1976, replies were obtained from 163 of these professional organizations. Clearly Canada was not strongly represented in this sample, only three provinces being involved with only four agencies reporting throughout this country. In spite of the undoubtedly unrepresentative nature of the Canadian sample, the four responding agencies from this part of the continent were merged with the U.S. sample for the statistical analyses reported in the CWLA study.

5. Norman B. Ackley, "Sealed Adoption Files: When to Open? A New Approach," *Conciliation Courts Review,* Vol. 17, No. 1 (June 1979). Judge Ackley is a judge of the Superior Court, Seattle, Washington.

6. Jeffrey C. Chang, *University of California (Davis) Law Review,* Vol. 12, No. 2 (1979), p. 377.

7. Richard Zeilinger, "The Need to Know vs. the Right to Know," *Public Welfare,* Vol. 37, No. 3 (Summer 1979), pp. 44-47.

8. William M. Evan, *Organization Theory,* 1976, p.171.

9. *Ibid.,* pp. 177-178 (emphasis added).

10. *Ibid.,* p. 179.

11. Cliff Picton, "Post-Adoption Support," *Adoption and Fostering,* 88, No. 2, 1977.

12. The following is an excerpt from a notice that appeared over the name of Margaret E. Edgar, a social service worker and former president of the Open Door Society of Montreal, Que., Canada. The note was published in *Adoption and Fostering,* 90, No. 4, 1977.

Across Canada adoption statistics show a decreasing number of placements and fewer social workers involved exclusively in adoption work. . . . It is hoped that with more time available to them adoption workers will be able to offer the on-going consultations and group discussions so often requested by adopting parents.

13. Janette Thompson, "Roots and Rights — A Challenge for Adoption," *The Social Worker/Le Travailleur Social,* Vol. 47, No. 1 (Spring 1979), pp. 13-15.

14. Janette Thompson, Joan Webber, Alice Stoneman and Dorothy Harrison, *The Adoption Rectangle: A Study of Adult Adoptees' Search for Birth Family History and Implications for Adoption Service.* Children's Aid Society of Metropolitan Toronto, June 1978.

15. C. Wright Mills, *The Sociological Imagination,* 1969, 1972, pp. 8-9.

16. John Triseliotis, *In Search of Origins,* 1973, p. 159.

17. Mary Thornton, "Keeping adoption records," *Adoption and Fostering,* 90, No. 4, 1977.

18. Margaret Kornitzer, "Finding Adoption Records," *Adoption and Fostering,* 87, No. 1, 1977.

Chapter 13

Adoptive Kinship Reformed: Compass for the Mainstream Family?

Adoptive Kinship Reformed

What does it take to achieve the goal of institutional reform? Because I do not consider the task of this book to provide specific proposals, but rather to raise and clarify the issues, I can afford a theoretical approach. I do not mean an approach dissociated from the problematics of a living reality, but one that builds on existing theory, especially on theory which seeks to explain the circumstances of adoptive kinship.

What is needed at this point is to identify basic parameters for thinking out the issues of adoptive kinship and its potential reform. Perhaps we can make a beginning with the parameters provided by the Shared Fate theory, but if it is to be of help we must keep in mind that this theory concerns itself almost exclusively with the micro-system of the parent-child relationship. However, we want to deal not with an interpersonal relationship but with a system of roles and of rules, a system we call a social institution. Unfortunately, sociology does not provide its practioners with the tools needed to "translate" readily what is known about a micro-system of social relationships into a macro-system of institutional arrangements. If we want to make use of what we have learned about adoptive parent-child relations for the operation of the institution of adoptive kinship we must fall back on a mode of reasoning less than fully satisfactory for this purpose, namely reasoning by analogy.

Let us therefore take the Shared Fate theory as model for the construction of a theory of adoptive kinship as institution. What needs to be translated into macro-social (institutional) terms are these findings which together make up the principal part of the Shared Fate theory.

When adoptive parents acknowledge the difference between their own parenthood and that of parents and children consanguineally related, they can more readily:
(1) put themselves empathically into the special place in which the adopted child finds him/herself. Such empathy is conducive to:
(2) readiness to listen to the child's questions about his/her background

even though such questions may be troublesome for the adoptive parent.

(3) Such readiness to listen and answer questions, however uncomfortable, enhances the child's trust in the parent and therefore the bonds between adopted child and adoptive parents.

It is this sequence from the Shared Fate theory that I propose to apply to the problem of similar theorizing about the institution of adoptive kinship. What I propose is that we think by way of analogies about equivalent statements that apply to the macro-system, i.e. to the institutional arrangements. To begin this kind of thinking let us consider the macro-social equivalent of the parent-child relationship. Since at least during the early child-rearing years that relationship involves superordination of the parents and subordination of the child, we may consider the analogous relationship of state and citizen.

In the case of the institution, the state is superordinate and the citizen subordinate, however much this super-subordination may be emphasized in autocratic, and muted in democratic, societies. With this structural equivalent in mind, let me develop what appear to be functional equivalents of the Shared Fate theory for the circumstances of the institution of adoptive kinship:

Institutional Equivalents of Adoptive Parent-Child Relations

In the micro-system of parent-child relationship we have found:	In the macro-system of the state-citizen relationship, it is posited:
Rejection-of-difference	The definition of adoptive kinship as the equivalent of consanguineal kinship is false and misleading
making for	probably making for
low empathy	a low degree of public understanding of or sympathy with the actual position of the adopted, especially among professionals responsible for the definition
making for	probably making for
low communication	sealed records of birth and adoption, contractual anonymity for birthparents, and unreliable statistical information because the whole of adoption has been officially obscured as a social fact
making for	probably making for
low trust or integration	lowered faith of the adopted in the political institutions of their society, seeing that as a class they are defined as beneficiaries while they are also victimized by the institutional arrangements created to serve them.

Let it be understood that at this stage such a hypothetical listing can only serve as a heuristic device, i.e., to stimulate thinking about this complex issue. I shall therefore merely suggest certain parameters that I regard as indispensable for thinking about the institutional reform of adoptive kinship:

1. If the definition of adoptive kinship as the equivalent of consanguineal kinship is false, and if from that false definition derive undesirable consequences, such as lack of public understanding of the issues, then a first priority ought to be the attempt to redefine the nature of adoptive kinship so as to conform to realities.

2. Since misunderstandings and distortions of the sealed records issue appear to have been supported by professional action and organization, it would seem incumbent on the professional apparatus of child welfare and law to make a concerted effort at clarifying public misconceptions. This would imply that after an agreed-upon redefinition of adoptive kinship, a public information program would explain past practices and likely directions of present ones. Thereby birthparents could be given warning of a changed point of view before they might be located in a search.

3. Are sealed records now to be opened? That cannot be done unless those in authority can first decide on the primary recipient of the service. Thus if three parties — birthparents, adoptive parents, and adoptees — are each equally deserving of the protection of the authorities, then action is not likely taken toward a statutory access to records by adult adoptees. Only when the adoptee as adult is regarded as the principal client that he/she was as child, can the decision to open records be made in the adoptee's favor as against that of other interested parties.

Let me say again that I do not presume to propose a particular pattern of reform. The task I set myself in this book was to identify the structural problems that have led to the unrest among the adopted. I believe that this unrest is not spurious, but very much connected with the way the institution has been constructed. It is now clear to me that the construction of adoptive kinship has been faulty and that many of the human beings who were to have been served by it may also have suffered considerable damage. What is therefore required is a concerted effort to rethink the institution and to provide legal and social arrangements which will fit the redefinition. Meanwhile, it is not sufficient to create a system for the future, but equally important to devise a bridge to the past. Millions of adult adoptees in the population of North America are looking to the public and the private law for relief.

Such relief can come more readily as functionaries in the areas of private and public law begin to see a different outline to the meaning of adoptive kinship. While new legal and administrative definitions must be devised, there is an image that will be helpful in that symbolic reconstruction: that of adoptive kinship as a compass for the mainstream family.

Compass for the Mainstream Family?

A viable institution must command moral authority and sufficient coercive power to assure compliance with its rules and way of life. As Chapter 11 had suggested, those central attributes of social institutions have been eroding over many years in the case of the family in the urban-industrial West. In the sense that little in the way of moral authority now commands familistic loyalties, and that there are no "elders" to enforce the individual's adherence to rules such as they are, the family system is de-institutionalized. It is now much more akin to a voluntary association in which the child-rearing roles and tasks are much less clearly prescriptive than they once were. In constructing the institution of adoptive kinship by legal and administrative contrivance, moral authority and coercive power necessarily came to reside in the legitimating and administering organizations rather than the family itself. This fact made adoptive kinship a secondary institution, that is, an arrangement that does not stand on its own feet but is basically supported by social administration and the legal apparatus.

While adoptive kinship is itself thus propped up by other more powerful institutions, it may be serving in turn to prop up traditional kinship values. Closeness, durability, loyalty — those virtues of the traditional kinship system were institutionally transplanted to the system of adoptive kinship. If adoptive kinship serves that kind of function in the society as a whole it is less a legal fraud than a cultural hoax. It is then a hoax in which the entire society is deluded into thinking that the old virtues are not dead but live on in the purer sacrificial structure of adoptive kinship. Thus if some of its members must suffer because of a faulty and inconsistent institutional underpinning, the damage done may be made understandable and perhaps even justified because of a larger cause. Perhaps in the end the cause is not that of the children, but that of society as a whole. Perhaps it is assumed that the participants in the drama of adoptive kinship can somehow resurrect the archaic past that is gone forever.

My critics are likely to retort by asking about my alternative. Do I want to see a situation in which the adoptive family becomes a voluntary association, when it lacks the roots of a common ancestry which at least the consanguineal family has? Do I want to see its members confused by dual loyalties? Let my answer be in terms of *Shared Fate*. I propose that, rather than a reminder of the archaic past, the adoptive family has the potential to be a compass for the creative development of the mainstream family of the future.

When one inspects the demographic development of the family in the West, it becomes evident that along a number of parameters it is moving in the direction structurally given in the adoptive family. Thus the family of the mainstream exhibits much mobility, a fact endemic with the adoptive family. The midstream family of the urban-industrial West is becoming smaller, approaching the 1-2 child family of adoption. The gender equality given in the situation of involuntarily childless adopters, i.e., the lack of a biological division of labor, is also approximated in the changing ideology of male-female relations in the mainstream family. The latter shows a tendency for delayed marriage, suggesting that the ages of parents in consanguineal families will come closer to the ages of parents in adoptive familes, holding age of child constant. With divorce and remarriage creating numerous stepparent households, increasing numbers of persons will experience and act in parent-child relationships which provide no common ancestry for the members, and which instead will confront them with complex and overlapping loyalty demands. Thus here, too, exists the approximation to characteristics of adoptive kinship.

With such structural similarities exposed, it becomes easier to explain in what sense the adoptive family can be considered a compass for the family of the mainstream. If the adoptive family can be creatively supported by a Shared Fate approach, why not the mainstream family? Granted that some of the conditions of life for its members are very different from those of the adoptive family, they have some powerful common points of reference. Both types of family have to contend with drastic social changes that have in the past half century created enormous intergenerational conflicts. Perhaps it is not insignificant that the clinical helpers who have concerned themselves principally with the family have again and again recognized that where the traditional rules of conduct are weak or disappearing, new mechanisms of social solidarity must be created. And in that context, they have almost invariably identified authenticity, empathy, and communication as the essentials. The Shared Fate theory shows that the claims concerning these mechanisms are not unwarranted. Authenticity, empathy, and communicative abilities become substitutes for traditional supports for those anxious to make their families more cohesive.

Genuine institutional reform would free the adoptive family from the artificial props that currently try to enforce the loyalty of its children grown to adulthood. Such reform would thus incorporate the insight that only those free to leave can freely stay. In that sense the reform of adoptive kinship has implications also for the wellbeing of the mainstream family.

Chapter 14

Postscript 1985:
Clarifying Some Misconceptions

No book should be unassailable; and the more complex its story, the more it must draw the critique of its readers. But systematic critique is not the same as misreading a book's thesis. When the latter occurs, an author must come to the defense of the work. *Adoptive Kinship* represents the culmination of some three decades of research and writing; whether or not one likes what the book has to say, one ought not to misconstrue its message.

In this postscript chapter I must try to clarify two misconceptions that have been woven around the message of my work and its implications. These misconceptions might be of little importance, and therefore not needing this kind of clarification, were it not for an unusual set of events: they are currently the object of public policy debates. Thus the defense of my work is necessary if these debates are to be carried on without reliance on claims that misconstrue the Shared Fate approach to adoption.

Misconceptions in Law

Let me first draw the reader's attention to a policy-oriented paper published in 1983 by Professor Albert Hubbard,[1] a member of the Faculty of Law at the University of Ottawa ("Marriage Prohibitions, Adoption and Private Acts of Parliament: The Need for Reform"). Like *Adoptive Kinship,* Hubbard's learned and incisive paper refers in its subtitle to a "need for reform." Furthermore, a major part of his paper is devoted to a discussion of the judicial interpretation of adoption laws in Canada. And, as if to parallel the subject matter of my book even more, a central issue in Professor Hubbard's argument concerns "marriage prohibitions" between close relatives by adoption, especially between adoptive parents and their adopted children, and between adopted siblings without a common biological parentage. While he has made no reference to my work and may in fact not have known it when he wrote his, there are surprising similarities in interest and wording. But these similarities are only superficial, for Professor Hubbard advocates in the strongest possible terms, and with much legal erudition, that biologically unrelated siblings, who have become siblings through legal adoption, should be allowed to marry each other. As for adoptive parents marrying their adopted children, Hubbard concedes that such a step might not be advisable.

Now this thesis about the rights of adoptive brothers and sisters to become marriage partners clearly runs counter to the ideas developed in *Adoptive Kinship* (see especially Chapter 8). Nevertheless, I would not have been moved to write a rejoinder in this postscript if it had not been for an important legislative step which during 1984 and 1985 was being considered by a Committee of the Canadian Parliament.[2] This Senate Committee[3] had before it a bill which sought "to consolidate and amend the laws prohibiting marriage between related persons." In that context this bill also dealt with the marriage of persons related solely by way of legal adoption. (For the information of my American readers, I should here explain that in Canada the laws of adoption and their adjudication belong to the powers vested in the several provinces. Questions of incest, however, and thus the permissible and impermissible associations for marriage, are reserved to federal law.) Professor Hubbard's argument quite correctly shows that it is the variations and contradictions between provincial adoption laws, and these laws and the federal statutes, that now confound any reasonable adjudication of marriage requests by persons related through legal adoption. Not only does Professor Hubbard's proposed solution try to create clarity by calling for a uniform pattern of provincial adoption laws, but it invokes a definition of incest based strictly on "blood" relationship. Such a definition of incest would exclude from its prohibition any marriages proposed between persons related purely by legal adoption.

Professor Hubbard is clearly very knowledgeable in matters of family law, including marriage and adoption, no doubt a reason why the Senate Committee asked for his advice in the matter of the bill "to consolidate and amend the laws prohibiting marriage between related persons." But he seems less well-informed about the intricacies of the *policies* that have been developed to administer adoption in the several provinces. Thus, while he recognizes that there exist movements among the adopted for legal access to the records of their origins, and while he does not seem to object to such interests, he also states firmly that adopted persons should be bound by the same incest and marriage prohibitions as are other people, based on "blood" relationship. In other words, while Professor Hubbard would permit biologically unrelated siblings who are brother and sister by legal adoption to marry each other, he would forbid them to marry their biological siblings who might either have remained with the birthparents or have been adopted into a different family. Fair enough in principle, but how would such a prohibition be realized and enforced in circumstances in which adoption records are sealed and in which each provincial jurisdiction has different birth registers? Unlike the situation in England, where adopted persons have long had the right to inquire of the Registrar of Births at Somerset House whether a marriage they are contemplating is within permissible degrees, no such arrangement has been instituted in any jurisdiction in Canada, nor would it be feasible without the creation of uniform and centralized records of birth and of adoption. Similar limitations apply to the multiplicity of states and their separate jurisdictions in the United States of America. Note that Professor Hubbard would free the adopted from the current marriage prohibitions based on adoption, because they already have another prohibition based on consanguinity. But the latter prohibition is in most instances not enforceable and, even if the adopted wished to abide by it, they could in the vast majority of instances not do so because of the current practice of sealing adoption records. It is simply not possible to determine to whom one is biologically related if one is legally adopted and removed from knowledge of one's birth kin.

Aside from such blatant errors, Professor Hubbard's position paper and his testimony before the Senate Committee[4] appear to be based on the premise that, since social values are drastically changing away from familism and more and more toward individualism, individuals should as far as possible be allowed to do what they wish, *ergo* marry their siblings by adoption if they so wish. In *Adoptive Kinship* I have argued for open records to allow adopted adults access to knowledge about their forebears, but I have also argued against marriage by adopted persons within the same adoptive family, because such extreme individualism would rend the boundary and, indeed, the meaning of *family* in adoption. It would thus not only undermine the institution of adoption as a variant of the modern family, but would likewise undermine with it the social ground on which the adopted person's *familial* identity is based.

As if Professor Hubbard's erudite but potentially destructive proposals were not enough of an assault on everything in the Shared Fate approach to adoption, he has quite perversely made use of the argument of "difference" between birth status and adoption status. (But I am giving him the benefit of the doubt in speaking of his view of "difference" as based on *status;* that is how the Shared Fate approach understands "difference.") To show how Professor Hubbard seems to understand "difference" in the context of adoption, let me quote from his testimony before the Senate Committee. Here he refers to various depositions from religious bodies concerned with the marriage bill, among them a deposition from the United Church of Canada:

> There is then a quotation which reads:

> > Adoptive siblings should be prohibited from marrying. In adoptive families, most children are raised to think of each other as brother and sister. It is crucial to their sense of need of being wanted and belonging within the family circle. To permit marriage between adoptive siblings would emphasize the belief that they are somehow "different" from the rest of the family. It would be giving legal sanction to incest just as much as if they were genetically related.

> I would suggest, Madam Chairman, that *adopted children are different,* and that adopted children, if they do not know it, ought to know it. It is now considered the best social policy to disclose to children at the earliest possible moment the fact that they are adopted so that they know they are adopted......[5]

Professor Hubbard's thesis is not only that these adoptees are individualists who should be allowed to marry within the family if they so wish, but that they should be allowed to do so precisely *because they are different.* The ordinary rules for other humans evidently need not apply to the adopted, which makes them strange visitors from outer space. Professor Hubbard's "reform" formula would make the adopted into atomized individuals without the social ground of a family of orientation. Rather than seeing the adopted as "different" from other members of the adoptive family, the Shared Fate approach places them, and all other members of the nuclear unit, into *the same boat of collective difference as a family*. Thus the Shared Fate approach to adoption law reform, in contrast to Professor Hubbard's, sees the differences inherent in adoptive kinship as based on cultural and historical circumstances, and not on the peculiar characteristics of individuals. Accordingly the Shared Fate approach seeks to secure both the cohesion of the adoptive family *and* the freedom of its adult children to obtain any and all available records of their past. What the Hubbard approach has done is to confound this meaning of "freedom" to spell "freedom to marry adoptive siblings," thereby endangering that most lasting social bond of the fragile nuclear family, namely the social bond between siblings. Professor Hubbard's errors of judgment and reasoning would be of little consequence if they were not serving a legislative committee of Canada's Parliament to determine the future of adoptive kinship in this country.

Misconceptions in Social Work

As if the attitude toward secrecy in adoption had come to a 360 degree turn there has of late been a movement in social work for "open adoption". Among the spokesmen for this new outlook two familiar names stand out: Annette Baran and Reuben Pannor. In 1976 they laid down their original premise in an article entitled "Open Adoption."[6] Because of that article's relatively conservative point of view and its subsequent radical alteration, it seems appropriate to quote from the former position briefly:

> . . . the authors have been studying the problems associated with sealed records in adoptions for the past two years. This inquiry has led into many areas, including the re-evaluation of past practices and the consideration of new approaches for the present and future.
>
> In addition to a new appraisal of the concepts of anonymity and confidentiality as epitomized by the sealed record, there is also a need to develop a wider range of options for parents who can neither raise their own children nor face the finality of the traditional relinquishment and adoptive placement process. The concept of open adoption should be considered as an alternative that can meet the needs of some children. *An open adoption is one in which the birth parents meet the adoptive parents, participate in the separation and placement process, relinquish all legal, moral, and nurturing right to the child, but retain the right to continuing contact and to knowledge of the child's whereabouts and welfare.*[7]

Subsequently, in this article, the authors show that in a number of other societies, typically preliterate and folk societies, there existed what the anthropologist Jack Goody has called "kinship fostering." This kind of fostering meant that, while the child knew who the biological parents were, he/she would readily be reared in the household of one or more blood relatives. Such kinship fostering is, however, not fully applicable to the circumstances of modern urban society in which the extended family is at best a rather unreliable network of relatives who may at times meet, who may aid each other if need be, but who cannot be thought of as a working community. In folk societies the extended family households are in close proximity, no more than a village away, and the child's domestic care in no way precludes his or her visiting in the several households of the extended kin, including that of the birthparents. As everyone of us knows from experience, the geographic mobility on this continent is such that the kind of proximity of kin network relations required for true kinship fostering has become inapplicable, except for some relatively isolated rural communities such as are found among the Mennonites or the Hutterite colonies. The analogy between the plan for "open adoption" and the folk society's "kinship fostering" patterns is therefore, in my view, false. Nevertheless, the argument in these authors' paper is well worth pursuing:

> In the United States, indications are that past adoption practices were more open. There has been a tendency to deny the value of these practices and to consider them as irregular and unprofessional, but they worked well and deserve reconsideration. It was not unusual before World War II for a couple to take in a pregnant unwed woman, care for her through the pregnancy and delivery, and then adopt her child. A close connection developed between the couple and the unwed mother, which permitted the mother to relinquish her baby confidently, knowing she was providing the child with a home she approved of and felt a part of.
>
> There is no evidence that this practice caused any later problems for either the birth or adoptive parents. Neither is there evidence that birth parents came back to harass the adoptive families. The adoptive parents could tell the child of its birth heritage convincingly and with first-hand knowledge and understanding. There was an openness in such situations, and a good feeling was transmitted to the adoptee. This approach expressed the principle that a mother had the right to choose the substitute parents for her child, and that their caring for her was an indication of how they would care for her child. *Such a principle is still recognized in the many states that have laws distinguishing between agency and independent adoptions. Independent adoptions are predicated on the belief that birth parents have the right to choose those who will raise their children.*[8]

Then the authors show that the closed adoption pattern had been built around, or at least justified on, the basis of protecting the child from bias against the status of illegitimacy. Now that this bias has been in large measure overcome and single mothers are more often than not keeping their offspring rather than give them up for adoption, it is to be noted that this change also has increased the "numbers of such children on the welfare rolls, in and out of foster placement, or under protective services . . . ." This development leads Baran and Pannor to a modern justification for open adoption:

> The young single mothers who have an emotional attachment – whether positive or negative – to their children desperately need a new kind of adoptive placement in which they can actively participate. They want the security of knowing they have helped provide their children with a loving, secure existence and yet have not denied themselves the possibility of knowing them in the future.[9]

But for all the authors' optimistic view of this innovative step in adoption, their concluding note is suitably conservative:

> *Open adoption is not a panacea and should not be considered a suitable procedure for all birth or adoptive parents.* It is, however, a viable approach in specific situations and can offer an acceptable solution to an otherwise insoluble problem. If open adoption is to be mutually satisfactory and beneficial, adoption agencies must be willing to expend greater efforts over longer periods of time. The professional skills available are more than equal to the task. However, what is currently lacking in the profession is the willingness to consider adoption that allows the birth mother a continuing role in her child's life. Perhaps the clear definition of this need will lead to the consideration of open adoption as an alternative.[10]

However much I may differ with some of Baran and Pannor's reasoning in this article, I felt at the time it appeared that it made a valuable suggestion. It seemed to me reasonable to develop what they call "open adoption" around the children moved from their own or foster homes after they had gained well-established memories of these homes. It seemed proper for the evolving programs of "permanency planning." What I questioned was whether this would be a desirable avenue to adoption generally, and I was satisfied with their answer, that open adoption was not to be seen as a panacea, that it was not to be an all-or-nothing arrangement. Now, however, the authors have reversed themselves. In an article entitled "Open Adoption as Standard Practice"[11] the authors place "closed adoption" and "open adoption" in opposition to each other, no longer on a continuum of possible and desirable arrangements. Moving beyond open adoption in selected cases they have, with this new article, called for an end to all closed adoptions. In their more recent piece they bring to bear no new information, either from clinical practice or from research, to support this much more radical position. Instead, they try to lean on my work in defense of their radical proposition for "open adoption as standard practice":

Crucial to an understanding of the need for open adoption is what Kirk [1964] refers to as the basic need to understand that adoptive kinship is not the same as consanguineous kinship. He correctly points out that the dogma of "no differences" leads to unnecessary inequities, felt injustices, and serious social tensions. He offers a detailed examination of the difference between biological parenthood and adoptive parenthood, pointing out the importance of being able to fully accept the difference."[12]

As readers of *Adoptive Kinship* have observed, I have quoted from the authors' book, *The Adoption Triangle,* with respect and consider its conclusions very important. I believe that their article "Open Adoption" is a valid inference from their earlier work, but I cannot see where my statement, quoted in their 1984 paper, supports this latest, all-or-nothing, doctrinaire call for "open adoption as standard practice." The fact that the adoptive family is different from the family based on consanguineal parenthood calls for openness in adoption, but openness in adoption is not synonymous with "open adoption."

Most problematic for me is the fact that these authors, who know my work well, should have so greatly misread its message. Is there any lesson in the fact that one's work can and will be misconstrued? I think so; it is probably that one should let most such events pass by more or less unnoticed, unless of course the misconceptions were to lead to changes in public policies. In the case of the Hubbard and the Baran and Pannor articles there is indeed a possibility of such public policy changes. That is why I have felt it necessary to provide this rejoinder in the postscript to the new edition of *Adoptive Kinship.*

NOTES

1. Albert Hubbard, Q.C., "Marriage Prohibitions, Adoption and Private Acts of Parliament: The Need for Reform", *McGill Law Journal,* Vol. 28, No. 2, 1983
2. The Standing Senate Committee on Legal and Constitutional Affairs
3. American readers unacquainted with the organization of Canada's Parliament should understand that, while the lower house, the House of Commons, is made up of elected members, the upper house, the Senate is made up of appointed members. These appointments are made by the Prime Minister of the party then in power.
4. Tuesday, May 22, 1984, Issue No. 9, Second proceedings on: Bill S-13, "An Act to consolidate and amend the laws prohibiting marriage between related persons".
5. *ibid,* 9:8 (emphasis added)
6. Annette Baran, Reuben Pannor, and Arthur D. Sorosky, "Open Adoption", *Social Work,* March 1976
7. *ibid,* p. 97 (emphasis added)
8. *ibid,* p. 98 (emphasis added)
9. *ibid,* p. 98
10. *ibid,* p. 100 (emphasis added)
11. Reuben Pannor and Annette Baran, "Open Adoption as Standard Practice", *Child Welfare,* Vol. LXIII, No. 3, May-June 1984
12. *ibid.,* p. 248

Bibliography

Ackley, N.B., "Sealed Adoption Files: When to Open? A New Approach," *Conciliation Courts Review,* Vol. 17, No. 1; June 1979.

Bain, K. and M.M. Eliot, "Adoption as a National Problem," *Pediatrics,* Vol. 20, No. 2; 1957.

Benet, M.K., *The Politics of Adoption.* New York: The Free Press/ Macmillan; 1976.

Berelson, B., *Content Analysis in Communications Research.* New York: The Free Press; 1952. Summarized in Gardner Lindzey (ed.), *Handbook of Social Psychology,* New York: Addison-Wesley; 1954.

Boas, F., "The Central Eskimo," in *Sixth Annual Report/ Bureau of Ethnology.* United States Government Printing Office; 1888.

Bohman, M., *Adopted Children and Their Families.* Stockholm: Proprius; 1970.

Braithwaite, R.B. *Scientific Explanation.* New York: Harper & Row; 1953, 1960.

Brenner, R., *A Follow-up Study of Adoptive Families.* New York: Child Adoption Research Committee; 1951.

Brieland, D., "An Experimental Study of the Selection of Adoptive Parents at Intake," Child Welfare League of America; May 1959.

Brooks, L.M. and E.C. Brooks, *Adventuring in Adoption.* Chapel Hill: University of North Carolina Press; 1939.

Brown, F., "What Do We Seek in Adoptive Parents," *Social Casework;* April 1951.

Burgess, L.C., *The Art of Adoption.* Washington, D.C.: Acropolis Books; 1976.

Bynner, W., *The Way of Life According to Laotzu. An American Version.* John Day Co.; 1944.

Cannon, W.B., *The Wisdom of the Body.* New York: Norton; 1939, 1963.

Calhoun, A.W., *A Social History of the American Family.* 3 Volumes. Cleveland: Arthur K. Clark; 1918, 1945.

Carroll, J.F.X., "The Acceptance or Rejection of Differences Between Adoptive and Biological Parenthood by Adoptive Applicants as Related to Various Indices of Adjustment/ Maladjustment." Unpublished Ph.D. dissertation, Department of Sociology, Temple University; 1968.

Chang, J.C., "A Step Towards Resolving the Adoption Records Controversy: The Adoption Agency as the Key to Unlocking Sealed Identities," *University of California (Davis) Law Review,* Vol. 12, No. 2; Summer 1979.

Children's Home Society of California, "The Changing Faces of Adoption," Report of Research Project; 1977.

Cicourel, Aaron V., *Method and Measurement in Sociology*. New York: Free Press; 1964.

Cottrell, L.S., Jr., "The Adjustment of the Individual to His Age and Sex Roles," *American Sociological Review*, Vol, 7, No. 5; 1942.

Day, C., "Access to Birth Records: General Register Office Study," *Adoption and Fostering*, Vol. 98, No. 4; 1979.

Dembroski, B.G. and D.L. Johnson, "Dogmatism and Attitudes Toward Adoption," *Journal of Marriage and the Family;* Vol. 31, No. 4, November 1969.

Department Committee on the Adoption of Children, *Adoption of Children*. London: H.M. Stationery Office; 1970. *Report of the Departmental Committee on the Adoption of Children*. London: H.M. Stationery Office; 1972.

Dewey, M., *Dewey Decimal Classification and Relative Index*. Lake Placid Club, N.Y.: Forest Press; 1876, 1965.

Dinitz, S., R.R. Dyes and A.C. Clarke, "Preference for Male and Female Children: Traditional or Affectional?," *Marriage and Family Living*, Vol. XVI, No. 2; 1954.

Dunning, R.W., "A Note on Adoption among the Southampton Island Eskimo," *Man*, Vol. LXII (November):163-68; 1962. *Preliminary Sociological Report on the Southampton Island Eskimo Community*. Ottawa: Northern Research Coordination Centre, Department of Northern Affairs; 1957.

Evan, S., "The Unmarried Mother's Indecision About Her Baby as a Mechanism of Defense," paper given under the auspices of the National Association on Service to Unmarried Parents at the National Conference of Social Work, Philadelphia, Pa. (mimeo) May 23; 1957.

Evan, W.M., *Organization Theory*. New York: John Wiley & Sons; 1976. "Some Approaches to the Sociology of Law," in *Law and Sociology*. New York: Free Press; 1962.

Fanshel, David, "An Upsurge of Interest in Adoption," *Children*; September-October 1964.

Firth, R., *We, the Tikopia*, London: George Allen and Unwin; 1936.

Fisher, F., *The Search for Anna Fisher*. New York: A. Fields; 1973.

Glaser, B.G., and A.L. Strauss, *The Discovery of Grounded Theory: Strategies for Qualitative Research*. Chicago: Aldine; 1967.

Goffman, E., *Asylums*. Chicago: Aldine; 1962.

Goode, W.J., "A Theory of Role Strain," *American Sociological Review*, Vol. 25, No. 4; 1960.

Grey, E., and R.M. Blunden, *A Survey of Adoption in Great Britain*. London: H.M. Stationery Office; 1971.

Harrington, J.D., "The Courts Contend with Sealed Adoption Records," *Public Welfare*, Vol. 38, No. 2; Spring 1980. "Legislative Reform Moves Slowly," *Public Welfare*, Vol. 37, No. 3, Summer; 1979.

Hepworth, H.P., *Foster Care and Adoption in Canada*. Ottawa: Canadian Council on Social Development; 1980.

Her Majesty's Stationery Office, *Children Act 1975;* 1975.

Hofstadter, R., *The American Political Tradition*. New York: Knopf; 1959.

Hughes, E.C., "Mistakes at Work," *The Canadian Journal of Economics and Political Science*, Vol. 17, No. 3; August 1951. "The Study of Occupations," in Merton et al. (eds.), *Sociology Today*. New York: Basic Books; 1959.

Isaac, R.J., "Children Who Need Adoption," *The Atlantic Monthly;* November 1963.

Jaffee, B. and D. Fanshel, *How They Fared in Adoption*. New York: Columbia University Press; 1970.

Jonassohn, K., "On the Use and Construction of Adoption Rates," *Journal of Marriage and the Family*, Vol. 27, No. 4, November, 1965.

Jones, M.A., *et al*, *The Sealed Adoption Record Controversy — Report of a Survey of Agency Policy, Practice and Opinions*. Child Welfare League of America; July 1976.

Jourard, S.M., *Personal Adjustment*. New York: Macmillan; 1963.

Kaplan, A., *The Conduct of Inquiry*. San Francisco: Chandler; 1964.

Kennedy, Lucile, "Why Do We Need Adoption Agencies?," *National Parent-Teacher;* April 1957.

Kirk, H.D., "Some Aspects of the Problems Caused by Weakened Social Ties." Unpublished Sociology Honors thesis, The City College of New York; 1948. "Community Sentiments in Relation to Child Adoption." Unpublished Ph.D. dissertation, Cornell University; 1953. "A Dilemma of Adoptive Parenthood: Incongruous Role Obligations," *Marriage and Family Living*, Vol. XXI, No. 4; November 1959. "Guarding the Ramparts: Reader Reactions to a Magazine Article Challenging a Social Work Prescription," *The Social Worker* (Canada); June-July 1962. "The Impact of Drastic Change on Social Relations," in G.K. Zollschan and W. Hirsch (eds.), *Explorations in Social Change*. Boston: Houghton Mifflin; 1964. *Shared Fate: A Theory of Adoption and Mental Health*. New York: The Free Press; 1964. "Are Adopted Children Especially Vulnerable to Stress?" (with Jonassohn, K. and Fish, A.D.), *Archives of General Psychiatry*, Vol. 14, March 1966. "Shared Fate as Theory of Adoption and as Theory of Human Community," *Proceedings of the World Conference on Adoption and Foster Care*, Milan, 1972. *Halifax Children* (with Jonassohn, K.), University of Waterloo, 1973. "Toward a Taxonomy of Social Discontinuities," in Zollschan, G.K. and Hirsch, W. (eds.), *Social Change*, Cambridge, Mass.: Schenkman Publishing Co.; 1976.

Kornitzer, M., *Child Adoption in the Modern World*. London: Putnam; 1952. "Finding Adoption Records," *Adoption and Fostering*, 87, No. l; 1977.

Kuhn, T.S., *The Structure of Scientific Revolutions*. Chicago: University of Chicago Press; 1962.

Lasswell, H.D., "Describing the Contents of Communications," in B.L. Smith, H.D. Lasswell, and R.D. Casey (eds.), *Propaganda, Communication, and Public Opinion*. Princeton, N.J.: Princeton University Press; 1946.

Lasswell, H.D., N. Leites, *et al., Language of Politics: Studies in Quantitative Semantics*. New York: Stewart; 1949.

Leeding, A., "Access to Birth Records," *Adoption and Fostering*, 89, No. 3; 1977.

Leslie, G.R., *The Family In Social Context*. New York: Oxford University Press 1967, 1973.

Littner, N., "The Natural Parents," in Shapiro (ed.), *A Study of Adoption Practice*, 1955.

Louisiana Department of Public Welfare, *How to Adopt a Child in Louisiana;* 1950.

Lowie, R., "Adoption-Primitive," *Encyclopedia of the Social Sciences*, Vol. I, 459-60. New York: The MacMillan Co.; 1930.

Maas, H.S., Discussion of H.D. Kirk's "A Dilemma of Adoptive Parenthood," *Marriage and Family Living*, 21, No. 4, 1959.

Maddox, B., *The Half-Parent: Living With Other People's Children*. New York; Evans; 1975.

Malinowski, B., "Myths in Primitive Psychology," *Magic, Science and Religion*. Doubleday Anchor; 1948, 1954.

Marcus, C., *Adopted?*, Vancouver: International Self-Counsel Press; 1979.

Martinson, F.M., *Family in Society*. New York: Dodd, Mead; 1970.

McWhinnie, A.M., *Adopted Children: How They Grow Up*. London: Routledge & Kegan Paul; 1967.

Mills, C.W., *The Sociological Imagination*. New York: Oxford University Press; 1959, 1972.

Mitchell, G.D. (ed.), *Dictionary of Sociology*. London: Routledge and Kegan Paul; 1968.

Opler, M.E., "Themes as Dynamic Forces in Culture," *American Journal of Sociology*, Vol. 51, No. 3; 1945.

Orwell, G., "England, Your England" Part I of "The Lion and the Unicorn," in the *Collected Essays, Journalism and Letters*, Vol. II, 1968.

Parsons, T., "The Law and Social Control," in M. Evans (ed.), *Law and Sociology*. New York: Free Press; 1962.

Paton, J., *TheAdopted Break Silence*. Acton: Life History Study Center; 1954.

Picton, C., "Post-Adoption Support," *Adoption and Fostering*, 88, No. 2; 1977.

Pierce, S., "Law, Marriage and Family — A Socio-legal Enquiry Into The Institutionalization of Adoptive Relationships in Canada." Unpublished Honours paper, Department of Sociology, University of Waterloo; 1972.

Polier, Hon. J.W., "Adoption and Law," *Pediatrics,* Vol. 20, No.2, August 1957.

Robertson, D.C., "Parental Socialization Patterns in Interracial Adoption." Unpublished Ph.D. dissertation, Department of Sociology, University of California, Los Angeles; 1974.

Schapiro, M., *A Study of Adoption Practice.* Child Welfare League of America; 1955.

Schechter, M.S., "Observations on Adopted Children," *Archives of General Psychiatry,* Vol. 3; July 1960.

Silverman, A.R., and Feigelman, W., "Some Factors Affecting the Adoption of Minority Children," *Social Casework* 58, 1977.

Simon, R.J., and H. Alstein, *Transracial Adoption.* New York: John Wiley & Sons; 1977.

Sorosky, A.D., A. Baran, and R. Pannor, *The Adoption Triangle.* New York: Anchor; 1978.

Thompson, J., "Roots and Rights — A Challenge for Adoption," *The Social Worker/Le Travailleur Social,* Vol. 47, No. 1; Spring 1979.

Thompson, J., J. Webber, A. Stoneman, D. Harrison, *The Adoption Rectangle: A Study of Adult Adoptees' Search for Birth Family, History and Implications for Adoption Service.* Children's Aid Society of Metropolitan Toronto; June 1978.

Thornton, M., "Keeping Adoption Records," *Adoption and Fostering,* 90, No. 4; 1977.

Thunen, M., "Ending Contact with Adoptive Parents: The Group Meeting," *Child Welfare,* Vol. XXXVII, No. 2; 1958.

Toussieng, P.W., "Realizing the Potential in Adoptions," *Child Welfare;* June 1971. "Thoughts Regarding the Etiology and Psychological Difficulties in Adopted Children," *Child Welfare;* February 1962.

Triseliotis, J. *In Search of Origins.* London: Routledge and Kegan Paul; 1973.

United Nations Department of Social Affairs, *Study on Adoption of Children,* 1953.

United States Children's Bureau, *Protecting Children in Adoption,* Report of a Conference, 1955.

Vincent, Clark E., *Unmarried Mothers.* New York: Free Press; 1961.

Wadlington, W.J. III, "The Adopted Child and Intra-Family Marriage Prohibitions," *Virginia Law Review,* Vol. 49, April 1963.

Weckler, J.E., "Adoption on Mokil," *American Anthropologist,* Vol. LV, No. 4; 1953.

Weinstein, E.A., "Adoption," *International Encyclopedia of the Social Sciences.* New York: Macmillan/Free Press; 1968.

Wheelis, A., *The Quest for Identity.* New York: Norton; 1958.

Williams, R.M., Jr., *American Society.* New York: Knopf; 1951.

Wittenborn, J.R., *The Placement of Adoptive Children,* Springfield, Ill., Charles C. Thomas; 1957.

Woodworth, R.S., *Heredity and Environment.* Social Science Research Council Bulletin #47; 1941.

Young, L., *Out of Wedlock.* New York: McGraw-Hill; 1959.

Zeilinger, R., "The Need to Know vs. the Right to Know," *Public Welfare,* Vol. 37, No. 3, Summer 1979.

Zollschan, G.K., and W. Hirsch, *Explorations in Social Change.* Boston: Houghton Mifflin; 1964.

Index

A Note on the Author

H. David Kirk was born in 1918 into a Jewish family in the Rhineland, West Germany. The family name was Kirchheimer, anglicized when the parents took the three sons to the United States in 1938. In 1934 David had left Germany to finish high school in England. Later, in America, he earned a B.S. degree at the City College of New York. During 1948 to 1953 he was a graduate student at Cornell University, where he was also an instructor and held a research fellowship from the United States Public Health Service. This enabled him to undertake the study of community values concerning illegitmacy, infertility, and adoption, and it led to his Ph.D. dissertation. Although adoption has been his longest-term interest, this interest arose out of the larger issues of human dislocation, belongingness, loyalty, and community, issues of which his boyhood experiences made him aware.

In 1954 he joined the faculty of McGill University's School of Social Work, and a year later he was able to initiate the cross-national survey of adoptive families. From the various studies of that decade there resulted Kirk's first book, *Shared Fate*. A second book, *Adoptive Kinship,* appeared in 1981, supplementing the ideas developed in the earlier one by an analysis of adoption laws and policies. Professor Kirk is currently a member of the Department of Sociology at the University of Waterloo and the Faculty of Law, University of Victoria. He has lectured on adoption in Canada, the United States, Great Britain, Denmark, Germany, Italy, and Israel. He is the adoptive father of four, now in their thirties.

Also from Ben-Simon Publications:
A New and Enlarged Edition of Shared Fate

For eighteen years, from 1964 to 1982, the first edition of this important book remained in hard-cover. Now it has been re-issued in paperback, with a new preface and a fascinating new postscript chapter. In that chapter David Kirk looks back on his earliest learning experiences as an adoptive father, in particular his daughter Francie's development as an artist. It is she who has designed and drawn the cover of this new edition of *Shared Fate.*

Ben-Simon Publications
P.O. Box 318
Brentwood Bay, B.C.
Canada V0S 1A0